Grammar Sense 3

SECOND EDITION

TEACHER'S BOOK

AUTHOR
Katharine Sherak

OXFORD

UNIVERSITY PRESS

198 Madison Avenue
New York, NY 10016 USA

Great Clarendon Street, Oxford, OX2 6DP, United Kingdom

Oxford University Press is a department of the University of Oxford.
It furthers the University's objective of excellence in research, scholarship,
and education by publishing worldwide. Oxford is a registered trade
mark of Oxford University Press in the UK and in certain other countries

General Manager, American ELT: Laura Pearson
Publisher: Stephanie Karras
Associate Publishing Manager: Sharon Sargent
Managing Editor: Alex Ragan
Director, ADP: Susan Sanguily
Executive Design Manager: Maj-Britt Hagsted
Electronic Production Manager: Julie Armstrong
Sr. Designer: Yin Ling Wong
Image Manager: Trisha Masterson

Publishing and Editorial Management: hyphen S.A.

ISBN: 978 0 19 448940 9 Teacher's Book 3 with Online Practice pack
ISBN: 978 0 19 448944 7 Teacher's Book 3 as pack component
ISBN: 978 0 19 448928 7 Online Practice as pack component
Printed in China

This book is printed on paper from certified and well-managed sources

Contents

Welcome to Grammar Sense

A Sensible Solution to Learning Grammar

Grammar Sense Second Edition gives learners a true understanding of how grammar is used in authentic contexts.

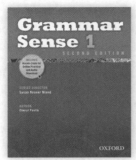 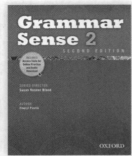 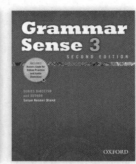 

With Grammar Sense Online Practice

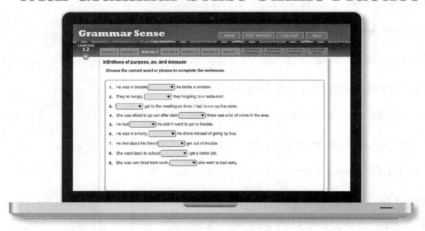

- **Student Solutions:** a **focus on Critical Thinking** for improved application of grammatical knowledge.

- **Writing Solutions:** a **Writing section in every chapter** encourages students to see the relevance of grammar in their writing.

- **Technology Solutions:** *Grammar Sense Online Practice* provides additional practice in an easy-to-use **online workbook**.

- **Assessment Solutions:** the Part Tests at the end of every section and the Grammar Sense Test Generators allow **ongoing assessment**.

Each chapter in *Grammar Sense Second Edition* follows this format.

The Grammar in Discourse section introduces the target grammar in its natural context via high-interest readings.

A GRAMMAR IN DISCOURSE

You Snooze, You Win at Today's Workplace

A1 Before You Read

Discuss these questions.

How much sleep do you get each night? Do you usually get enough sleep? Why or why not? Do you ever take naps?

A2 Read

CD1 T2 Read this magazine article to find out how some businesses are helping their tired employees.

> Exposure to **authentic readings** encourages awareness of the grammar in daily life: in textbooks, magazines, newspapers, websites, and so on.

You Snooze, You Win at Today's Workplace

It's early afternoon and lunch is over. You're sitting at your desk and plowing through paperwork. Suddenly you're fighting to keep your eyes open. The
5 words on your computer are zooming in and out of focus, and your head is beginning to bob in all directions. A nap sounds good right about now—so does a couch or reclining armchair.
10 Well, a growing number of companies are beginning to accept the idea of sleeping on the job. No, it's not a dream. Employees are increasingly sleeping less and working longer
15 hours at the office. Some employers, therefore, are warming up to the idea that a midday nap helps increase productivity, creativity, and safety.

Some companies are now providing
20 tents in quiet areas of their offices. Each one contains a sleeping bag, a foam pad, an MP3 player, eye shades, and yes, an alarm clock. In Japan, some firms have "nightingale rooms"
25 where employees are encouraged to take "power naps," and nap salons are springing up around the globe in cities like London, Amsterdam, Tokyo, and New York.

fact, it sometimes leads
till, that doesn't stop
according to Professor
und that "they're
r cars, in the bathroom,
oms. Others are trying to
in their cubicles.
the phone to their ear,
o write or read

Adapted from *The Christian Science Monitor*

bob: to move repeatedly up and down
cubicle: a small enclosed area
dismissal: telling an employee that he or she is fired
plow through: to force one's way through

productivity: the amount of work you can do in a certain time
snooze: to nap
warm up to: to begin to like

> **Pre- and post-reading tasks** help students understand the text.

A3 After You Read

Write *T* for true or *F* for false for each statement.

__T__ 1. Tired workers produce fewer products.

_____ 2. Some employers provide special napping areas.

_____ 3. People need to sleep a total of five hundred hours a year.

_____ 4. One study shows that most adults get eight hours of sleep per night.

_____ 5. Most companies do not encourage napping.

_____ 6. Employees only nap at the office.

The Form section(s) provides clear presentation of the target grammar, detailed notes, and thorough practice exercises.

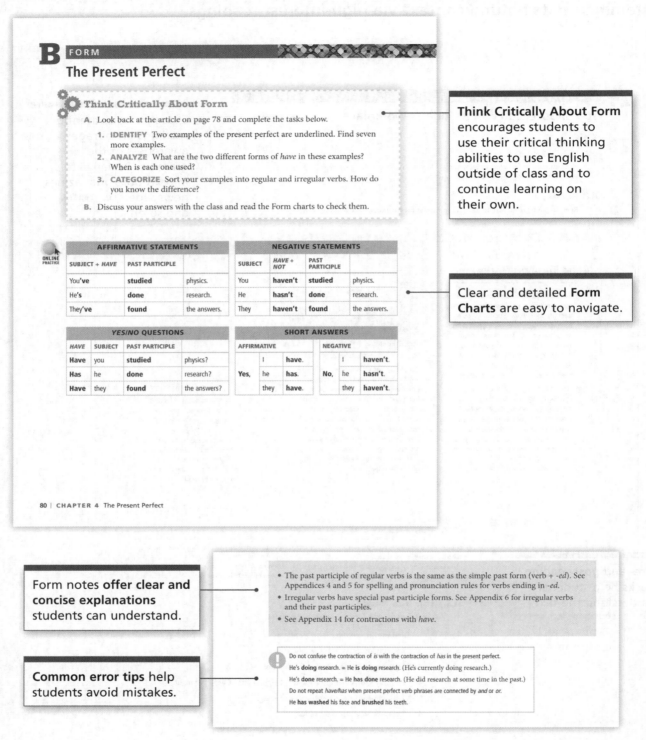

B FORM

The Present Perfect

Think Critically About Form

A. Look back at the article on page 78 and complete the tasks below.

1. **IDENTIFY** Two examples of the present perfect are underlined. Find seven more examples.
2. **ANALYZE** What are the two different forms of *have* in these examples? When is each one used?
3. **CATEGORIZE** Sort your examples into regular and irregular verbs. How do you know the difference?

B. Discuss your answers with the class and read the Form charts to check them.

Think Critically About Form encourages students to use their critical thinking abilities to use English outside of class and to continue learning on their own.

ONLINE PRACTICE

AFFIRMATIVE STATEMENTS		
SUBJECT + HAVE	PAST PARTICIPLE	
You've	studied	physics.
He's	done	research.
They've	found	the answers.

NEGATIVE STATEMENTS			
SUBJECT	HAVE + NOT	PAST PARTICIPLE	
You	haven't	studied	physics.
He	hasn't	done	research.
They	haven't	found	the answers.

YES/NO QUESTIONS			
HAVE	SUBJECT	PAST PARTICIPLE	
Have	you	studied	physics?
Has	he	done	research?
Have	they	found	the answers?

SHORT ANSWERS						
AFFIRMATIVE			NEGATIVE			
	I	have.		I	haven't.
Yes,	he	has.	No,	he	hasn't.
	they	have.		they	haven't.

Clear and detailed **Form Charts** are easy to navigate.

Form notes **offer clear and concise explanations** students can understand.

- The past participle of regular verbs is the same as the simple past form (verb + -ed). See Appendices 4 and 5 for spelling and pronunciation rules for verbs ending in -ed.
- Irregular verbs have special past participle forms. See Appendix 6 for irregular verbs and their past participles.
- See Appendix 14 for contractions with *have*.

Common error tips help students avoid mistakes.

Do not confuse the contraction of *is* with the contraction of *has* in the present perfect.

He's **doing** research. = He **is doing** research. (He's currently doing research.)

He's **done** research. = He **has done** research. (He did research at some time in the past.)

Do not repeat *have/has* when present perfect verb phrases are connected by *and* or *or*.

He **has washed** his face and **brushed** his teeth.

The Meaning and Use section(s) offers clear and comprehensive explanations of how the target structure is used, and exercises to practice using it appropriately.

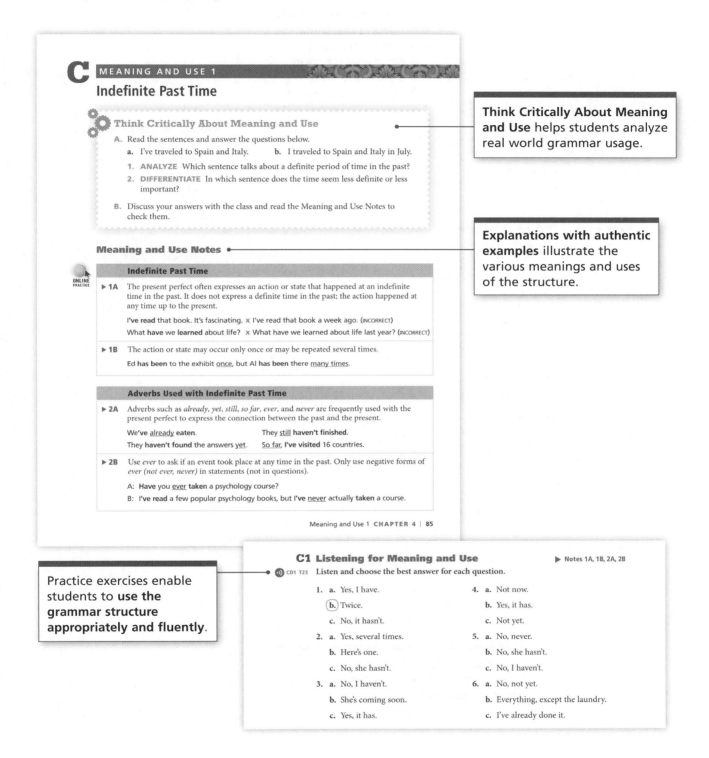

C MEANING AND USE 1

Indefinite Past Time

Think Critically About Meaning and Use

A. Read the sentences and answer the questions below.

    a. I've traveled to Spain and Italy.   b. I traveled to Spain and Italy in July.

    1. **ANALYZE** Which sentence talks about a definite period of time in the past?

    2. **DIFFERENTIATE** In which sentence does the time seem less definite or less important?

B. Discuss your answers with the class and read the Meaning and Use Notes to check them.

Think Critically About Meaning and Use helps students analyze real world grammar usage.

Meaning and Use Notes

ONLINE PRACTICE

Explanations with authentic examples illustrate the various meanings and uses of the structure.

Indefinite Past Time

▶ **1A** The present perfect often expresses an action or state that happened at an indefinite time in the past. It does not express a definite time in the past; the action happened at any time up to the present.

    I've read that book. It's fascinating. X I've read that book a week ago. (INCORRECT)

    What **have** we **learned** about life? X What have we learned about life last year? (INCORRECT)

▶ **1B** The action or state may occur only once or may be repeated several times.

    Ed **has been** to the exhibit <u>once</u>, but Al **has been** there <u>many times</u>.

Adverbs Used with Indefinite Past Time

▶ **2A** Adverbs such as *already, yet, still, so far, ever,* and *never* are frequently used with the present perfect to express the connection between the past and the present.

    We've <u>already</u> eaten.   They <u>still</u> **haven't** finished.

    They **haven't** found the answers <u>yet</u>.   <u>So far</u>, **I've visited** 16 countries.

▶ **2B** Use *ever* to ask if an event took place at any time in the past. Only use negative forms of *ever (not ever, never)* in statements (not in questions).

    A: **Have** you <u>ever</u> **taken** a psychology course?

    B: **I've read** a few popular psychology books, but **I've** <u>never</u> actually **taken** a course.

Meaning and Use 1 **CHAPTER 4** | 85

Practice exercises enable students to **use the grammar structure appropriately and fluently.**

C1 Listening for Meaning and Use   ▶ Notes 1A, 1B, 2A, 2B

CD1 T23 Listen and choose the best answer for each question.

1. a. Yes, I have.
    b. Twice.
    c. No, it hasn't.

2. a. Yes, several times.
    b. Here's one.
    c. No, she hasn't.

3. a. No, I haven't.
    b. She's coming soon.
    c. Yes, it has.

4. a. Not now.
    b. Yes, it has.
    c. Not yet.

5. a. No, never.
    b. No, she hasn't.
    c. No, I haven't.

6. a. No, not yet.
    b. Everything, except the laundry.
    c. I've already done it.

Special sections appear throughout the chapters with clear explanations, authentic examples, and follow-up exercises.

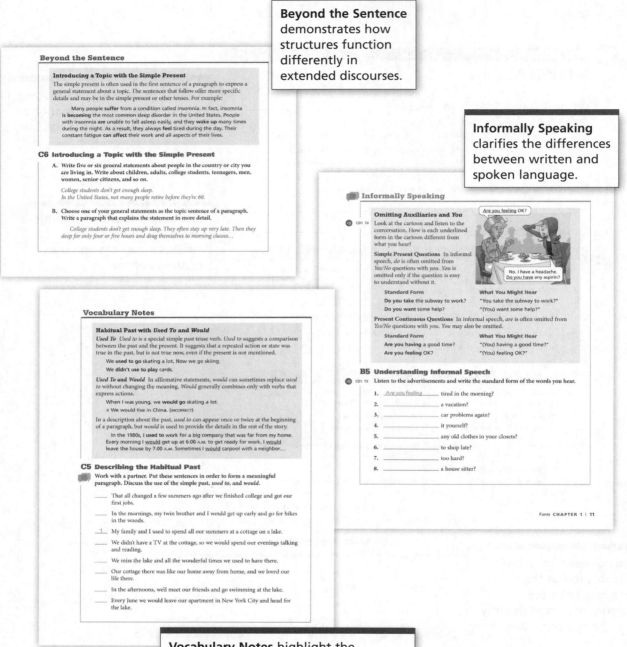

Beyond the Sentence demonstrates how structures function differently in extended discourses.

Beyond the Sentence

Introducing a Topic with the Simple Present
The simple present is often used in the first sentence of a paragraph to express a general statement about a topic. The sentences that follow offer more specific details and may be in the simple present or other tenses. For example:

Many people **suffer** from a condition called insomnia. In fact, insomnia **is becoming** the most common sleep disorder in the United States. People with insomnia **are** unable to fall asleep easily, and they **wake up** many times during the night. As a result, they always **feel** tired during the day. Their constant fatigue **can affect** their work and all aspects of their lives.

C6 Introducing a Topic with the Simple Present

A. Write five or six general statements about people in the country or city you are living in. Write about children, adults, college students, teenagers, men, women, senior citizens, and so on.

College students don't get enough sleep.
In the United States, not many people retire before they're 60.

B. Choose one of your general statements as the topic sentence of a paragraph. Write a paragraph that explains the statement in more detail.

College students don't get enough sleep. They often stay up very late. Then they sleep for only four or five hours and drag themselves to morning classes…

Informally Speaking clarifies the differences between written and spoken language.

Informally Speaking

Omitting Auxiliaries and *You*
CD1 T4 Look at the cartoon and listen to the conversation. How is each underlined form in the cartoon different from what you hear?

Are you feeling OK?

No. I have a headache. Do you have any aspirin?

Simple Present Questions In informal speech, *do* is often omitted from *Yes/No* questions with *you*. *You* is omitted only if the question is easy to understand without it.

Standard Form	What You Might Hear
Do you take the subway to work?	"You take the subway to work?"
Do you want some help?	"(You) want some help?"

Present Continuous Questions In informal speech, *are* is often omitted from *Yes/No* questions with *you*. *You* may also be omitted.

Standard Form	What You Might Hear
Are you having a good time?	"(You) having a good time?"
Are you feeling OK?	"(You) feeling OK?"

B5 Understanding Informal Speech
CD1 T5 Listen to the advertisements and write the standard form of the words you hear.

1. _Are you feeling_ tired in the morning?
2. _____ a vacation?
3. _____ car problems again?
4. _____ it yourself?
5. _____ any old clothes in your closets?
6. _____ to shop late?
7. _____ too hard?
8. _____ a house sitter?

Form CHAPTER 1 | 11

Vocabulary Notes

Habitual Past with *Used To* and *Would*
Used To *Used to* is a special simple past tense verb. *Used to* suggests a comparison between the past and the present. It suggests that a repeated action or state was true in the past, but is not true now, even if the present is not mentioned.

We **used to go** skating a lot. Now we go skiing.
We **didn't use to play** cards.

Used To* and *Would In affirmative statements, *would* can sometimes replace *used to* without changing the meaning. *Would* generally combines only with verbs that express actions.

When I was young, we **would go** skating a lot.
x We would live in China. (INCORRECT)

In a description about the past, *used to* can appear once or twice at the beginning of a paragraph, but *would* is used to provide the details in the rest of the story.

In the 1980s, I **used to** work for a big company that was far from my home. Every morning I **would** get up at 6:00 A.M. to get ready for work. I **would** leave the house by 7:00 A.M. Sometimes I **would** carpool with a neighbor…

C5 Describing the Habitual Past
Work with a partner. Put these sentences in order to form a meaningful paragraph. Discuss the use of the simple past, *used to*, and *would*.

___ That all changed a few summers ago after we finished college and got our first jobs.

___ In the mornings, my twin brother and I would get up early and go for hikes in the woods.

_1_ My family and I used to spend all our summers at a cottage on a lake.

___ We didn't have a TV at the cottage, so we would spend our evenings talking and reading.

___ We miss the lake and all the wonderful times we used to have there.

___ Our cottage there was like our home away from home, and we loved our life there.

___ In the afternoons, we'd meet our friends and go swimming at the lake.

___ Every June we would leave our apartment in New York City and head for the lake.

Vocabulary Notes highlight the connection between the key vocabulary and grammatical structures.

The Writing section guides students through the process of applying grammatical knowledge to compositions.

WRITING
Write an Article for Your School's Online Newspaper

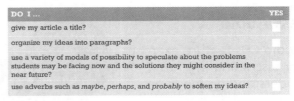

Think Critically About Meaning and Use

A. Work with a partner. Read each situation. Choose the sentence that is the most certain.

1. The key is missing.
   a. It may be on the table.
   b. It must be on the table.
   c. It ought to be on the table.

2. A letter has just arrived.
   a. It can't be from Mary.
   b. It must not be from Mary.
   c. It might not be from Mary.

3. Thomas is doing his homework.
   a. He might finish by four o'clock.
   b. He could finish by four o'clock.
   c. He won't finish by four o'clock.

4. The answer is 25.
   a. That may not be right.
   b. That couldn't be right.
   c. That might not be right.

5. The doorbell is ringing.
   a. It has to be the mail carrier.
   b. It should be the mail carrier.
   c. It ought to be the mail carrier.

6. My car is at the service station.
   a. It won't be ready soon.
   b. It will probably be ready soon.
   c. It ought to be ready soon.

B. Discuss these questions in small groups.

1. **GENERATE** Look at sentence 1. Imagine you know for sure that the key is _not_ on the table. What two modal forms could you use to replace _must be_?

2. **PREDICT** Look at sentence 6a. What might the speaker say next to support the idea?

> Integrating grammar into the writing process helps students **see the relevance of grammar to their own writing.**

Edit

Find the errors in this paragraph and corre

A migraine is a severe headache that can
sufferers often experience symptoms such as
vision. However, there are other symptoms th
coming. You maybe sensitive to light, sound,
The good news is that treatment must often

> Editing exercises focus students on **identifying and correcting problems** in sentence structure and usage.

Write

Imagine that you are the health editor of your school's online newspaper. Write an article discussing ways that students might stay fit while they are studying at your school. Use modals and phrasal modals of present and future possibility.

1. **BRAINSTORM** Think about all the problems that students face and the solutions that you might include. Use these categories to help you organize your ideas into three or four paragraphs.
   - **Problems:** Why might students find it difficult to stay fit while they are studying (e.g., sitting for too many hours, study/sleep habits, food)?
   - **Solutions/Advice:** What are some of the things that students might do to stay fit (e.g., exercise, eat properly, get enough sleep)?
   - **Conclusion:** What may happen if they don't follow your advice? What benefits might they experience if they follow your suggestions?

2. **WRITE A FIRST DRAFT** Before you write your first draft, read the checklist below and look at the examples on pages 146–147. Write your draft using modals of possibility.

3. **EDIT** Read your work and check it against the checklist below. Circle grammar, spelling, and punctuation errors.

DO I ...	YES
give my article a title?	
organize my ideas into paragraphs?	
use a variety of modals of possibility to speculate about the problems students may be facing now and the solutions they might consider in the near future?	
use adverbs such as _maybe_, _perhaps_, and _probably_ to soften my ideas?	

4. **PEER REVIEW** Work with a partner to help you decide how to fix your errors and improve the content. Use the checklist above.

> Collaborating with classmates in **peer review** helps students improve their own grammar skills.

Assessment

PART 1
TEST | The Present, Past, and Future

Choose the correct word or words to complete each sentence.

1. What _____ at his corporate job?

   a. your father does   **c.** does your father do

   b. do your father   **d.** does your father

2. Passengers used to wait on long lines before the airlines _____ electronic check-in machines.

   a. introduce   **c.** introduced

   b. used to introduce   **d.** introducing

3. In what city _____ going to be?

   a. the next Olympic games will   **c.** will the next Olympic games

   b. are the next Olympic games   **d.** the next Olympic games are

What is expressed in each sentence? Choose the correct answer.

4. I'm living with John this semester.

> **Part Tests** allow ongoing assessment and evaluate the students' mastery of the grammar.

Teacher's Resources

Teacher's Book

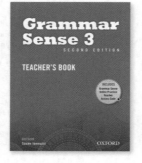

- Creative techniques for presenting the grammar, along with troubleshooting tips, and suggestions for additional activities

- Answer key and audio scripts

- Includes a *Grammar Sense Online Practice* Teacher Access Code

Class Audio

- Audio CDs feature exercises for discriminating form, understanding meaning and use, and interpreting non-standard forms

Test Generator CD-ROM

- Over 3,000 items available!

- Test-generating software allows you to customize tests for all levels of Grammar Sense

- Includes a bank of ready-made tests

Oxford
Teachers' Club

Grammar Sense Teachers' Club site contains additional teaching resources at www.oup.com/elt/teacher/grammarsense

ONLINE PRACTICE

Grammar Sense Online Practice is an online program with all new content. It correlates with the *Grammar Sense* student books and provides additional practice.

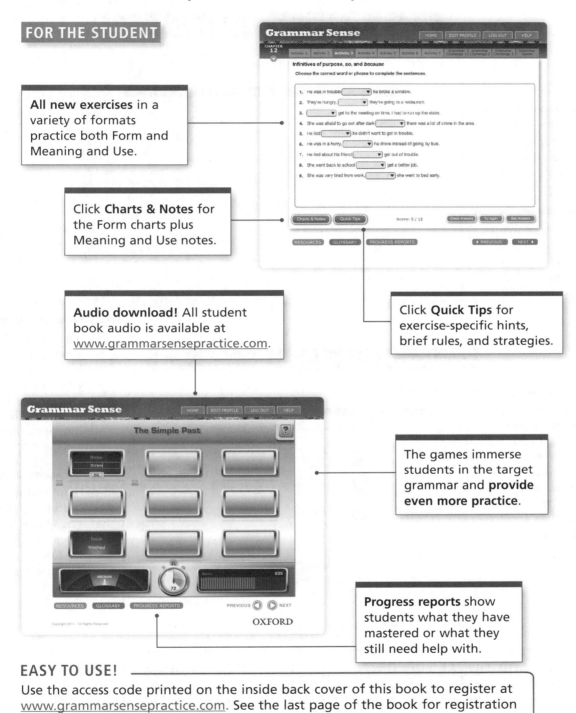

All new exercises in a variety of formats practice both Form and Meaning and Use.

Click **Charts & Notes** for the Form charts plus Meaning and Use notes.

Audio download! All student book audio is available at www.grammarsensepractice.com.

Click **Quick Tips** for exercise-specific hints, brief rules, and strategies.

The games immerse students in the target grammar and **provide even more practice**.

Progress reports show students what they have mastered or what they still need help with.

EASY TO USE!

Use the access code printed on the inside back cover of this book to register at www.grammarsensepractice.com. See the last page of the book for registration instructions.

Flexible enough for use in the classroom or easily assigned as homework.

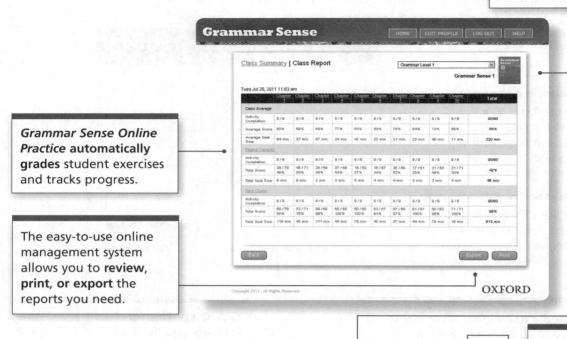

Grammar Sense Online Practice **automatically grades** student exercises and tracks progress.

The easy-to-use online management system allows you to **review, print, or export** the reports you need.

You can **access all** *Grammar Sense Online Practice* **activities**, download the student book audio, and utilize the additional student resources.

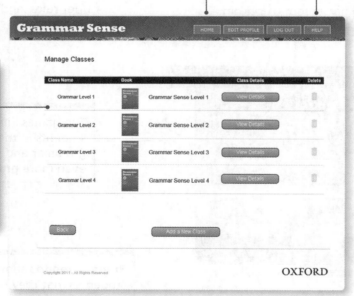

The **straightforward online management system** allows you to add or delete classes, manage your classes, plus view, print, or export all class and individual student reports.

Click Help for simple, step-by-step support that is **available in six languages**: English, Spanish, Korean, Arabic, Chinese, and Japanese.

FOR ADDITIONAL SUPPORT
Email our customer support team at grammarsensesupport@oup.com and you will receive a response within 24 hours.

FOR ADMINISTRATOR CODES
Please contact your sales representative for an Administrator Access Code. A Teacher Access Code comes with every Teacher's Book.

Teacher's Book Introduction
Susan Iannuzzi

About the Teacher's Book

THE CHAPTERS

- **Overview:** Each chapter of the Teacher's Book begins with an overview of the grammar presented in the Student Book chapter. It enables the teacher to focus on the main points covered in the chapter, and highlights difficulties students may have with the structures.

- **Grammar in Discourse:** This section provides directions to help the teacher effectively teach the Before You Read, Read, and After You Read activities in the Student Book. It suggests creative ways to activate background knowledge, offers innovative reading strategies, and gives tips on checking comprehension.

- **Form:** This section offers two alternative ways to teach the inductive Think Critically About Form exercises: Method 1 for students who are unfamiliar with the structure and may need extra support, and Method 2 for students who are already familiar with the structure and may be able to work more independently. The section also contains step-by-step instructions for presenting the Form Charts, and directions for utilizing the Special Sections such as Informally Speaking.

- **Meaning and Use:** This section offers advice on teaching the inductive Think Critically About Meaning and Use exercises. It also provides step-by-step instructions for presenting the Meaning and Use Notes and directions for using the Special Sections such as Vocabulary Notes and Beyond the Sentence.

- **Trouble Spots:** These notes, placed at strategic points throughout the Teacher's Book, alert the teacher to problems that students may have with the grammar. They suggest how to address these problems effectively, and, where relevant, direct the teacher to parts of the Student Book that clarify or offer practice of the grammar point.

- **Cultural Notes:** These occasional notes give background about American culture that students typically do not know, and that may help their understanding of the topic in the Student Book. The teacher can relay this information to students as appropriate.

- **Writing:** This section provides step-by-step instructions for guiding students through each stage of the scaffolded writing task at the end of each chapter.

AT THE BACK OF THE BOOK

- **Student Book Audioscript:** A complete audioscript is available for every listening activity in the Student Book.

- **Student Book Answer Key:** The Teacher's Book contains the answers to all the Student Book exercises. (The answers are not available in the Student Book.)

Teaching Techniques for the Grammar Classroom

TEACHING STUDENTS AT THE HIGH-INTERMEDIATE TO ADVANCED LEVEL

Students at this level will have already been exposed to most of the forms as well as some of the meanings and uses of the structures presented in the Student Book. They may still need to focus on form issues in more complex clauses and verb phrases, such as word order, agreement, and multiple auxiliary verbs. They may also be interested in the finer details of meaning and use, such as the distinction between the present perfect and present perfect continuous, the use of stative verbs in continuous forms, or the subtle differences in meaning and use between gerunds and infinitives. *Grammar Sense 3* provides students at this level with the necessary guidance and a wealth of exercises to practice and expand their grammar knowledge.

PRESENTING THE FORM SECTIONS

Think Critically About Form Exercises

One of the most challenging aspects of teaching grammar is finding clear and concise ways to present new forms to students. The Think Critically About Form exercise in each chapter is a series of inductive tasks in which students work on *identifying* the target structure and its most important structural features. In these exercises, students are asked to return to the reading text in the Grammar in Discourse section of the chapter, and follow the steps to recognize or systematically analyze key aspects of the form (such as the number of different parts in a structure, the addition of suffixes, word order, agreement, and so on). This serves as an introduction to the structural features illustrated and explained in the Form Charts, which students may then consult to check their answers.

Form Charts

In chapters with particularly challenging structures, you may need to help students work through and internalize the information in the Form Charts before they start on the form exercises. The following is a compilation of some of the most successful techniques for guiding students through this section. Choose appropriate techniques based on your teaching style, class size, class level, and students' previous experience with the grammar point. Most importantly, vary the techniques you use to accommodate the different learning styles of your students—some students may prefer to read and discuss every example in the chart before moving on to the exercises, while others may need to study the material less intensively.

Whole Class Techniques

1. After students have finished the Think Critically About Form exercise, ask them to close their books. Elicit examples of the target grammar from the reading text by asking questions that will produce the target grammar. When possible, personalize your questions. For example, to elicit possessive pronouns, hold up a book and ask, *Whose book is this?* with the aim of eliciting responses such as *It's his. It's mine.* When students answer, write their responses on the board. If a student gives an incorrect response (e.g., *It is her.*), you should still write it on the board. Incorrect answers are as valuable as correct ones, because they can be used to focus students' attention on the structure. Likewise, if a student answers correctly but uses a different structure than the one you wish to focus on (e.g., *It's her book.*), write this answer on the board and ask if anyone knows an alternative response (e.g., *It's hers.*). Write students' responses on the board, then have them open their books to the Form Charts and find sentences that use the same structures as those on the board.

2. To focus more closely on the various parts of a structure, copy the chart headings onto the board, or construct other types of contrastive charts (e.g., *-s/-es/-ies*, or singular/plural, etc.). Elicit examples from the reading text to illustrate each point, or ask students to create

their own examples. Have individual students come to the board and fill in the charts. Then ask the rest of the class to decide if their examples are correct or not, and to explain why.

3. After students have finished the Think Critically About Form exercise, ask them to silently review the Form Charts for a few minutes. Assess their understanding of the charts by asking questions about the form. For example, for *Yes/No* questions in the present tense, you might ask *Where is the subject? What word does the question begin with? How many* Yes/ No *question forms are there?* In this way, you will be able to judge whether students have fully understood the form of the target grammar.

Pair or Group Work Techniques

1. Divide students into pairs or small groups. Assign each group a Form Chart and ask them to read and study the information. Then ask each group in turn to present the form in their chart to the rest of the class. Students can use their own example sentences to aid their presentation, in addition to those provided in the book.

2. Divide students into pairs or small groups. Write two correct sentences and one incorrect sentence on the board. (Make sure the error is one of *form*, not meaning and use.) Tell students that one sentence is incorrect. Ask them to work together to identify the incorrect sentence by looking at the Form Charts. Some students may know the answer without using the charts, but ask them to point to the information or example in the chart that shows why it is incorrect. This insures that they know how to interpret the charts.

PRESENTING THE MEANING AND USE SECTIONS

Think Critically About Meaning and Use Exercises

Once students have grasped the form of a given structure, the next challenge is to find creative and engaging ways to help them understand the meaning and use. The Think Critically About Meaning and Use exercises do just this by offering carefully constructed examples, often in the form of minimal pairs, and asking students to use contextual cues to draw inferences about key aspects of meaning and use. These inductive tasks serve as an introduction to the features of meaning and use that are further elucidated in the Notes that follow.

Meaning and Use Notes

Students need to read and absorb the Meaning and Use Notes before starting the exercises. What follows are some techniques for helping students work through the Meaning and Use Notes. Regardless of the technique you choose, it is important that you have a clear understanding of the scope of the Meaning and Use Notes before you present them. In some instances, a particular structure may have multiple meanings and uses, but the chapter will not address all of them. In Levels 1 and 2, certain meanings and uses of structures are omitted to avoid overwhelming the students with too much information, while in Level 3, basic meanings and uses may be de-emphasized in order to focus on more complex issues.

Whole Class Techniques

1. Give students an opportunity to read and ask questions about the Meaning and Use Notes. Check their understanding by writing several original sentences on the board and asking them to match the meaning and use in each sentence to the Meaning and Use Notes. With more advanced students you can include a few incorrect sentences among the examples and have students identify correct and incorrect meanings and uses. Before you do this, be sure you have a firm grasp of the meaning and use you are focusing on so you can clearly explain why the examples you provided are correct or incorrect.

2. If there are several Meaning and Use Notes, or if you think students will find the content challenging, have them read and demonstrate their understanding of one Note at a time. Once they have read the Note, elicit sentences that demonstrate the meaning and use of the

Note they just read. For example, to elicit examples of *must be* and *must feel* to show understanding of someone's feelings (Student Book 3, page 154, Note 4B), make up sentences such as *I didn't eat dinner last night. I ran ten miles yesterday.* Ask students to respond. This should elicit sentences such as *You must be hungry. You must feel exhausted!*

Pair or Group Work Techniques

1. Divide students into pairs or small groups. Assign each pair or group a Note and ask students to study it. Then ask each pair or group to present their Note to the rest of the class. Students can create their own example sentences to aid their presentation, in addition to those provided in the book. Again, be sure you fully understand the meaning and use in question so you can tell students whether their examples are correct or incorrect and, most importantly, *why* they are correct or incorrect.

2. Divide students into pairs or small groups. Have each pair or group read one Note and create two example sentences to illustrate the information presented in the Note. Ask each pair or group to come to the front of the class to explain the Note and write their example sentences on the board. Ask the class if the sentences are correct examples of the information in the Note. If not, call on individual students to suggest alternate correct sentences.

General Teaching Techniques

Grammar Sense contains a wealth of exercises covering all four skills areas: reading, writing, listening, and speaking. Depending on your students, curriculum, and time frame, these exercises can be taught in many ways. Successful grammar teaching requires skillful classroom management and teaching techniques, especially in the areas of elicitation (drawing information from students), grouping procedures (groups, pairs, or individuals), time management (lengthening or shortening exercises), and error correction (peer or teacher correction, correction of spoken or written errors).

ELICITATION

Elicitation is one of the most useful teaching techniques in the grammar classroom. In essence, elicitation draws information out of the students through the use of leading questions. This helps students to discover, on their own, information about grammar forms as well as meanings and uses. For example, to elicit the difference in meaning between a gerund and an infinitive when used after the verb *stop*, write the following sentences on the board: *Ed stopped to eat cake. Alan stopped eating cake.* Then, in order to elicit the difference in meaning between the two sentences, ask questions such as, *In which sentence did Ed eat cake? Which sentence suggests that Ed is on a diet?* These questions require students to analyze what they know about the grammar and make inferences about meaning.

Knowing when to elicit information can be difficult. Too much elicitation can slow the class and too little elicitation puts students in a passive position. Avoid asking students to judge whether something sounds natural or acceptable to them because, as non-native speakers, they will not have the same intuitions about English as native speakers.

GROUPING STUDENTS

Group work is a valuable part of language learning. It takes away the focus from the teacher as the provider of information and centers on the students, giving them the opportunity to work together and rely on each other for language acquisition. Shyer students who may be less likely to speak out in class have an opportunity to share answers or ideas. Your class level will inform how you approach group work. Be sure to circulate among groups to monitor the progress of an activity, particularly at lower levels, and to answer any questions students cannot resolve on their own. Although students at the higher levels are more independent and can often manage their own groups, be attentive to the activities at hand, ready to offer feedback and keep everyone on-task. In classes where the level of students is uneven, try varying the composition of the groups to make the learning process interesting for everybody. Sometimes you can pair up a higher-level student with a lower-level student to give him or her an opportunity to help another classmate. However, other times you may want to group all the higher-level students together and offer them additional, more challenging activities. It is useful, especially in discussion activities, to conclude with a culminating task in which one or more students report back something (results, a summary) to the rest of the class using the target structure. This helps to refocus the class on the structure and provide a conclusion to the activity.

TIME MANAGEMENT

Some exercises are divided into steps, making it possible to shorten an activity by assigning part of it for homework or by dividing the class into two groups and assigning half the items to each group. Similarly, exercises can be lengthened. Many of the exercises in *Grammar Sense* require students to ask for or offer real-life information. You can ask students to create additional sentences within these activities, or have them do an activity again with a different partner. If your class does an activity well, ask them to focus on other aspects of the form, for example, transforming their affirmative sentences into negative ones, and vice-versa.

CHECKING EXERCISES

How you check exercises with students will depend on the level you are teaching. Having students check their answers in pairs or groups can be an effective technique, because it makes students revisit their work and resolve with other students the mistakes they have made. With lower levels, this requires careful teacher supervision. It is also possible at all levels to check exercises as a class, elicit corrections from students, and offer necessary feedback. It is often useful, especially for correcting editing exercises, to use an overhead projector. Be careful not to single out students when correcting work. Aim instead to create a supportive atmosphere whereby the class learns through a group effort.

CORRECTING ERRORS

Students can often communicate effectively without perfect grammar. However, in order to succeed in higher education or the business world, they need to demonstrate a high level of grammatical accuracy, and to understand that even a small change in form can sometimes result in a significant change in meaning. As students become aware of this, they expect to be corrected. However, their expectations as to how and when correction should be offered will vary. Many teachers have difficulty finding the optimal amount of correction—enough to focus students on monitoring errors, but not so much as to demoralize or discourage them. It is important to target specific types of errors when correcting students, rather than aiming to correct everything they say or write. The focus of the current lesson and your knowledge of your students' strengths and weaknesses will dictate whether you focus on form, pronunciation, meaning, or appropriate use. Discuss error correction with your students and determine how *they* would like to be corrected. Aim to combine or vary your correction techniques depending on the focus of the lesson and the needs of your students.

Spoken Errors

There are a variety of ways to correct spoken errors. If a student makes an error repeatedly, stop him or her and encourage self-correction by repeating the error with a questioning (rising) tone, or by gesturing. Develop a set of gestures that you use consistently so students know exactly what you are pointing out. For example, problems with the past tense can be indicated by pointing backwards over your shoulder, future time can be indicated by pointing your hand ahead of you, and third person can be shown by holding up three fingers. (Be careful not to choose gestures that are considered offensive by some cultures.) If your students feel comfortable being corrected by their peers, encourage them to help each other when they hear mistakes. Another option is to keep track of spoken errors during an activity, and then at the end elicit corrections from the class by writing the incorrect sentences you heard on the board. This way, students are not singled out for their mistakes, but get the feedback they need.

Written Errors

It is important to encourage students to monitor their written errors and learn strategies to self-correct their writing. Establish a standard set of symbols to use when marking students' work. For example, *pl* for *plural, agr* for *agreement, s* for *subject, v* for *verb*. When you find an error, do not correct it, but instead mark it with a symbol. Students will have to work out the exact nature of their error and correct it themselves. This will reduce your correction time and encourage students to learn for themselves by reflecting on their errors. Peer correction is another useful technique by which students can provide feedback on a partner's work. In order for it to be effective, give students clear and limited objectives and do not expect them to identify all the errors in their classmate's work. Note that students may be resistant to peer correction at first, and nervous about adopting others' mistakes. But once they develop trust in one another, they will be surprised at how much they can learn from their classmates.

1

The Present

Overview

The simple present is used to describe actions or states that have a general, habitual, and unchanging sense (e.g., *I work at the library.*). The present continuous is used to describe events that are happening now or around now and don't last forever (e.g., *They are eating lunch.*). Note that stative verbs (e.g., *know, believe, have*) are sometimes difficult for students because some of these verbs are not generally used in the present continuous (e.g., *know*), and others have a different meaning in the present continuous than in the present simple (e.g., *I have a car.* vs. *I am having a good time.*).

Form: The key challenges are remembering

- the *-s/-es* for third-person singular (*he, she,* and *it*) in the simple present.
- the *do* auxiliary in simple present questions and negatives (e.g., *Do you work on weekends? I don't sleep enough.*).
- the *be* auxiliary and the *-ing* ending of the main verb in the present continuous.

A GRAMMAR IN DISCOURSE

You Snooze, You Win at Today's Workplace

A1: Before You Read

- Give students five minutes to discuss the questions in their book in pairs.
- Call on several students to share their answers.
- Then ask *How do you feel when you don't get enough sleep?* Allow students to share their responses.
- Ask the class if they know the meaning of the expression "You snooze, you lose." If they don't ask them if they know the meaning of the

word "snooze" (to sleep, to nap). Now have the students try to guess the meaning of the expression. If they still don't understand, explain that this is a saying that means if you sleep late or don't pay attention, you might miss an opportunity for success.

- Ask students why they think the title of the article is "You Snooze, You Win at Today's Workplace." (Sleeping at work can refresh people and make them more productive workers.)

A2: Read

- Before students start reading, ask them to scan the article to find the sentence that describes the average American company's attitude toward napping at work (paragraph 7, line 52 . . . *napping on the job is not yet acceptable.*).
- Ask students whether the title of the article seems to support this attitude. (It does not.)

Cultural Notes

Explain that the trend in many workplaces across Europe, Great Britain and the States is to work more than the typical eight-hour day. Because of this, many employees are tired all the time.

La-Z-Boy is a well-known furniture company that specializes in recliners. The name La-Z-Boy is often used as a synonym for the word *recliner* (e.g., *My grandfather sits on his La-Z-Boy all day and watches TV.*).

A3: After You Read

- Have students answer the true/false questions individually and mark the places in the article where they found their answers.
- Ask them to compare answers with a partner.
- Circulate and note any problematic items; then go over these with the whole class.
- As a follow-up activity, write the following questions on the board and have students

discuss them in pairs: *Should employers permit employees to nap at work? Do you ever nap at work? Do you know anybody who naps at work?* (Students may have differing views of daytime resting.)

- Then bring the class together and have students share views.

B) FORM

The Simple Present and the Present Continuous

THINK CRITICALLY ABOUT FORM

Method 1
(For students not familiar with the structure)

- **1. IDENTIFY** Tell students to look at the underlined words in line 2 of the article *(You're sitting)*. Elicit the verb form (the present continuous). Ask how many parts the verb has (two: *be* and verb + *-ing*). Have students go through the article to find six more verbs in the present continuous.

- Call on individual students for the present continuous verbs, and have them write these verbs in one column on the board. Remind students that some of the verbs are negative and some don't have the auxiliary right before the main verb, e.g., line 2, *You're sitting at your desk and plowing.* Ask one of the students to label the column *Present Continuous.*

- Have students find the simple present verb underlined in line 7 *(sounds)* and ask them to tell you how many parts this verb has (one: base form of verb + *-s* for third-person singular). Tell students to find six more verbs in the simple present and have them write them in another column on the board. Have one student label this column *Simple Present.*

- Ask students to examine the two lists of verbs on the board and tell you the differences in form. Students should notice the following: Present continuous consists of *be* in the simple present tense (*am, is,* or *are*) and verb + *-ing,* whereas the simple present consists of the base form of the verb for the entire conjugation except for third-person singular, which takes an *-s/-es* ending.

- **2. COMPARE AND CONTRAST** Ask students to find a negative simple present verb (*they're not,* line 26; *doesn't stop,* line 29). Elicit how many parts the verb has. (*They're not* has two parts: *be* and *not. Doesn't stop* has three parts: *do* and *not* and verb.) Make sure students understand the difference in form by pointing out that *be* in the negative simple present consists of *be* and *not,* and other verbs consist of *do* and *not* and verb.

- Then ask students to find one negative present continuous verb (*are not getting,* line 20). Elicit how many parts the verb has (three parts: *be* and *not* and verb + *-ing*).

- **3. GENERATE** Ask students to work in pairs to change the sentences to *Yes/No* questions. Have two students write their answers on the board (*a. Does the average American sleep six hours a night? b. Are Americans sleeping less?*). Elicit or offer feedback as necessary.

- Explain that the simple present verb *sleep* requires the *do* auxiliary as a helping verb to form a question. The present continuous verb *are sleeping* only requires inverting the subject and the auxiliary *be* to form a question.

- Point out that in the simple present the verb *be* only requires inverting the subject and *be* to form a question (e.g., *Maria is tired.* becomes *Is Maria tired?*). It does not need the *do* auxiliary like other verbs.

Method 2
(For students familiar with the structure)

- Have students work in pairs to complete the activities.

- Give students a few minutes to refer to the charts to check their answers and review the structures.

- Call on students to go over the exercises. Discuss any disagreements and have students make any necessary corrections.

FORM CHARTS

- Have students read the simple present charts. As they read, write the following on the board in a column: *Affirmative Statement, Negative Statement, Yes/No Question, Short Answer,* and *Information Question.* Leave room after each category for example sentences.

- Allow students to ask any questions. Then call on a student for a new affirmative statement in the simple present (e.g., *I email my sister every night.*). Write this sentence next to *Affirmative Statement* on the board and elicit the other forms listed.

- Have students read the present continuous charts and repeat the procedure above for a new present continuous affirmative statement.

- Then have students write two *Yes/No* questions in the simple present using the verbs *be* and *want*.

- Have some students share examples on the board. Make sure students remember to use the *do* auxiliary for sentences with *want* and to just invert the subject and the verb *be*.

Informally Speaking: Omitting Auxiliaries and *You* (p. 11)

- Choose two students to read the text in the speech bubbles. Then tell the class you will play the recording and that they should listen to how the underlined form in the cartoon is different from what they hear. If needed, play the recording more than once.

- Have students point out the differences. (The cartoon reads *Are you feeling OK?* and *Do you have any aspirin?* whereas on the recording this is read *You feeling OK?* and *You have any aspirin?*) Explain that the form on the recording is considered more informal spoken English. Point out that the form in the cartoon is standard English and students should use this form when writing and speaking, although they may hear native speakers using the informal form.

C MEANING AND USE 1

Contrasting the Simple Present and the Present Continuous

THINK CRITICALLY ABOUT MEANING AND USE

- **1.–2. ANALYZE** Have students answer the questions.

- Call on individual students to explain the answers. (For question 1 the answer is b. The conversation is in the present continuous, describing something happening right now. The answer to question 2 is a. The conversation is in the simple present, describing a repeated action or a routine.)

- Ask the students to think of two more questions in the present continuous and simple present using the same verb (e.g., *What do you eat for breakfast? What are you eating?* or *What do you usually read? What are you reading?*). One sentence should be about something happening at the moment and another about a repeated action or a routine.

- Have students write their questions on the board, and then go over them as a class.

MEANING AND USE NOTES

- Divide the board into two columns and label them *Simple Present* and *Present Continuous*.

- Put the class into groups (or pairs if the class is small) and assign each group one of the Notes.

- Ask each group to read the Note and prepare to teach the explanation to the class. Tell each group to paraphrase the explanation and write original sentences, based on the examples, that clearly illustrate the particular aspect of meaning and use.

- For the group presentations, have one student present the explanation and another write the sentences in the correct columns. Have students check for any errors. Answer any questions.

Trouble Spots

Meaning and Use Note 2B explains a potentially challenging aspect of the present continuous: the extended present. Point out that with this usage, the activity is not happening right now but it is in progress over a period of time *around* now. Emphasize the underlying principle of the present continuous: The action is changing, not permanent. Direct students to the time expressions, such as *this week* and *these days*, which stress the temporary nature of the activity.

Beyond the Sentence: Introducing a Topic with the Simple Present (p. 16)

This section gives students practice with the meaning and use of grammar as it functions naturally in extended discourse such as paragraphs and conversations.

- Tell students to read the Note. Call on one student to summarize it.

- Have students examine the verbs in bold and tell you how many tenses were used in the passage (two—simple present and present continuous).

- Ask students which verbs refer to unchanging, habitual situations (*suffer, are, wake up, feel, can affect*) and which verb refers to a changing, "in progress" situation (*is becoming*).

D MEANING AND USE 2

Verbs with Stative Meanings vs. Verbs with Active Meanings

THINK CRITICALLY ABOUT MEANING AND USE

- Have students underline the verb in each sentence.

- **1.–2. CATEGORIZE** Then on the board make two columns titled *Actions* and *States/Conditions*. Ask students to tell you the two verbs that should go in the *Actions* column (*use* and *do*) and the three verbs that should go in the *States/Conditions* column (*have, be,* and *feel*). Write the verbs in the appropriate columns.

Trouble Spots

In general, because stative verbs express unchanging states or conditions, they do not typically occur in the continuous (e.g., *know, believe,* and *have*). However, avoid telling students that stative verbs *never* use the continuous or that they *always* use the simple present. There are times, as students will see later in the chapter, when we want to stress that a state or condition is temporary (e.g., *My kids are being so good today.*), when a stative verb is used actively (e.g., *I'm tasting the soup to see if it's too hot.*), or when we use stative verbs to stress emotion (e.g., *I'm just loving this book!*). (See Informally Speaking on page 22 of the Student Book for more information.) In these cases, the present continuous is used.

MEANING AND USE NOTES

By now, students should have begun to see that stative verbs express a more permanent meaning than active verbs because they refer to a condition or state and are therefore usually used in the simple present. However, students should also realize that some stative verbs can be used in the present continuous with active meanings that are different from the stative meaning (e.g., *I have a pen. I'm having lunch.*).

- Give students time to read through the Notes and ask questions.

- Then write the following verbs on the board: *know, taste, have, feel, weigh, sound.*

- Put students into pairs and have them write one sentence in the simple present for each of the verbs in the list above. Then tell them to write four new sentences putting the verbs in the present continuous. Point out that two of the verbs cannot be put in the present continuous.

- Combine the pairs into groups of four and have them compare their sentences. Put the following questions on the board and have the groups answer them:

  Which two verbs cannot be put into the present continuous? (know, sound)
  Why not? (These are stative verbs that cannot be used as action verbs.)
  Can you think of other examples of such stative verbs? (e.g., mean, believe, need, seem, own, mind, appreciate)
  Compare the meaning of the verbs in the present continuous sentences and the simple present sentences. Do they differ? (Yes, the meanings differ. Note that for the verb feel, if both sentences refer to physical sensations [e.g., I feel OK. He is not feeling well today.] then there is no difference in meaning. See Note 3. But if the sentence has an active verb, then the meaning of feel is different [e.g., She is feeling the fabric to see if she likes it.] Feel means touch.).

  Refer students to Notes 2A, 2B 2C, and 3 to check their answers.

- Bring the class together to go over the answers to the questions. Then call on students to read their sentences for the different verbs and tenses. Note any problematic ones and write them on the board. Try to elicit corrections from students. Answer any outstanding questions and discuss any disagreements.

Informally Speaking: Expressing Emotions in the Continuous (p. 22)

- Choose two students to read the text in the speech bubbles. Then tell the class you will play the recording and that they should listen to how the underlined form in the cartoon is different from what they hear. If needed, play the recording more than once.

- Have students point out the differences. (On the recording the present continuous is used for the stative verbs *love* and *hate*, and in the cartoon the present simple is used.) Explain that the form on the recording is considered more informal English. Point out that the form in the cartoon is standard English and students should use this form when writing and speaking, although they may hear native speakers using the informal form.

WRITING

THINK CRITICALLY ABOUT MEANING AND USE

- Have students do A individually. Then, in small groups, have them compare answers and discuss any differences.

- Have them stay in groups and do B.

- As a class, review any difficult items from A. Then elicit answers to B:

  1. COMPARE AND CONTRAST ("I'm writing a book" means that someone is writing a book in the extended present (i.e., at this period of time). "I write books" implies that the person earns his or her living from being a writer. The person may or may not be writing a book at the present time but he or she has probably has written one or more books in the past and expects to write more in the future.)

  2. PREDICT (Answers will vary. Some examples are: 1. *It's a novel about a girl's life in Puerto Rico*; 3. *She repairs computers, and she*

loves her job; 5. *We're learning about modern French culture at the moment.*)

WRITE

The purpose of this activity is to give students practice in using the simple present and present continuous by writing a profile for a social networking site.

1. Brainstorm

As a class, start a brainstorm on the board about life as a new college or university student. Write the brainstorming categories on the board, and elicit the kinds of details that students might write about. Have students work individually to make brainstorming notes on being a new student at a college or university.

2. Write a First Draft

Before students begin writing, make sure they have read the checklist in the Edit section. Also have them look at the example on page 26. Remind students to use the best points from their brainstorming notes to write their profile.

3. Edit

Direct students to read and complete the self-assessment checklist on page 26. Ask for a show of hands for how many students gave all or mostly *yes* answers. If desired, ask students to comment on some of the errors they found.

4. Peer Review

Pair students and direct them to read each other's work. Ask students to answer the questions in the checklist and discuss them. Give students suggestions of helpful feedback: e.g., *You haven't said anything about your schedule. Could you add information? / You wrote* I be going *here. Those are the right verbs, but do we want to use* be *or another form of* be?

5. Rewrite Your Draft

Students should consider their partners' comments from the peer review and rewrite as necessary. Encourage students to proofread their work again before turning it in.

2 The Past

Overview

The simple past and the past continuous are often used together to clarify the order of past events. The past continuous can give background information to completed events in the simple past (e.g., *I was sleeping when the phone rang.*). The meaning and use of these verb forms can be confusing for students because the choice of form depends entirely on context. For example, to emphasize that an activity was completed, the simple past is used (e.g., *She drove home.*). However, in order to emphasize that the activity was in progress, the past continuous is used (e.g., *She was driving home.*).

Form: Students will likely continue to make errors with irregular simple past verb forms. Refer them to the list of irregular verbs in Appendix 6 of the student book.

A GRAMMAR IN DISCOURSE

A Night to Remember

A1: Before You Read

- Give students some examples of important news events (e.g., the collapse of the Berlin Wall in 1989, the death of Princess Diana in 1997, etc.) and write them on the board.

- Elicit a few other important recent news events and write them on the board. Put students into groups. Have them discuss where they were and what they were doing at the time these events happened.

A2: Read

- Ask students if they have seen the movie or know the history of the *Titanic*. Ask if anyone can give a brief summary of what happened to the ship. If no one can, provide a summary

yourself. (The *Titanic* was a luxury transatlantic passenger ship. The engineers who built the ship thought it was unsinkable, but on its first voyage from Britain to New York, it hit an iceberg and sank.)

- Explain key vocabulary such as *iceberg, crew* and *crash* as necessary.

- Tell students to read the excerpt individually. Have them note what each person or group of people was doing when the *Titanic* hit the iceberg.

- Divide students into small groups and have them compare their answers.

- Write the phrase *When the Titanic hit the iceberg* on the board. Call on each group to name one thing that was happening when the ship hit the iceberg. Write each answer on the board so that it completes the sentence (*one of the ship's officers was standing watch, the night baker was making rolls,* etc.).

- Ask a student to read the sentences on the board out loud.

A3: After You Read

- Have students do this exercise individually and mark the places in the text where they found the answers.

- Ask them to compare answers with a partner.

- Circulate and note any difficult or problematic items. Then go over these with the whole class.

- As a follow-up activity, write these questions on the board and have students discuss them in groups: *Do you think most of the passengers were frightened when the* Titanic *hit the iceberg? Why or why not? Do you think the crew was frightened? Why or why not? Do you know why so many of the passengers and crew of the* Titanic *died?* (They died because there weren't enough lifeboats.) *What do you think people have learned from the* Titanic *disaster?* (Better engineering and construction methods, better emergency preparation.)

The Simple Past, the Past Continuous, and Time Clauses

THINK CRITICALLY ABOUT FORM

Method 1
(For students not familiar with the structure)

- **1. IDENTIFY** Point out the underlined verb *banged* in the excerpt. Elicit how many parts this verb has (one: verb + *-d/-ed* for past tense). Explain that this is the regular form of the simple past.

- Ask students to call out three other regular simple past verb forms from the excerpt. Write them on the board in a column labeled *Regular Simple Past.*

- Point out the underlined word *was* in the excerpt. Elicit that *was* is the simple past of the verb *be*. Explain that *was* is an irregular simple past verb form. Tell students that irregular simple past verb forms must be memorized. Refer students to Appendix 6 in the Student Book for a list of irregular verbs.

- Call on students to find three irregular simple past verb forms in the excerpt and write them on the board in a column labeled *Irregular Simple Past.*

- **2. RECOGNIZE** Tell students to look at the circled verb form in the excerpt *(were watching)*. Elicit the name of this form of the verb (the past continuous) and ask how many parts the verb has (two: *was/were* and verb + *-ing*). Explain that with the past continuous, only the verb *be* is in the past. Elicit the past forms of the verb *be (was, were)* and write them on the board with their appropriate subject pronouns *(I/he/she/it was; you/we/they were).*

- Ask students to find six past continuous verb forms in the excerpt. Call on individual students for examples. Write them on the board in a column labeled *Past Continuous.*

Remind students that in some cases a single subject and auxiliary verb can be used for several main *-ing* verbs (e.g., line 29: *While they were playing and laughing*).

- Ask students to sort the verbs into two lists, singular and plural. Elicit that the verb *were watching* is plural—the subject is *they;* the verb *was standing watch* is singular—the subject is *George Thomas Rowe.*

- **3. ANALYZE** If necessary, ask students *What is a clause?* (a group of words that has a subject and verb). Direct students to the clause *while they were talking,* line 30. Explain that this is a time clause and that time clauses in this excerpt begin with *when, while,* and *before.*

- Ask students to find and mark some of the time clauses in the excerpt. Then elicit which form, the simple past or past continuous, is connected to each type of time clause. (*When* and *before* are connected to the simple past; *while* is connected to the past continuous.)

- Ask students if the time clauses come before or after the main clause they are connected to. (Some come before and some come after.)

Method 2
(For students familiar with the structure)

- Have students work in pairs to complete the activities.

- Give students a few minutes to refer to the charts to check their answers and review the structures.

- Call on students to go over the exercise. Discuss any disagreements and have students make any necessary corrections.

FORM CHARTS

- Read the simple past and past continuous example sentences in the charts out loud.

- Put students into groups and give each group a different set of four verbs (both regular and irregular, e.g., *sleep, walk, play, think*). Have each group write two sentences for each verb, one in the simple past and one in the past continuous (e.g., *Tamara slept on the couch. The baby was sleeping when we arrived.*). Each group should have a total of eight sentences.

- Circulate and offer feedback as necessary.

- Give students time to read through the remaining charts.
- Then have groups exchange sentences and put the other group's sentences into the negative (e.g., *Tamara didn't sleep on the couch. The baby was not sleeping when we arrived.*), and create information questions (e.g., *Where did Tamara sleep? Who was sleeping when you arrived?*) and *Yes/No* questions with short answers (e.g., *Did Tamara sleep on the couch? Yes, she did. No, she did not. Was the baby sleeping when you arrived? Yes, she was. No, she was not.*). Refer students to the charts to help them create the various structures.
- Have the groups exchange their questions again and check the structures the other group wrote. Answer any questions.
- If necessary, do a quick review of time clauses and main clauses. The main clause (also known as an independent clause) is a clause that can stand by itself (e.g., *My mother called me.*). A time clause is a dependent clause that cannot stand by itself. For example, the time clause *While you were sleeping* is not a complete sentence. It depends on the main clause for additional information. When you connect a time clause with a main clause, you get a complete sentence (e.g., *While you were sleeping, my mother called me.*).
- Have students read the sentences in the charts and note the time clauses, the main clauses, and the use of commas.
- Write several new sentences with time clauses on the board without commas:

  Before our teacher came into the room we were talking.

  While we were studying yesterday someone was listening to music outside.

  They were reading when someone turned off the light.
- Elicit the correct punctuation (commas are needed in the first two sentences: after *room* and after *yesterday*). Remind students that when the time clause precedes the main clause, there should be a comma after the time clause (e.g., *Before our teacher came into the room, we were talking.*).

Trouble Spots

Irregular past tense verbs are sometimes difficult even for more advanced students because their formation is not rule governed. The only way to learn the different forms of these verbs is to memorize them. Quizzes, spelling bee type games, and drills on these forms can help students remember them.

C MEANING AND USE 1

Contrasting the Simple Past and the Past Continuous

THINK CRITICALLY ABOUT MEANING AND USE

- **ANALYZE** Give students a minute to examine the two pairs of sentences and answer the question.
- Call on individual students to explain the difference between the sentences (Completed event: 1a and 2a; Unfinished event: 1b and 2b).
- Have students work in pairs to write a new pair of sentences, using a different verb, in the simple past and the past continuous.
- Call on several pairs to share their sentences with the class. Elicit the difference in meaning between the pairs of sentences.

MEANING AND USE NOTES

- Divide students into groups and assign one of the Notes to each group.
- Ask each group to read the Note and prepare to teach the explanation to the class. Tell each group to paraphrase the explanation and write new examples that clearly illustrate the particular aspect of meaning and use.
- Circulate as the groups work, answering questions and pointing out any problems in their example sentences.
- Ask one of the students in each group to present the explanation while another student writes the example sentences on the board. Ask the rest of the class if the paraphrase is accurate and if the example sentences are correct. If not, work together as a class to improve them.

Vocabulary Notes: Habitual Past with *Used To* and *Would* (p. 39)

These Notes remind students that both *used to* and *would* are used to talk about a repeated action that was true in the past but is no longer true now. The key difference between the two is that *would* is not used with states, but *used to* is.

- Tell students they are going to write sentences about things they used to do at different times in their lives, but no longer do. Write the following on the board: *When I was five, I . . . , When I was in high school, I . . . , etc.* Have students write four activities for each category. Remind students to start a description with *used to,* and then use *would* to provide details.

- Correct students if they use *would* with verbs that do not express action, and remind them to use *used to* instead.

- Finally have students write two sentences about things they didn't use to do. Remind students of the form change from *used to* to *use to* with negatives (e.g., *I didn't use to sleep late.*).

Beyond the Sentence: Using the Simple Past in Discourse (p. 40)

This section is intended to give your students practice with the meaning and use of grammar as it functions naturally in extended discourse such as paragraphs and conversations.

- Point out that a time expression indicates the verb tense. A time expression is usually necessary when there is a change in tense. For example, *I called Jill last weekend* shows past tense, and then, *She's back at work now* indicates a change to present.

- Ask students to read the two passages, paying close attention to the time expressions (*last week* in paragraph 1; *last weekend, this morning,* and *now* in paragraph 2). Talk about the tense changes in both paragraphs. (Paragraph 1 starts with the present and changes to the past. Paragraph 2 starts with the past and changes to the present.)

- Answer any outstanding questions.

D MEANING AND USE 2

The Simple Past and the Past Continuous in Time Clauses

THINK CRITICALLY ABOUT MEANING AND USE

- **1.–3. ANALYZE** Ask students to read the example sentences and questions in their book.

- Explain to students that before they answer the questions, they will show the meaning of the verbs in the example sentences with time lines.

- Draw a time line on the board like this:

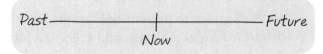

- Copy sentence a on the board and underline the verbs. Mark on the time line where the verbs in the sentence would fall sequentially.

a.

They <u>were talking</u> about the passengers when they suddenly <u>felt</u> the vibration.

were talking

Past ~~~~~~×————|————Future
felt Now

- Ask two students to copy sentences b and c on the board, underline the verbs, and draw time lines beneath them. See the models below.

b.

Some people <u>were sleeping</u> while others <u>were playing</u> cards.

were sleeping

Past ~~~~~~~~~~~|————Future
were playing Now

c.

When the bell <u>rang</u>, he <u>yelled</u> to his assistant.

rang yelled

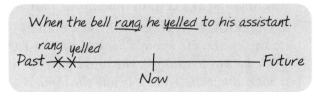

- Elicit corrections and suggestions from the class if the two students need help.
- Ask students to compare the three time lines and answer the three questions in the exercise.
- Come together as a class to check the answers and go over any problem areas (1. c; 2. a; 3. b).

MEANING AND USE NOTES

- Divide students into groups. Assign each group one Note to read and prepare to present to the class. Ask the students to draw a time line to accompany one of the sample sentences. Then have them write an original sentence and draw a time line to show its meaning.

- Ask each group to present the sample sentence with time line to the class, and then write the additional example sentence on the board. Have the group call a student from a different group to draw a time line for the new sentence. Allow the group to correct the time line if necessary. Offer assistance if students have any problems.

- Once every group has presented, offer additional examples if necessary, and answer any outstanding questions.

WRITING

THINK CRITICALLY ABOUT MEANING AND USE

- Have students do A individually. Then, in small groups, have them compare answers and discuss any differences.
- Have them stay in groups and do B.
- As a class, review any difficult items from A. Then elicit answers to B:

  1. COMPARE AND CONTRAST (Changing "were building" to "built" signifies that the action was completed. The original sentence [with "were building"] suggests that the action was ongoing at a certain time in the past.)

  2. GENERATE (Answers will vary. Some examples are: *He wrote a book about the* Titanic *while he was teaching at the university; He wrote a book about the* Titanic *before the famous movie came out; He became famous after he wrote a book about the* Titanic.)

WRITE

The purpose of this activity is to give students practice in using the simple past, past continuous, and habitual past with *used to* and *would* by writing an essay about a memorable experience from their childhood.

1. Brainstorm

As a class, start a brainstorm on the board about memorable childhood experiences. Write the brainstorming categories on the board, and elicit the kinds of details that students might write about. Have students work individually to make brainstorming notes on childhood memories.

2. Write a First Draft

Before students begin writing, make sure they have read the checklist in the Edit section. Also have them look at the example on page 48. Remind students to use the best points from their brainstorming notes to write their narrative essay.

3. Edit

Direct students to read and complete the self-assessment checklist on page 48. Ask for a show of hands for how many students gave all or mostly *yes* answers. If desired, ask students to comment on some of the errors they found.

4. Peer Review

Pair students and direct them to read each other's work. Ask students to answer the questions in the checklist and discuss them. Give students suggestions of helpful feedback: e.g., *Did you go to the beach just once or every year? What verb tense do we use if you only went once? What about if you went every year?*

5. Rewrite Your Draft

Students should consider their partners' comments from the peer review and rewrite as necessary. Encourage students to proofread their work again before turning it in.

3 Future Forms

Overview

Several future forms can be used to express future time. This chapter introduces the future continuous (e.g., *She will be working late.*) and reviews the four future forms: *will* (e.g., *I will do it tomorrow.*), *be going to* (e.g., *We are going to travel all summer.*), present continuous (e.g., *I am seeing a movie tonight.*), and simple present (e.g., *The bus leaves at 3:30.*). The choice of form depends on the context of the sentence. Frequently, more than one form is acceptable. Therefore, it is helpful to students to focus on areas where the choice of form indicates a clear difference in meaning and where specific rules for use exist.

Form: Students may find it confusing to use the simple present and the present continuous for future events (e.g., *My flight leaves at 6:00 tomorrow. Relatives are visiting me this weekend.*).

A GRAMMAR IN DISCOURSE

Trend Forecasters Predict Future

A1: Before You Read

- Elicit or explain the meaning of *forecasters* (people who predict what will happen in the future based on evidence).
  Then put the students into pairs to discuss the questions.

- Bring the class back together and have each pair of students share some of the predictions they came up with.

A2: Read

- Before students read, elicit or explain the meaning of *trend* (a currently popular idea or behavior). Then ask them to read the article to find out what two experts predict for the future.

- Divide students into three groups. The article discusses predictions about health, technology, and lifestyles. Assign one set of predictions to each group to paraphrase and present to the class.

- Have the other students agree or disagree with the predictions, and explain why.

A3: After You Read

- Have students do this exercise individually and mark the places in the text where they found the answers. Explain any new vocabulary.

- Ask students to compare answers with a partner.

- Circulate and note any difficult or problematic items. Then go over these with the whole class.

- Call on students to tell you which products and trends they chose.

- As a follow-up activity have each student write down one unique prediction about the future on a piece of paper.

- Then have students exchange papers with the person sitting next to them and write a response to the prediction. Tell them to explain if they agree or disagree with it.

- When they finish, have students get back their original papers and read their partner's opinions. Call on students to share their responses.

B FORM

The Future Continuous and Review of Future Forms

THINK CRITICALLY ABOUT FORM

Method 1
(For students not familiar with the structure)

- **1. IDENTIFY** Write the three future forms from the article (*be going to, will,* and *future* *continuous*) at the head of three separate columns on the board. Elicit one example of each future form from the article (e.g., *are going to buy, will enable,* and *will be buying*) and write them in the appropriate columns.

- Elicit the form of *be going to* (*am/is/are going to* + verb), *will* (*will* + verb), and the future continuous (*will be* + verb + *-ing*) for each example.

- Have students work individually to find other examples of each form in the article, and then have them compare lists with a partner.

- Ask three students to complete the columns on the board, one student for each form.

- **2. GENERATE** Ask students which other tense can be used to express the future (the simple present; e.g., *The train leaves at 10:00 A.M.*).

Method 2
(For students familiar with the structure)

- Have students work in pairs to answer the questions.

- Give students a few minutes to refer to the charts to check their answers and review the structures.

- Call on students to go over the exercise. Discuss any disagreements and have students make any necessary corrections.

FORM CHARTS

- Tell students to read the affirmative and negative statements in the future continuous charts.

- Call students to the board to write two new future continuous sentences, one affirmative and one negative, using two different verbs.

- Have students look at the examples in the other future continuous charts. Then call on them to change the new sentences they created to *Yes/No* questions and information questions.

- Tell students to close their books for a review of future forms. Write the names of the five future forms (*future continuous, future with* be *going to, future with* will, *present continuous as future,* and *simple present as future*) on the board. Read an example sentence from the charts for each form and call on individual students to tell you which form was used.

- Alternatively, divide students into groups and give them one example sentence for each type of future form on separate slips of paper. Have one student in each group read the sentence to the other group members and ask them to identify the type of future form used. Then have them open their books to confirm their answers.

C) MEANING AND USE 1

Contrasting *Will* and the Future Continuous

THINK CRITICALLY ABOUT MEANING AND USE

- Tell students to underline the future forms in each sentence (*I'll pick up* and *I'll be picking up; he'll be eating* and *he'll eat*).

- **1.–2. ANALYZE** Have students discuss Questions 1 and 2 with a partner, and then call on students to give their answers to the class (1. 1b describes a plan and 1a describes a promise; 2. 2a refers to an activity in progress and 2b refers to the beginning of an activity).

MEANING AND USE NOTES

- Help students understand that the essential difference between the future with *will* and the future continuous is that the future continuous indicates that the action will be in progress at a future time, whereas *will* indicates the start of an action in the future.

- To emphasize the difference between the forms, tell students to read the Notes. Have them pay careful attention to Note 2, which points out that *will* has a special meaning in the first person—to make a promise.

- Answer questions students have about any of the Notes. Then write new examples of paired sentences on the board—one with the future with *will* and one with the future continuous: *Kelly will drive to work at 8:00. Kelly will be driving to work at 8:00.* Ask students to explain the difference in meaning. (In the first, Kelly will *start* driving at 8:00; in the second, she will already be on the road at that time.)

D) MEANING AND USE 2

Contrasting *Be Going To*, the Present Continuous as Future, and the Simple Present as Future

THINK CRITICALLY ABOUT MEANING AND USE

- Ask students to examine the three sentences and explain in what situation they might hear each of them.

- **1.–2. EVALUATE** Have students answer the two questions in the exercise (1. a and c; 2. b).

- Give students a few minutes to refer to the Notes to check their answers.

- Go over the answers as a class. Discuss any disagreements and answer any questions students may have.

MEANING AND USE NOTES

- Explain that sometimes we can use different future verb forms to express the same meaning, but other times we have to use one specific form.

- Tell students to read the Notes. Then test their understanding by writing the following sentences on the board and asking which sentences are correct or incorrect and why.

    They're going to go camping soon. (Correct—future plan.)

    I begin my classes in two days. (Correct—set schedule.)

    *She's winning the race tomorrow. (Incorrect—this sentence describes a prediction, so the present continuous as future cannot be used.)

    He's having dinner at our house on Thursday. (Correct—future plan.)

- Tell students to work in pairs to create a two-line dialogue incorporating each of the correct sentences above (e.g., *Is Dave doing anything special this week? He's having dinner with us Thursday.*). Have each pair read them to the class and explain why the specific future form was used for each of the four dialogues.

- Next have the pairs write two new dialogues using any of the future forms. Refer them to the Notes as necessary.

- Then have the pairs share their dialogues on

E) MEANING AND USE 3

Contrasting *Will*, the Future Continuous, and *Be Going To*

THINK CRITICALLY ABOUT MEANING AND USE

- **1. IDENTIFY** Have students read each pair of sentences and underline the future verb forms.

- **2.–3. ANALYZE** Have students discuss questions 2 and 3 with a partner. Then bring the class together and call on students for the answers (2. 2a and 2b; 3. 1a and 1b).

- Discuss any disagreements and have students make any necessary corrections.

MEANING AND USE NOTES

- Have students read the explanation in Note 1B and remind them that the choice between *will*, the future continuous, and *be going to* can depend on the level of formality of the context. To reinforce this, write the following sentences on the board and call on students to tell you a possible context for each sentence.

    Experts say that humans will walk on Mars by 2050. (newspaper article or news report)

    Mommy, we're going to go on a field trip tomorrow. (child talking to parent)

    Mr. Vice President, what will the President discuss in his speech tomorrow? (journalist to politician)

    Will you be joining us for dinner this evening? (one business acquaintance to another)

  Point out that in more formal contexts *will* or the future continuous are sometimes used.

- Divide the class into groups and assign each group one of the remaining Notes.

- Ask each group to read their Note and prepare to teach the explanation to the class. Tell each group to paraphrase the explanation and write original sentences, based on the examples, that clearly illustrate the particular aspect of meaning and use.

- For the group presentations, have one student present the explanation and one write the new example sentences. Elicit and offer feedback as necessary.

Beyond the Sentence: Repeating Future Forms in Discourse (p. 71)

This section is intended to give students practice with the meaning and use of grammar as it functions naturally in paragraphs and conversations.

- Make sure that students understand the basic idea that *be going to* or the future continuous is used to introduce a topic, and *will* or present continuous as future are used in the sentences that follow to supply detail.

WRITING

THINK CRITICALLY ABOUT MEANING AND USE

- Have students do A individually. Then, in small groups, have them compare answers and discuss any differences.
- Have them stay in groups and do B.
- As a class, review any difficult items from A. Then elicit answers to B:

  1. ANALYZE (All of A's questions are in the simple past. All of B's responses use future forms.)

  2. EVALUATE (3, 6 [speaker uses future to explain why something was done in past]; 1 [speaker uses future for a sudden decision to do something in the near future in response to something that happened in the past].)

WRITE

The purpose of this activity is to give students practice in using *be going to, will*, the future continuous, and future time clauses by writing a blog post about life in the future.

1. Brainstorm

As a class, start a brainstorm on the board about what the future might be like in fifty years. Write several brainstorming categories on the board, and elicit the kinds of details that students might write about. As necessary, make suggestions to the class about topics they may want to write about, such as health, daily activities, and technology. Have students work individually to make brainstorming notes on the future in fifty years.

2. Write a First Draft

Before students begin writing, make sure they have read the checklist in the Edit section. Also have them look at the example on page 74. Remind students to use the best points from their brainstorming notes to write their blog.

3. Edit

Direct students to read and complete the self-assessment checklist on page 74. Ask for a show of hands for how many students gave all or mostly *yes* answers. If desired, ask students to comment on some of the errors they found.

DO I...	YES
organize my ideas into paragraphs?	☐
use *be going to* and *will* for predictions and expectations?	☐
use the future continuous for expectations and future activities in progress?	☐
use future time clauses to show the order of future events?	☐
use expressions like *I think*, *maybe*, and *probably* to show that I am speculating?	☐

4. Peer Review

Pair students and direct them to read each other's work. Ask students to answer the questions in the checklist and discuss them. Give students suggestions of helpful feedback: e.g., *The order of events is unclear here. Can you think of a time word or phrase that could help the reader understand when this event happened?*

5. Rewrite Your Draft

Students should consider their partners' comments from the peer review and rewrite as necessary. Encourage students to proofread their work again before turning it in.

4

The Present Perfect

Overview

Unlike the present and past tenses, which focus on one particular time period (e.g., *I live in Spain. I lived in Spain last year.*), the present perfect focuses on the link between the past and the present. The present perfect is used for a situation that started in the past and continues until now (e.g., *I have lived in Spain for ten years.*), or for a situation with no definite time specification that could have occurred any time up to the present (e.g., *I have lived in Spain.*).

Form: Mastery of the present perfect involves learning and remembering the spelling of many irregular past participles. Refer students to Appendix 6 of the Student Book. Give quizzes on the most common irregular past participles to help students learn them.

A GRAMMAR IN DISCOURSE

The Questions That Stump the Scientists

A1: Before You Read

- Explain that the article is about scientific discoveries and areas scientists still want to explore. Give students an example of something that scientists haven't figured out, such as how to cure the common cold, or why dinosaurs became extinct.

- Divide students into small groups to discuss the questions in their books. Remind them that there are no right or wrong answers.

- Have students share their ideas together as a class.

A2: Read

- Before students read, elicit or explain the meaning of the verb *to stump* (to make someone unable to answer). Look at the word

in context of the title of the article. Elicit what the title means (the questions that scientists are not able to answer).

- Tell students to read the first paragraph and explain what they think the main idea of the article is. (Although there have been many important scientific discoveries, there are still many more to be made.) Then point out that the article will explore three areas of science: memory, matter, and life on other planets.

- Organize a jigsaw reading. First, divide students into three groups and assign one of the three areas to each group. Ask students to read and discuss their section and then write a one- or two-sentence summary.

- When students finish, send one member of each group to another group so that there is at least one member representing each of the three areas. Each student will explain to the new group the section that he or she read.

A3: After You Read

- Have students do this exercise individually and mark the places in the text where they found the answers.

- Ask them to compare answers with a partner.

- Then bring the class together and ask students which statements are false (1, 3, 4, and 5). Call on individual students to turn them into true statements.

- As a follow-up activity put students into pairs and have them brainstorm some additional questions that have not yet been answered by scientists.

- Combine pairs into groups of four and let them share their ideas and discuss if they think the different questions will ever be answered (or if the questions maybe already have been answered).

The Present Perfect

THINK CRITICALLY ABOUT FORM

Method 1
(For students not familiar with the structure)

- As an introductory activity, write this sentence on the board: *I have visited India.*

- Underline *have visited* and elicit how many parts the verb has (two). Explain that this form is the present perfect and the parts of the verb are *have* (or *has*) and the past participle, in this case verb + *-ed.* If students don't know the term *past participle,* explain that it is a past verb form, like the past tense, but is used with *have* in the present perfect (e.g., *I walked.* vs. *I have walked.*). Explain that when the verb ends in *-ed,* this is a regular past participle. Elicit some more examples of regular verbs in the present perfect (e.g., *I have looked. She has lived. We have started.*).

- Now write this sentence on the board: *I have seen the Taj Mahal.*

- Underline *have seen* and explain that this form is also the present perfect, but the past participle does not end in *-ed.* Explain that this is called an irregular past participle and that these come in many forms. Elicit some additional examples of irregular verbs in the present perfect (e.g., *I have eaten a banana. This door has broken three times. I have told him the bad news.*). Tell students that the only way to learn irregular past participles is to memorize them. Refer students to Appendix 6 for lists of irregular verbs.

- **1. IDENTIFY** Direct students to the reading and have them call out the two underlined present perfect forms (*'ve come* and *have made*). Ask if the forms are regular or irregular. (Both verbs are irregular.) Then have students find seven more examples of the present perfect in the text. You may need to point out some of the irregular verbs.

- **2. ANALYZE** Elicit that *have* has two possible forms (*have* and *has*), and see if the students can find and explain them. (*Has* is only used for third-person singular.)

- **3. CATEGORIZE** On the board, draw two columns and label them *Regular Verbs* and *Irregular Verbs.* Elicit the difference between regular and irregular verbs. (Regular verbs have past participles that end in *-ed.* Irregular verbs have past participles that vary in form.) Then call students to come up to the board and write the examples of the present perfect they found in Question 1 in the appropriate columns. Elicit or offer corrections as necessary.

Method 2
(For students familiar with the structure)

- Have students work in pairs to answer the questions.

- Give students a few minutes to refer to the charts to check their answers and review the structures.

- Call on students to go over the exercise. Discuss any disagreements and have students make any necessary corrections.

FORM CHARTS

- Read the three example sentences in the first chart out loud as the students look at them in their books. Call on one student to identify the auxiliary (*have* or *has*), and on another student to identify the main verb (the past participle) in each sentence. Tell students to continue doing this in pairs until they have read all the examples in the charts.

- Ask students to write several new present perfect sentences: one affirmative, one negative, one *Yes/No* question with a short answer, and one information question.

- Call on several students to read their sentences. Make any necessary corrections.

Informally Speaking: Omitting *Have* and *You* (p. 84)

- Choose two students to read the text in the speech bubbles. Then tell the class you will play the recording and that they should listen to how the underlined form in the cartoon is different from what they hear. If needed, play the recording more than once.

- Have students point out the differences. (The cartoon reads *Have you seen any good movies lately?* On the recording the form is shortened to *Seen any good movies lately?*) Explain that the form on the recording is considered more informal English. Point out that the form in the cartoon is standard English and students should use this form when writing and speaking, although they may hear native speakers using the informal form.

C MEANING AND USE 1

Indefinite Past Time

THINK CRITICALLY ABOUT MEANING AND USE

- **1.–2. ANALYZE AND DIFFERENTIATE** Have students work in pairs to answer the questions (1. b; 2. a).
- Give students a few minutes to refer to the Notes to check their answers.
- Call on students to go over the answers. Discuss any disagreements and have students make any necessary corrections.

MEANING AND USE NOTES

- Ask students to read the Notes.
- Write other paired example sentences on the board to highlight the contrast in meaning between the present perfect and the simple past (e.g., *I've ridden on a motorcycle.* vs. *I rode on a motorcycle one time with my brother.*). Call on individual students to explain the difference. (The first sentence uses the present perfect because it refers to an indefinite time in the past. The second sentence uses the simple past because it refers to a specific time that is now completed.)
- Follow up this activity by having students write one present perfect sentence in their notebooks about foods they have eaten and one about places they have been to (e.g., *I've eaten Mexican food. I've visited Thailand.*).
- Have several students write their sentences on the board. Then, next to each sentence, have students write the same sentence in the simple

past. Remind students to specify a time, e.g., *last year, in 1980, in September.* Call on students to explain the difference in meaning between each pair of sentences.

D MEANING AND USE 2

Recent Past Time and Continuing Time up to Now

THINK CRITICALLY ABOUT MEANING AND USE

- **1.–3. EVALUATE** Have students read the example sentences and answer the questions with a partner.
- Call on students for answers to the questions (1. c; 2. a and b; 3. b). Have other students agree or disagree with the answers.

MEANING AND USE NOTES

- Tell students to read the Notes.
- Ask students how they know that the events in the example sentences in Note 1 are recent. (In some sentences there are clues such as *lately, recently,* and *just*; in other examples the context helps show that the event is recent—airport announcements mention recent arrivals; telephone recordings indicate that a call was just made; a ringing doorbell means that somebody has just arrived.)
- For the information in Note 2A, draw a horizontal time line like this:

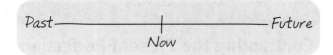

After you read each sentence in the Note out loud, ask students to tell you how to draw the events on the time line. The finished time line should look like this:

```
        1991                    2011
        (Born)                  (Now)
Past ─────┬──────────────────────┬───── Future
          ╲╱╲╱╲╱╲╱╲╱╲╱╲╱╲╱╲╱╲╱
                for 20 years
             ╲╱╲╱╲╱╲╱╲╱╲╱╲╱
                 since 1991
              ╲╱╲╱╲╱╲╱╲╱
                all my life
```

- Elicit from students that each of the sentences suggests the same thing: I still live here.

Trouble Spots

Many students have learned the meaning and use of *since* and *for* as part of the present perfect and may believe these words can be used only this way. Although *since* is used mostly with the present perfect, *for* is often used with other tenses (e.g., Simple past: *I lived in Japan for two years*. Future: *I'm going to study for an hour*.).

Vocabulary Notes: Adverbs That Express Recent Past Time (p. 91)

- Ask students to close their books.

- On the board, write three sentences from the Notes, one with *just*, one with *recently*, and one with *lately*. Ask students to explain the meaning of each adverb.

- Tell students to open their books and look at all six sentences. Have them note where the different adverbs can be positioned in a sentence, and how their meanings do not change. For example, these two sentences have the same meaning, but the adverb is placed differently in each one: *She's recently been away. She's been away recently.*

- Put students into groups and have them make up two sentences each with *recently* and *lately* in different positions. Circulate as the groups work and make sure they use the present perfect in the sentences.

E) MEANING AND USE 3

Contrasting the Present Perfect and the Simple Past

THINK CRITICALLY ABOUT MEANING AND USE

- **1.–2. ANALYZE** Have students read the two sets of sentences and note the verbs and other words that refer to time in the sentences. Do the first one with them (*I've worked; for three years; I love*). Then have them answer the questions.

- Call on individual students for the answers and to explain the meaning of the simple past and

present perfect in the sentences. (In 1a the person still works in Los Angeles. This is indicated by the use of the present perfect *'ve worked* and the use of the simple present in *I love my job*. In 1b the person no longer works there. This is indicated by the use of the simple past *worked* and *loved*. In 2a the speaker asks for an exact time of a past event, such as *last night* or *on March 5*, whereas in 2b the speaker wants to know only *if* the person has seen the movie, not when.)

- Discuss any disagreements and have students make any necessary corrections.

MEANING AND USE NOTES

Draw a horizontal time line on the board like this:

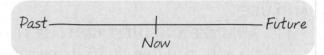

- Ask several students to come to the board to illustrate the verbs in the first few example sentences in Note 1. For the first pair of sentences (*She's been hardworking all her life. She was hardworking all her life.*), their time lines should look like this:

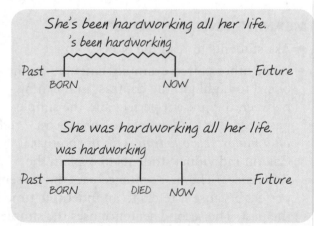

- Elicit feedback from the class to help the students at the board, and make corrections where necessary.

- Then have students read through the remaining two Notes in pairs and think up additional example sentences.

- Go over any questions regarding the explanations in the Notes. Then have students write their example sentences on the board. Elicit or offer feedback as necessary.

Beyond the Sentence: Introducing Topics with the Present Perfect (p. 97)

This section is intended to give your students practice with the meaning and use of grammar as it functions naturally in extended discourse such as paragraphs and conversations.

- Make sure that students understand the basic idea—that the present perfect introduces the general idea, and that the simple past is used in the sentences that follow to supply details about specific past events.

- To supplement this activity, bring in a short newspaper article in which the present perfect and simple past are used together. Try to find a short article of high interest, such as a story about a local hero, that does not have complex vocabulary.

- Give students copies of the article to read individually.

- Divide students into small groups or pairs and have them discuss the main idea of the article.

- Tell students to underline the verbs in the article and explain why the simple past or present perfect was used. For example, *John Doe <u>has</u> always <u>been</u> a hero in his neighborhood. Last year, the town <u>named</u> him their bravest resident.* The second sentence offers specific details by using the simple past to indicate definite past time.

- If possible, show the article on an overhead projector and go over the answers. Otherwise, ask students to look at their handouts. Call on students to read the verbs they underlined, identify the simple past or present perfect, and explain why each one was used.

WRITING

THINK CRITICALLY ABOUT MEANING AND USE

- Have students do A individually. Then, in small groups, have them compare answers and discuss any differences.

- Have them stay in groups and do B.

- As a class, review any difficult items from A. Then elicit answers to B:

1. PREDICT (Answers will vary. Some examples are: If speaker doesn't intend to go, he or she might add: "Unfortunately, I'm really busy at work this month, so I probably won't be able to go. If speaker intends to go, he or she might add: " . . . but I have plans to see it on Sunday.")

2. APPLY (If *just* is used, then the speaker means that he or she has finished the work in the recent past–say, a few minutes ago. In other words, answer b would be correct.)

WRITE

The purpose of this activity is to give students practice in using the present perfect and other verb tenses by writing a newspaper article about a recent event in their community or country.

1. Brainstorm

As a class, start a brainstorm on the board about something interesting that has happened recently. Ask questions to elicit specific details about the event, such as where it happened, who was involved, and how it might affect the students or other people. Then have students choose their own event and work individually to make brainstorming notes about what happened.

2. Write a First Draft

Before students begin writing, make sure they have read the checklist in the Edit section.

3. Edit

Direct students to read and complete the self-assessment checklist on page 100.

4. Peer Review

Pair students and direct them to read each other's work. Ask students to answer the questions in the checklist and discuss them. Give students suggestions of helpful feedback: e.g. *Should you use* have *or* has *with the subject of this sentence? / When did the action occur? Did it finish in the past, or is it still going on now?*

5. Rewrite Your Draft

Students should consider their partners' comments from the peer review and rewrite as necessary. Encourage students to proofread their work again before turning it in.

5 The Present Perfect Continuous

Overview

Like the present perfect, the present perfect continuous can be used to describe an activity that began in the past and continues up to now (e.g., *I have lived here since May. I have been living here since May.*). The focus on the ongoing activity, however, is often stronger in the present perfect continuous than in the present perfect (e.g., *I've been thinking about you.* vs. *I've thought about you.*). The present perfect continuous is also used to describe an activity that has recently ended (e.g., *I need a drink of water because I've been running.*). Students may need help identifying the subtle differences between the present perfect continuous and present perfect.

Form: Remind students that verbs with stative meanings are not usually used with continuous forms.

A GRAMMAR IN DISCOURSE

Longer Life in the Blue Zones

A1: Before You Read

- Before students discuss the questions, ask them if they personally know any people in their 70s, 80s, or even 90s. These could be grandparents, neighbors, etc.

- If students do know older people, ask them to think about the kinds of lives they lead. Write the following questions on the board for students to discuss in small groups: *Do they live alone? How is their health? Are they active? How are their lives different from when they were younger?*

- Ask students to discuss the Before You Read questions in small groups. Remind them to think about the lives of the older people they have just discussed.

- As an additional question, ask students *Why do some people live longer than others?*

- Have a student from each group summarize their answers for the class.

A2: Read

- Before students read the article, have them preview it by reading the title, the first sentence of every paragraph, and the conclusion.

- Call on a variety of students to predict some of the factors that Dan Buettner believes help people live longer, healthier lives.

- Have students read the article.

Cultural Notes

There is an increasing focus on the elderly in many countries as the percentage of older people in the population increases—a change brought about largely by improved health care, higher standards of living, and a lower birthrate. It is common to see seniors who are physically active and continuing to work. Some countries are concerned that this increase in elderly population will put a strain on support systems like social security, pensions, and health care. Others worry that there will not be enough young people to fill the workforce as people retire.

A3: After You Read

- Have students do this exercise individually and mark the places where they found the answers.

- Ask them to compare answers with a partner.

- Circulate and note any difficult or problematic items. Then go over these with the whole class.

- As a follow-up, write these questions on the board for the students to discuss in pairs: *Has this article changed the way you feel about getting older? Does getting older seem more positive or negative now than it did before you read the article?* Bring the class together and have students share their ideas.

The Present Perfect Continuous

THINK CRITICALLY ABOUT FORM

Method 1

(For students not familiar with the structure)

- **1. IDENTIFY** Write the underlined verb from the article *(has been traveling)* on the board. Do not underline the separate parts yet. Ask students to find five more examples of the present perfect continuous in the article. Then ask students to write them on the board.

- **2. RECOGNIZE** Refer students back to the original example on the board. Elicit and underline the auxiliaries (there are two: *has* and *been*) and point out the ending of the main verb *(-ing)*. Then ask several students to come up and underline the auxiliaries and the *-ing* in the examples they wrote on the board for question 1.

- **3. ANALYZE** Ask students to identify the two forms of *have* in the examples written on the board *(have* and *has)*. Elicit when each form is used *(has* for third-person singular, *have* for all other forms).

Method 2

(For students familiar with the structure)

- Have students work in pairs to answer the questions.

- Give students a few minutes to refer to the charts to check their answers and review the structures.

- Call on students to go over the exercise. Discuss any disagreements and have students make any necessary corrections.

FORM CHARTS

- Ask individual students *What have you been doing since our class started? What have you* not *been doing since our class started?* This should elicit responses such as *I've been learning grammar. I haven't been watching TV.*

- Write the students' responses on the board, even if the form is incorrect. Then have students look at the charts and correct any incorrect forms.

- Ask students to silently read the *Yes/No* questions, short answers, and information questions in the charts.

- Put students into pairs and have them ask and answer a new *Yes/No* question using a time expression and the verb *exercise* (e.g., *Have you been exercising these days? Yes, I have.*) and a new information question using a time expression and the verb *eat* (e.g., *What have you been eating lately?*). If necessary, elicit appropriate time expressions.

- Call on a few students to share their answers.

Informally Speaking: Omitting *Have* (p. 108)

- Choose two students to read the text in the speech bubbles. Then tell the class you will play the recording and that they should listen to how the underlined form in the cartoon is different from what they hear. If needed, play the recording more than once.

- Have students point out the differences. (On the recording, you don't hear the auxiliary *have. Have you been going* in the cartoon is read *You been going* and *I've been writing* is read *I been writing.*) Explain that the form on the recording is considered more informal English. Point out that the form in the cartoon is standard English and students should use this form when writing and speaking, although they may hear native speakers using the informal form.

C MEANING AND USE 1

Focus on Continuing or Recent Past Activities

THINK CRITICALLY ABOUT MEANING AND USE

- **1.–3. ANALYZE** Have students read the example sentences and answer the questions in pairs. Remind them to look for words in the sentences that indicate whether the action is continuing *(still, for months)* or has been recently completed.

- Bring the class together to go over the answers (1. b, she is still searching; 2. a, the person is reaching a conclusion; 3. c, the person has finished knitting).

MEANING AND USE NOTES

- Show students how to illustrate the first example sentence in the Notes on a time line on the board.

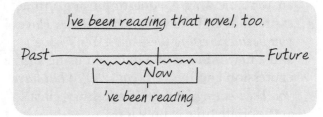

- Ask several students to come to the board to draw a time line for the other two sentences in Note 1. (The time sequence, showing the past continuing toward the future, should be similar to the time line for the first sentence.)

- Tell students to compare the time lines on the board with the explanation in the Note.

- Then have students read the other two Notes.

- To check their understanding of all the Notes, write the following sentences on the board. Tell students to indicate which Note the example refers to.

  I'm tired. I've been driving for three hours. (continuing activity)

  I'm glad we reached you. We've been trying to call you for two hours. (recent past activity)

  I've been planning to see you, but I haven't had time. (excuse)

  You look great. I can see that you've been exercising. (conclusion)

D) MEANING AND USE 2

Contrasting the Present Perfect Continuous and the Present Perfect

THINK CRITICALLY ABOUT MEANING AND USE

- **1.–2. EVALUATE** Give students a few minutes to analyze the two pairs of sentences.

- Ask which pair of sentences expresses the same meaning and which pair expresses different meanings (2a and 2b indicate that the action is still happening; 1a suggests that the action is still happening, whereas 1b indicates that it is finished).

- **3. INTERPRET** Ask students to look at 1a and 1b and decide who has probably finished the book (Vera), and who is probably still reading the book (Kathy).

Trouble Spots

Students may not fully understand the distinction between the present perfect and the present perfect continuous. Remind them that they both indicate a connection between the past and the present but with this difference: The continuous is more likely to refer to an action still in progress, whereas the present perfect can indicate that the action is finished (e.g., *I've been working for ten hours today, and I need to stop now.* vs. *I've worked a lot of hours this week, and I'm glad it's the weekend*.).

If the level of your class allows it, point out that sometimes the nature of the verb itself gives rise to the difference in meaning between the two verb tenses as in sentence pair 1 in Think Critically About Meaning and Use. Verbs such as *read* and *build* are processes that result in an accomplishment, e.g., a book is read or a building is built. As a result, use of the present perfect continuous shows that the process or action is still in progress, whereas use of the resent perfect indicates completion or accomplishment.

MEANING AND USE NOTES

- Have students read Note 1A and examine the sentence pairs. Ask *Is there a difference in meaning between these two sentences?* (No, there is no real difference.)

- Do the same with the sentence pairs in Notes 1B and 2, where the sentences do indicate a difference in meaning. After the students read each Note and examine the sentence pairs, ask *What is the difference in meaning between these two sentences?* (In Note 1B, the continuous indicates stronger emotion. In Note 2, the present perfect suggests that the activity was completed sometime in the past, whereas the present perfect continuous suggests that the activity is still happening or was very recently completed.)

- To check students' comprehension of the material after the caution note, write the following sentences on the board and ask students to tell you which one is correct, which one is incorrect, and why.

We've taken the bus to school three times this week. (Correct.)

*I've been eating pizza twice since I came here. (Incorrect—the present perfect continuous usually does not indicate how many times an action is repeated.)

Beyond the Sentence: Connecting the Past and the Present in Discourse (p. 116)

This section is intended to give your students practice with the meaning and use of grammar as it functions naturally in extended discourse such as in paragraphs and conversations.

- Tell students that the example conversation shows much of what they have learned about connecting past events to the present.

- Ask students to read the conversation and decide why each verb form in bold is used. (*I've been working* and *I've known* are situations that started in the past and that are continuing into the present; *did you know* has an end point and *got married* is a completed action in the past; *you've been married* started in the past and continues in the present; *celebrated* and *spent* are completed actions.)

- Go over any difficult or problematic items with the whole class.

WRITING

THINK CRITICALLY ABOUT MEANING AND USE

- Have students do A individually. Then, in small groups, have them compare answers and discuss any differences.

- Have them stay in groups and do B.

- As a class, review any difficult items from A. Then elicit answers to B:

  1. EVALUATE (Conversation A.)

  2. DRAW A CONCLUSION (In the original statement ["Cheryl has been going to Vancouver on business"], we understand that she has been to Vancouver a number of times in the recent past; she may or may not be there now. In the changed sentence ["Cheryl has gone to Vancouver on business"], it's clear that Cheryl is currently in Vancouver, but we have

no idea whether or not she has been there before or whether or not she goes there as part of her regular business activity.)

WRITE

The purpose of this activity is to give students practice in using the present perfect continuous and other verb tenses by writing a letter to the editor expressing their opinion on whether their country is taking care of its elderly population.

1. **Brainstorm**

   As a class, start a brainstorm on the board about your country's elderly population. Ask students to name several aspects of life that elderly people are usually concerned with, such as the cost and quality of medical care and how to enjoy retirement. Ask students to discuss what kinds of programs exist that address these concerns, and write one or two of their ideas on the board for each topic of concern. Have students work individually to add to the brainstorming notes about how the elderly are cared for in your country.

2. **Write a First Draft**

   Before students begin writing, make sure they have read the checklist in the Edit section. Remind students to use the best points from their brainstorming notes to write their letter.

3. **Edit**

   Direct students to read and complete the self-assessment checklist on page 120. Ask for a show of hands for how many students gave all or mostly *yes* answers.

4. **Peer Review**

   Pair students and direct them to read each other's work. Ask students to answer the questions in the checklist and discuss them. Give students suggestions of helpful feedback: e.g. *Is this the right form of* have? / *Did this action finish in the past, or is it still happening now?*

5. **Rewrite Your Draft**

   Students should consider their partners' comments from the peer review and rewrite as necessary. Encourage students to proofread their work again before turning it in.

The Past Perfect and the Past Perfect Continuous

Overview

The past perfect is used to show events in the past that happened before a specified past time or event (e.g., *I had eaten my lunch when she called me.*). The past perfect continuous is used to emphasize that an activity was in progress before a specified past time or event (e.g., *I had been eating my lunch when she called me.*). Sometimes students mistakenly think that the past perfect and past perfect continuous express events that were in the very distant past, when in fact, they simply show the relationship between past events, regardless of how long ago they occurred.

Form: Point out to students that the past perfect form of *have* is *had had* (e.g., *I had had a very busy day and was happy to finally be in bed.*).

A GRAMMAR IN DISCOURSE

Wild Thing

A1: Before You Read

- Tell students they will read about a woman's attempt to challenge herself. Ask what the expression *to challenge oneself* means (to attempt something very difficult in the hope of achieving it). Point out that the word *challenge* is used as both a verb and a noun (*to challenge oneself* and *to face a challenge*).

- Ask a few volunteers to give examples of challenges (e.g., *running a marathon, climbing a mountain, getting a degree*).

- Divide students into small groups and give them ten minutes to discuss the questions.

- Ask a member of each group to give one reason some people like to face great challenges. Write these on the board and leave them there for the After You Read discussion.

Cultural Notes

Outward Bound is a worldwide not-for-profit organization that creates opportunities for young people to experience outdoor adventures such as rock climbing, hiking, camping, and mountain climbing. The philosophy behind the organization is that young people are capable of realizing their potential only by facing challenges.

A2: Read

- Ask students to guess what an outdoor educational program might be. Don't confirm or correct their answers just yet, as they will check their guesses when they read the excerpt.

- Tell students to read the excerpt and mark all the reasons the writer gives for participating in Outward Bound.

- Put students into pairs to compare answers.

- Call on each pair to name one item from their list and write it on the board. Leave these answers on the board for the After You Read discussion.

A3: After You Read

- Ask students if they guessed correctly what an outdoor educational program is. Ask why the woman wanted to challenge herself by joining Outward Bound. (She wanted to break away from the "I-could-never-do-that" category.)

- Ask if her reasons for challenging herself were similar to any of the reasons listed on the board from the Before You Read discussion.

- Ask students to answer the true/false questions individually and then compare answers with a partner. Remind them to note the places in the excerpt where they found their answers.

- Call on individual students to give their answers and have them support their answers with information from the article.

- As a follow-up activity, ask students *Has anyone participated in a program like Outward Bound?* If yes, ask them to share their experience. Otherwise, ask *If given the opportunity, would you like to participate in a program like Outward Bound? Why? Why not?*

B) FORM

The Past Perfect and the Past Perfect Continuous

THINK CRITICALLY ABOUT FORM

Method 1
(For students not familiar with the structure)

- **1. IDENTIFY** Ask students to look at the underlined example of the past perfect in the excerpt. Point out that this is the negative form, and elicit the affirmative form *(had eaten)*. Write this on the board.
- Elicit the form of the past perfect *(had + past participle)*.
- Have students work in pairs to find four more past perfect verbs in the excerpt, and call on a volunteer to write the verbs on the board in their full forms *(had + past partiple)*.
- Ask students for the contracted form of *had* in the past perfect *('d)*. Locate an example in the text *(I'd admired)* and elicit the full form *(I had admired)*.
- **2. COMPARE AND CONTRAST** Write the past perfect continuous example sentence on the board *(She had been searching for a way to challenge herself.)* next to the list of the past perfect verbs. Underline the two auxiliaries *(had been)* and circle the main verb *(searching)*.
- Elicit the differences in form between the past perfect and the past perfect continuous. Point out *been* and the *-ing* ending on the main verb in the past perfect continuous.

Method 2
(For students familiar with the structure)

- Have students do the exercise in pairs.
- Give students a few minutes to refer to the charts to check their answers and review the structures.

- Call on students to go over the exercise. Discuss any disagreements and have students make any necessary corrections.

FORM CHARTS

- Put students into pairs and assign them roles of Students A and B. Explain that they will quiz each other on the forms in the charts: Student B will close his or her book and listen to Student A read a sentence from the charts in the past perfect. Student B will change the sentence to the past perfect continuous. Student A will then confirm that the answer was correct or tell Student B to try again:

  Student A: We had hiked for hours by then.

  Student B: We had been hiking for hours by then.

  Student A: Correct.

- Students should quiz each other for a few minutes on sentences from each chart (affirmative, negative, *Yes/No* questions, short answers, and information questions). When they finish, Student B will quiz Student A by reading the sentences in the past perfect continuous and eliciting the past perfect.

- As a final check, write the following sentences on the board and ask students if they are correct or incorrect and why.

  We had had a very big test when we saw you. (Correct.)

  *They had been liking baseball before they came to America. (Incorrect—*like* is a stative verb and isn't usually used in the continuous.)

  *My instructor had already wrote a letter to my advisor by the time I turned in my late assignments. (Incorrect—*written*, not *wrote*, is the past particle of *write.*)

Informally Speaking: Reduced Forms of *Had* (p. 129)

- Choose two students to read the text in the speech bubbles. Then tell the class you will play the recording and that they should listen to how the underlined form in the cartoon is different from what they hear. If needed, play the recording more than once.

- Have students point out the differences. (The cartoon reads *Dana had* whereas on the recording this is pronounced *"Dana'd"*). Explain that the form on the recording is considered more informal English. Point out that the form in the cartoon is standard English and students should use that form when writing and speaking, although they may hear native speakers using the informal form.

C   MEANING AND USE 1

The Past Perfect

THINK CRITICALLY ABOUT MEANING AND USE

- **1.–3. IDENTIFY AND RECOGNIZE** Have students work in pairs to answer the questions (1. a, *because a tree had fallen across my driveway*; b, *after she had enrolled*; c, *He'd been on a mountain climbing expedition*; d, *Although I'd been terrified*; 2. past perfect; 3. simple past).

- Give students a few minutes to refer to the Notes to check their answers.

- Discuss any disagreements and have students make any necessary corrections.

Trouble Spots

Students may expect the past perfect to always appear in a sentence with the simple past, which shows the later past event or time. Emphasize that the past perfect sometimes occurs without the simple past. Show students examples in which the second event or time is not indicated by the simple past but is nevertheless understood to be the later of the two events or times. For example: *At 11:00 A.M., I had already eaten a big breakfast and part of my lunch.* The action expressed by *had eaten* happened before 11:00 A.M. *By 2002, I had already studied two languages.* Studying the two languages happened before 2002.

MEANING AND USE NOTES

- Draw this time line on the board:

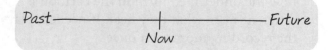

- Write the example sentences from Note 1A above the time line.

- Mark the time line to show the order of events in the sentence like this:

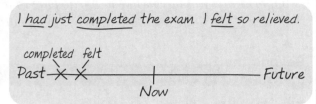

- Divide the class into groups and assign each group one Note.

- Ask each group to read the Note and prepare to teach the explanation to the class. Tell each group to paraphrase the explanation and write original sentences, based on the examples, that clearly illustrate the particular aspect of meaning and use. Tell students to use time lines in their explanations where helpful.

- For the group presentations, have one student present the explanation and another one write the new examples sentences and draw time lines. Elicit and offer feedback as necessary.

D   MEANING AND USE 2

The Past Perfect Continuous

THINK CRITICALLY ABOUT MEANING AND USE

- **ORGANIZE** Have students work in pairs to answer the question (1. a; 2. b).

- Give students a few minutes to refer to the Notes to check their answers.

- Discuss any disagreements and have students make any necessary corrections.

MEANING AND USE NOTES

- Divide students into three groups and assign one of the Notes to each group.

- Tell each group to read their Note and prepare to teach the explanation to the class. Each group should paraphrase the information and write an original sentence that clearly illustrates the meaning and use.

- Circulate as the groups work, helping with vocabulary for the paraphrase and pointing out any problems in the example sentences.

- As the groups present, ask the rest of the class if the example sentences are correct. If not, work together to improve them.

Beyond the Sentence: Adding Background Information in Longer Discourse (p. 139)

This section is intended to give students practice with the meaning and use of grammar as it functions naturally in extended discourse such as paragraphs and conversations.

- Ask students to read the example paragraph and guess what it is describing (a long and difficult plane trip).

- Elicit the mood-setting details that are expressed using the past perfect continuous and the past perfect (e.g., *We had been traveling for thirteen hours . . . ; The seat had been uncomfortable . . . ; I hadn't slept . . .*).

- As a follow-up to Exercise D5, Part B, have students underline the past perfect and past perfect continuous verbs they used in their paragraph. Ask them to explain why they used those forms when they did (to set the tone for the background of the event).

WRITING

THINK CRITICALLY ABOUT MEANING AND USE

- Have students do A individually. Then, in small groups, have them compare answers and discuss any differences.

- Have them stay in groups and do B.

- As a class, review any difficult items from A. Then elicit answers to B:

   1.–2. PREDICT (In sentence 4, if we changed *until* to *when*, then the answers to both a and b would be True; In sentence 8, if we changed *had been working* to *had worked*, both a and b would be True.)

WRITE

The purpose of this activity is to give students practice in using the past perfect, past perfect continuous and time clauses by writing an essay about a famous person's career.

1. Brainstorm

As a class, start a brainstorm on the board about famous people and some of the things that happen to them, such as winning awards, doing charity work, getting married, making speeches, having an accident or developing an illness, and so on. Write the topics on the board and elicit one or two details or examples for each. When students have the idea, ask them to choose an event from a famous person's life and to work individually to make brainstorming notes about what happened.

2. Write a First Draft

Before students begin writing, make sure they have read the checklist in the Edit section. Also have them look at the example on page 142. Remind students to use the best points from their brainstorming notes to write their essay.

3. Edit

Direct students to read and complete the self-assessment checklist on page 142. Ask for a show of hands for how many students gave all or mostly yes answers. If desired, ask students to comment on some of the errors they found.

4. Peer Review

Pair students and direct them to read each other's work. Ask students to answer the questions in the checklist and discuss them. Give students suggestions of helpful feedback: e.g., *Which event happened first? Would you use past perfect continuous for that or past perfect? / Part of this verb is missing. What auxiliary verb do you need to add?*

5. Rewrite Your Draft

Students should consider their partners' comments from the peer review and rewrite as necessary. Encourage students to proofread their work again before turning it in.

7 Modals of Possibility

Overview

This chapter introduces modals of present possibility, which are used to express guesses about present situations (e.g., *Jan must be sick again.*), and modals of future possibility, which are used for predictions about the future (e.g., *She should be here later.*). Note that some modals have more than one meaning. As in the examples above, *must* and *should* can function as modals of possibility. However, *must* can also function as a modal of obligation (e.g., *You must arrive on time.*), and the modal *should* can also function as a modal of advisability (e.g., *You should eat less junk food.*). Students are likely to be less familiar with the meaning and use of modals of possibility than these other forms. They may need help recognizing the subtle differences.

Form: Modals are followed by the base form of a verb. They never take the third-person *-s*, the *-ing* for continuous, or the *-ed* past tense endings. They do not require *do* for negation or questions.

A) GRAMMAR IN DISCOURSE

Could Too Much Exercise Hurt You?

A1: Before You Read

- Tell students that they will read an online post about fitness. Ask what it means to *stay fit* (to keep the body in good health and form). Point out the relationship between the word *fit* and *fitness*.

- Divide the class into three groups. Have the groups brainstorm answers to the question in the post and write their answers in a list. As needed, encourage students to think beyond their personal experiences in order to answer the question.

- Ask one student from each group to read a possible answer from their list aloud to the

class. Have members of the group explain any unclear ideas or answer questions the class might have about their answer.

Cultural Notes

Overexercising can be a problem for many children, too. Today, kids are being injured more often from excessive practice in sports, weight lifting, and running.

A2: Read

- Tell students to read the whole post once to find out what the author says about exercising too much.

- Have students note unfamiliar vocabulary.

- After they have read, clarify the meanings of unfamiliar words.

A3: After You Read

- Have students do this exercise individually and mark the places in the text where they found their answers.

- Ask them to compare answers with a partner.

- Circulate and note any problematic items. Then go over these with the whole class.

- Call on several students to tell you some of the problems of overexercising discussed in the article (poor immune systems, broken bones, etc.). Write these on the board.

- As a follow-up activity, write these questions on the board for the students to discuss in pairs: *Have you ever gotten sick after an intense period of exercise? What happened? Has reading this text helped you better understand what happened to you?* If students have not had this experience, ask them to discuss whether the text has changed the way they think about exercise.

- Bring the class together and have students share their ideas.

Modals of Present and Future Possibility

THINK CRITICALLY ABOUT FORM

Method 1

(For students not familiar with the structure)

- **1. IDENTIFY** Tell students to look at the underlined modal forms in the article *(should be, could have, may be showing)*. Ask them to find six more modals in the article. Call on students for examples and list these on the board. If necessary, remind them that *might* is also a modal.

- **2. CATEGORIZE** Make three columns, one labeled *be*, one labeled *be* + verb + *-ing*, and one labeled *other verbs*. Locate the first modal followed by *be* in the article and write this in the *Be* column *(should be)*. Then find the first modal followed by *be* + verb + *-ing* form, and write this in the second column *(may be showing)*. Finally, do the same with the first modal followed by a different main verb, putting it in the *other verbs* column *(could have)*.

- Have students work in pairs to find more modals and verbs that follow them, writing them in their notebooks in two columns like those on the board.

- Ask two volunteers to come up to the board to complete the two lists.

- Point to each item in the list *other verbs*. Ask students to identify each modal. Elicit that the verb that follows the modal is always in the base form (e.g., *might do, might have*).

Method 2

(For students familiar with the structure)

- Have students work in pairs to answer the questions.

- Give students a few minutes to refer to the charts to check their answers and review the structures.

- Call on students to go over the exercise. Discuss any disagreements and have students make any necessary corrections.

FORM CHARTS

- Give students some time to study the charts. Then write the following sentences on the board and call on students to tell you which form is used:

  That much exercise can't be good for you. (negative present modal)

  The Thompsons won't be walking tonight because of the rain. (negative future modal)

  Marcus has to be the fastest runner I've ever seen. (present modal)

  I might be buying a new bike next month. (future modal)

- Ask students how the negative statements are formed (the word *not* is put between the modal and the verb).

- Write these sample affirmative sentences on the board and have individual students come up to change them to the negative:

  She might be swimming this weekend. (She might not be swimming this weekend.)

  Steven could be taking a vacation with his brother. (Steven couldn't be taking a vacation with his brother.)

  Jen's garden must need a lot of attention. (Jen's garden must not need a lot of attention.)

- To check students' comprehension of the charts, ask whether the following sentences are correct:

  *There aren't any lights on. They mustn't be home. (Incorrect—*must not* has no contracted form as a modal of possibility.)

  *The baby isn't crying. He maybe sleeping. (Incorrect—the sentence requires modal + verb [*may be*], not the adverb *maybe*.)

- Ask students to compare the forms of *have to* and *have got to* with *ought to*. Elicit that *have to* and *have got to* change form for the third-person singular but *ought to* does not.

- Check students' comprehension of the Form Notes by asking whether the following sentences are correct:

  *It have got to be right. (Incorrect—*have* becomes *has* in third-person singular.)

  *She oughts to go with you. (Incorrect—*ought* never changes form.)

Trouble Spots

Students often confuse the phrasal modal *have got to,* which voices necessity (e.g., *I have got to finish my homework.*) with the verb *have got,* which means *have* (e.g., *I have got a lot of homework.*). On the board, write the sentence *I have a car.* Then write *I've got a car.* Explain that these sentences mean the same thing. Write the sentence *She has a motorcycle.* Then ask students to change this to the *have got* version *(She's got a motorcycle.).* Ask them to tell you what follows *has got* (a noun). Next, write the sentences *You've got to be hungry. She's got to know the answer.* Ask students to identify the phrasal modals (*you've got to* and *she's got to*). Underline them and ask students to tell you what follows the phrasal modals (the verbs in the base form, *be* and *know*).

C) MEANING AND USE 1

Modals of Present Possibility

THINK CRITICALLY ABOUT MEANING AND USE

- **1.–2. ANALYZE** Put students in pairs to examine the sentences and answer the questions (1. In a, c, and f the speaker is more certain; 2. In b, d, and e the speaker is less certain).

Less Certain

↕

More Certain

- Discuss the differences between the modals with the whole class. The meanings of modals vary from less certain to more certain, although the difference in meaning between each modal is not precise.

- Ask students to close their books.

- Draw a vertical line on the board and label it according to the model.

- Ask students where to put the six modals from the sample sentences as well as *ought to, have to,* and *have got to.*

- Ask students to open their books and examine the vertical line showing modals in Meaning and Use Note 1 to see if they accurately guessed their meanings.

MEANING AND USE NOTES

- Have students silently read the information in the Notes. Then call on students to form new sentences using modals. For example, for Note 2, if a student is absent and the reason is not known or obvious, call on students to guess where she or he is, using *could, might,* or *may.*

- For Note 3, ask students *When do you plan to finish your assignment?* (Make sure they answer using *should* or *ought to*).

- For Notes 4A and 4B, make statements such as *I didn't have breakfast this morning. I won a hundred dollars.* Ask students to make conclusions, such as *You must be hungry. You've got to be excited.*

Trouble Spots

In this chapter, students are learning only about modals of possibility. Students may occasionally be confused with other meanings of the same modals, for example, *must* for necessity and obligation (e.g., *I must take the final exam. You must not touch that.*). In the same way, the modal *should* could be confusing, since it also is used for advisability (e.g., *You should study more. You should call the doctor tomorrow.*).

D) MEANING AND USE 2

Modals of Future Possibility

THINK CRITICALLY ABOUT MEANING AND USE

- **1.–3. ANALYZE AND INTERPRET** Put students into pairs to examine the sentences and discuss the questions.

- Go over the questions with the whole class (1. In a and c the speaker is less certain; 2. In b and d the speaker is more certain; 3. a and c have about the same meaning).

- Ask students to close their books. Draw a vertical line on the board like the one in Note 1 of Meaning and Use 2. Ask students to tell you where to put the four modals from the sample sentences as well as *ought to* and *may.*

- Have students check the vertical line against Note 1.

MEANING AND USE NOTES

- Divide students into small groups and assign each group one of the modals from Note 1.

- Have them write one sentence predicting a future class activity (a field trip, a test, a visitor, a project) using their modal (e.g., *We may have a test on modals. I might pass it.*). Refer students to Notes 2–4 to help them.

- Have the groups write their sentences on the board, and ask the class if the modals are in the correct form. Then ask students to write the sentences in their notebooks and number them in order of future probability from less certain to more certain, the number 1 indicating the least certain.

- Have students number the sentences on the board. Point out that some sentences, such as those with *might* and *could,* will have an equal amount of certainty.

WRITING

THINK CRITICALLY ABOUT MEANING AND USE

- Have students do A individually. Then, in small groups, have them compare answers and discuss any differences.

- Have them stay in groups and do B.

- As a class, review any difficult items from A. Then elicit answers to B:

  1. GENERATE (*It can't be on the table. / It couldn't be on the table.*)

  2. PREDICT (Answers will vary. An example is: *The mechanic had to order a new part, and it won't be in until early next week.*)

WRITE

The purpose of this activity is to give students practice in using modals and phrasal modals by writing an article about staying fit for their school's online newspaper.

1. Brainstorm

As a class, start a brainstorm on the board about how to stay fit while in school. Write several brainstorming categories on the board and elicit one or two details for each. For example, students might have ideas about when and where to work out (*problems*), balancing a healthy lifestyle with having fun (*advice*), and popular ways to exercise (*solutions*). When students are comfortable with the task, have them work individually to make brainstorming notes about staying fit at school.

2. Write a First Draft

Before students begin writing, make sure they have read the checklist in the Edit section. Also have them look at the example on page 166. Remind students to use the best points from their brainstorming notes to write their article.

3. Edit

Direct students to read and complete the self-assessment checklist on page 166. Ask for a show of hands for how many students gave all or mostly *yes* answers. If desired, ask students to comment on some of the errors they found.

DO I ...	YES
give my article a title?	☐
organize my ideas into paragraphs?	☐
use a variety of modals of possibility to speculate about the problems students may be facing now and the solutions they might consider in the near future?	☐
use adverbs such as *maybe, perhaps,* and *probably* to soften my ideas?	☐

4. Peer Review

Pair students and direct them to read each other's work. Ask students to answer the questions in the checklist and discuss them. Give students suggestions of helpful feedback: e.g., *Are you certain about this idea? You might want to use a word that shows less certainty, like* might *or* may.

5. Rewrite Your Draft

Students should consider their partners' comments from the peer review and rewrite as necessary. Encourage students to proofread their work again before turning it in.

8 Past Modals

Overview

Past modals have a variety of meanings and uses. Similarly to modals of present and future possibility, modals of past possibility are used to make guesses about past situations (e.g., *You must have been tired after the long trip.*). The chapter also covers other uses of past modals, such as to express past ability (e.g., *I could have helped you.*), advice (e.g., *Thomas should have gone to bed early.*), obligation (e.g., *You shouldn't have lied to me.*), and regrets (e.g., *I shouldn't have spent so much money.*).

Form: Potential errors with past modals include leaving out the *have* auxiliary (e.g., **I could gone home.* Incorrect) or not using the past participle of the main verb (e.g., **She would have be happy.* Incorrect). Students may also be confused because the form resembles the present perfect, however, the meanings and uses of the two are unrelated.

A GRAMMAR IN DISCOURSE

The Really Early Birds

A1: Before You Read

- Bring in pictures of birds in flight to help explain the words *flap, lift,* and *glide.*
- Ask students to guess how birds are able to fly. Write their guesses on the board. Students will refer to them after they read.

A2: Read

- Tell the class to read the first paragraph of the article, and then ask students to predict what the article will talk about (how prehistoric birds first learned to fly).
- Organize a jigsaw reading of the rest of the article. Divide students into small groups and

have each group read one of the remaining paragraphs and write a one- or two-sentence summary.

- As the groups work, circulate and answer questions about unfamiliar vocabulary or concepts.
- When students finish their summary, assign them to new groups so that there is at least one member representing each of the paragraphs. Make sure the students discuss the paragraphs in chronological order.

A3: After You Read

- Ask students to do this exercise individually (students may need to reread the entire article first). Remind them to note the places in the article where they found their answers.
- Go over any difficult or problematic items with the whole class.
- As a follow-up activity, divide the students into small groups and ask them to choose a reporter, who will present the group's ideas to the class. Write this question on the board for the groups to discuss: *What are some of the ways that scientists might use their knowledge about prehistoric birds?*
- Call on the reporters to share with the class the most interesting or important ideas from their groups.

B FORM

Past Modals

THINK CRITICALLY ABOUT FORM

Method 1
(For students not familiar with the structure)

- **1. IDENTIFY** Read the underlined past modal in the article to the students (*may have gotten*), and ask them to identify the main verb (gotten), the modal (may), and the auxiliary (have).

- Write the form of past modals on the board (modal + have + past participle).

- Have students work in pairs to find six more past modals. Then ask students to tell you what they are. Have one student write these on the board.

- **2. COMPARE AND CONTRAST** Ask one student to identify two past modals with singular subjects and two with plural subjects in the article; then ask if there is a form difference (no). To confirm, ask students to find another singular past modal and another plural past modal and analyze the forms.

- **3. EVALUATE** If students can't answer this question, refer them to one of the examples on the list on the board. Point out the auxiliary have and the past participle form of the main verb.

Method 2
(For students familiar with the structure)

- Have students work in pairs to answer the questions.

- Give students a few minutes to refer to the charts to check their answers and review the structures.

- Call on students to go over the exercise. Discuss any disagreements and have students make any necessary corrections.

FORM CHARTS

- Tell students to close their books. On the board, write the sentence *I could pass the test.* Ask students to tell you how to change this to past time (*I could have passed the test.*). Write this sentence on the board and write *may have, might have, should have,* and *must have* in a list as it appears in the chart so students see the sentence with a variety of modals.

- Ask students to tell you the form of past modals and write this on the board (modal + have + past participle).

- Tell students to transform the example sentence to a negative statement (*I could not have passed the test.*) and a *Yes/No* question

(*Could you have passed the test?*) using all the modals on the board.

- Tell students to open their books to confirm their answers. Ask them to read the charts and bulleted notes.

- Tell students to close their books again. On the board, write the sentence *He ought to have come.* Ask students to identify the phrasal modal (*ought to*), the auxiliary (*have*), and the main verb (*come*). Then write the sentence *She has to have known.* Ask students to identify the phrasal modal (*have to*), the auxiliary (*have*), and the main verb (*known*). Tell students to open their books to check their answers.

- To check students' comprehension of the Form Notes, write the following sentences on the board and ask students if the form is correct. If it is incorrect, have students tell you how to correct it.

   She mights have gone to the store. (Incorrect—*might* doesn't change form.)
   Could you have asked for some help? (Correct.)
   Should have he taken the bus? (Incorrect—the subject should be before *have* in a question.)
   They had to been aware of the danger. (Incorrect—the auxiliary *have* should come before *been*.)

Trouble Spots
Past phrasal modals are more complex in form than other past modals. Point out that with the phrasal modal *have to*, we use *did* in questions, negatives, and short answers instead of changing the word order of the modal (e.g., *Did you have to leave?* rather than *Had you to leave?* Incorrect). For this particular phrasal modal, the form rules are an exception to modal rules.

Informally Speaking: Reducing Past Modals (p. 175)

- Choose two students to read the text in the speech bubbles. Then tell the class you will play the recording and that they should listen to how the underlined form in the cartoon is different from what they hear. If needed, play the recording more than once.

- Have students point out the differences. (The cartoon reads *should have,* whereas on the recording this is pronounced *"should-uv"*; and the cartoon reads *could have,* whereas on the recording this is pronounced *"could-uv"*.) Explain that the form on the recording is considered more informal English. Point out that the form in the cartoon is standard English and students should use this form when writing and speaking, although they may hear native speakers using the informal form.

C MEANING AND USE 1

Modals of Past Possibility

THINK CRITICALLY ABOUT MEANING AND USE

- **1.–2. EVALUATE** Divide students into small groups to discuss the sentences in their books and answer the questions.
- Call on one group to explain in which sentences the speaker is more certain (a and d) and in which sentences the speaker is less certain (b and c).
- Write the modals from the sentences on the board and have students close their books. Draw a vertical line on the board like the one in Meaning and Use Note 1. Ask students to tell you how to order the modals from the sentences on the vertical line according to degree of certainty.
- Ask students to open their books and examine the vertical line showing modals in Meaning and Use Note 1 to see if they accurately guessed the degrees of certainty.

MEANING AND USE NOTES

- Divide students into three groups and assign one of the remaining Notes to each group.
- Tell each group to read the Note and prepare to teach the information to the class. The groups should write two new sentences that clearly

illustrate the meaning and use of the modals in their assigned Note.
- Circulate as the groups work, pointing out any problems in their example sentences.
- Ask each group to present their Note, and have the rest of the class check if the example sentences are correct. If not, work together to improve them.

D MEANING AND USE 2

Other Functions of Past Modals

THINK CRITICALLY ABOUT MEANING AND USE

- **1.–3. EVALUATE** Have students work in pairs to answer the questions (1. b, c; 2. a; 3. c).
- Give students a few minutes to refer to the Notes to check their answers.
- Call on students to read the questions and answers aloud. Discuss any disagreements and have students make any necessary corrections.

MEANING AND USE NOTES

- Emphasize that *could have, should have,* and *ought to have* are used to talk about things that never happened but that had the possibility of happening or were supposed to happen. (Conversely, *shouldn't have* and *ought not to have* indicate that something *did* happen and that the speaker believes it was not supposed to or was not a good idea.)
- Call on different students to read each of the Notes 1, 2A, and 2B out loud. Then ask students to create original sentences following the examples.
- Call on individual students to read their sentences out loud. After each sentence, ask, *Did the person do it? Did the event actually happen?*
- Finally call on a student to read Note 3. Elicit more example sentences from the class and answer any questions.

THINK CRITICALLY ABOUT MEANING AND USE

- Have students do A individually. Then, in small groups, have them compare answers and discuss any differences.
- Have them stay in groups and do B.
- As a class, review any difficult items from A. Then elicit answers to B:

  1. EVALUATE (Sentence 6 expresses strong possibility.)

  2. ANALYZE (Sentence 7 expresses disbelief, and sentence 2 expresses impossibility.)

WRITE

The purpose of this activity is to give students practice in using past modals by writing a review of a movie, a TV show, or a short story.

1. Brainstorm

As a class, start a brainstorm on the board about the kinds of things that are usually written in a review. Select a movie or TV show that most of the students are familiar with and write the title on the board. Write the brainstorming categories on the board: *events, strong points, critique.* Elicit details about the movie or TV show that answer the questions on page 188. You might also want to discuss how a written review would be different for a movie, a TV show, and a short story. Write student ideas on the board. Have individuals choose their own subject to write about and to make brainstorming notes for their review.

2. Write a First Draft

Before students begin writing, make sure they have read the checklist in the Edit section. Also have them look at the example on page 188. Remind students to use the best points from their brainstorming notes to write their article.

3. Edit

Direct students to read and complete the self-assessment checklist on page 188. Ask for a show of hands for how many students gave all or mostly *yes* answers. If desired, ask students to comment on some of the errors they found.

DO I ...	YES
organize my ideas into paragraphs?	☐
use the simple past and other past forms, as appropriate, to summarize the story and say what I liked about it?	☐
use past modals to speculate about what could have happened or been done differently?	☐

4. Peer Review

Pair students and direct them to read each other's work. Ask students to answer the questions in the checklist and discuss them. Give students suggestions of helpful feedback: e.g., *I'm not sure what you thought about that part of the movie. Did you like it or not? Can you give any details that help show why you feel that way? / How else could the author have ended the story?*

5. Rewrite Your Draft

Students should consider their partners' comments from the peer review and rewrite as necessary. Encourage students to proofread their work again before turning it in.

9 Passive Sentences (Part 1)

Overview

Students usually know how to mechanically transform sentences from active to passive and vice versa; however, they often are not sure when to use the passive. The active voice is used when the focus in on the doer of the action, or the agent (e.g., *Maria completed the project on Monday.*). The passive voice is used when the focus is on the receiver of the action (e.g., *The project was completed by Maria on Monday.*). It is also possible for the passive to be used with no agent, when the doer of the action is unknown, unimportant, or obvious in the sentence (e.g., *The project was completed on Monday.*).

Form: Only transitive verbs (verbs that can be followed by a direct object) can be put in the passive voice. Intransitive verbs such as *come*, *sleep*, and *stay* do not take a direct object and cannot be made passive.

A GRAMMAR IN DISCOURSE

The Expression of Emotions

A1: Before You Read

- Ask students to look at the four pictures in the text and write the emotion they think each one portrays.

- Divide the students into groups to compare their responses. They will probably agree on what the expressions represent, laying the foundation for the idea in the excerpt that the expression of emotions is universal.

A2: Read

- Ask students to read the excerpt to find out if the expression of emotions is universal.

- Tell students to note the places in the reading that answer this question.

A3: After You Read

- Ask students to do this exercise individually and mark the places in the text where they found their answers.

- Ask them to compare answers with a partner.

- Circulate and note any problematic items. Then go over these with the whole class.

- As a follow-up activity, divide students into groups and ask them to choose a reporter.

- Write these questions on the board for the groups to discuss: *How could you use the information from the article in your daily life?* (e.g., to be aware when someone else is happy or angry; to cheer up another person, etc.); *Who else might find this information useful?* (psychologists, sociologists, and people who deal with cross-cultural communication); *Why?* (because it will allow them to see the similarities between people's behavior patterns throughout the world).

- Call on the reporters to share their group's answers with the class.

B FORM

The Present and Past Passive

THINK CRITICALLY ABOUT FORM

Method 1
(For students not familiar with the structure)

- **1.–2. CATEGORIZE** Write the underlined example from the excerpt on the board (*are found*) and ask students how the passive is formed (*be* + past participle) and what tense the verb *be* is in (present). Ask them if the subject is singular or plural (plural).

- Tell students to find three more passives in the simple present. Students may need help limiting their search to the simple present form of the passive since other passive forms appear in the reading as well.

- Ask two students to make two lists on the board, one labeled *Singular* and the other *Plural*. Ask one student to write the singular present passive verbs and another to write the plural present passive verbs in the appropriate columns. Ask other students if they agree.

- Follow the same procedure for the past passive. Write the example on the board *(was noted)*. Elicit the form. (The tense is formed with *was* or *were* + past participle.)

- Have students find three more examples of singular or plural past passives and sort them into columns labeled *Singular* and *Plural*.

- **3. APPLY** Ask students to look at the two sample sentences in Question 3 and note the forms used. Then have them find one example of each form in the text. Go over these with the class, providing any necessary clarification.

Method 2

(For students familiar with the structure)

- Have students work in pairs to answer the questions.

- Give students a few minutes to refer to the charts to check their answers and review the structures.

- Call on students to go over the exercise. Discuss any disagreements and have students make any necessary corrections.

FORM CHARTS

- Ask students to read the charts to themselves. Then ask one student to explain the form in each chart and another to read the example sentences out loud.

- Check students' comprehension of each form by asking *What is the auxiliary verb? (be)* and *What is the past participle?*

- Introduce the concept of agent and receiver: First ask a student to drop his or her book on the floor. Ask *What did he/she do?* Elicit the sentence *He/She dropped the book.* Write the sentence on the board and underline *He/She*.

Explain that the student is the doer of the action, also called the agent.

- Circle *the book*. Explain that the book received the action, so it is the receiver.

- Ask students to put the sentence into the passive *(The book was dropped.)*.

- Point out that it is possible to include the agent in the sentence by adding the phrase *by him/her*.

- Once students understand the meaning of *agent* and *receiver*, call on individuals to add a different *by* + noun phrase to the end of some of the sentences in the charts (e.g., *The directions were explained* by the police officer. *Was the study published* by the academic journal?).

C) MEANING AND USE 1

Changing Focus from Active to Passive

THINK CRITICALLY ABOUT MEANING AND USE

- Have students read the sentences.

- **1. EVALUATE** Ask if each pair of sentences has about the same meaning or different meanings (about the same).

- **2.–3. ANALYZE** Have students determine the focus in the active and passive sentences. Students should notice that 1a and 2a focus more on the noun that is performing the action or causing something to happen, and 1b and 2b focus more on the noun that is receiving the action.

- Tell students to read the explanations in Notes 1A and 1B to check their answers.

MEANING AND USE NOTES

- Have students close their books and write the two sets of sentences from Note 2 on the board.

- Call on individual students to explain the focus of each set of sentences. (In the first one, the focus is on the word *we* and what *we* did. In the second set, the focus is on the results of the storm and the things that were affected by it.) Have students open their books to Note 2 to confirm their answers.

Vocabulary Notes: Verbs with No Passive Forms (p. 201)

If you think it is necessary, remind your students how to determine whether a verb is transitive or intransitive.

- On the board, write these partial phrases using transitive verbs with write-on lines in place of the nouns:

  Mark eats _____.
  We like _____.
  They are watching _____.

- Read each partial phrase out loud and ask students to suggest a noun to make a complete sentence. Then call on students to identify the subject and object of each sentence.

- Then do the same with phrases using intransitive verbs:

  We arrived _____.
  He died _____.
  She slept _____.

- Students will discover that these verbs can not be followed by an object. These verbs are called intransitive verbs and they cannot be made passive.

- Refer students to Appendix 7 in the Student Book for a list of common intransitive verbs.

- Introduce transitive stative verbs. These are verbs that take noun objects but are not usually put into the passive. Remind students that they learned about stative verbs, such as *become* and *have*, in Chapter 1.

- Write the following sentence on the board, and ask students if it is correct:

  *The car is had by Mary. (Incorrect— transitive stative verbs are not usually used in the passive.)

is *a former employee*; 2. Sentence 2a is more impersonal and indirect because we do not know who is making the request).

- Give students a few minutes to refer to the Notes to check their answers.

- Call on students to read the questions and answers out loud. Discuss any disagreements and have students make any necessary corrections.

MEANING AND USE NOTES

- Divide students into small groups and assign one of the Notes to each group.

- Tell each group to read the Note and prepare to teach the information to the class. Each group should paraphrase the information and write two original sentences that clearly illustrate the meaning and use.

- Circulate as the groups work, helping as necessary.

- As the groups present, ask the rest of the class if the example sentences are correct. If not, work together to improve them.

Beyond the Sentence: Keeping the Focus (p. 206)

This section is intended to give your students practice with the meaning and use of grammar as it functions naturally in extended discourse such as paragraphs and conversations.

- Ask students to read the example sentences.

- Have them draw an arrow from the subject pronoun in the second sentence (in both sentence pairs, *it*) to the noun it refers to in the first sentence (in both sentence pairs, *his wallet*). This will underscore how the focus is maintained across the two sentences.

D MEANING AND USE 2

Reasons for Using the Passive

THINK CRITICALLY ABOUT MEANING AND USE

- 1.–2. ANALYZE AND EVALUATE Have students work in pairs to answer the questions (1. In 1b the agent is unknown; in 1a the agent

WRITING

THINK CRITICALLY ABOUT MEANING AND USE

- Have students do A individually. Then, in small groups, have them compare answers and discuss any differences.

- Have them stay in groups and do B.

- As a class, review any difficult items from A. Then elicit answers to B:

  1. EVALUATE (Including the agent in 3 and 5 is a signal that that the information is important, as it makes it clear who performed the specific actions. In both 3 and 5, the agents are high-level authority figures [the manager in 3 and a company's board of directors in 5], so the information is significant to anyone interested in the events.)

  2. COMPARE AND CONTRAST (In 6, the agent is obvious [people in general believe something about a candidate for president]. In 2, the agent is unimportant [or else it would have been mentioned]; the sentence might be part of an announcement suggesting that students should report to the gym now if they want their photo to be taken.)

WRITE

The purpose of this activity is to give students practice in using present and past passives by writing an email to your professor about a lab project.

1. Brainstorm

As a class, start a brainstorm on the board about the steps, actions, and problems that happen during a typical lab project. For example, suggest that students are growing two plants under different conditions. Write several brainstorming categories on the board, such as *actions taken, problems, solutions,* and *future actions.* Elicit the kinds of details that students might write about, such as the expected results, the actual results, things that went wrong, and how students might change the project if they did it again. Have students work individually to make brainstorming notes about the review they plan to write.

2. Write a First Draft

Before students begin writing, make sure they have read the checklist in the Edit section. Also have them look at the example on page 210. Remind students to use the best points from their brainstorming notes to write their email.

3. Edit

Direct students to read and complete the self-assessment checklist on page 210. Ask for a show of hands for how many students gave all or mostly *yes* answers. If desired, ask students to comment on some of the errors they found.

DO I ...	YES
use active sentences to focus on who or what is performing an action?	☐
use passive sentences to talk about a process or to focus on the receiver or result?	☐
omit the agent in passive sentences when it is unimportant, unknown, or obvious or when I want to avoid blame?	☐

4. Peer Review

Pair students and direct them to read each other's work. Ask students to answer the questions in the checklist and discuss them. Give students suggestions of helpful feedback: e.g., *What do you want to focus on, the person doing the action or the object receiving the action? / Do we need to know the agent in this sentence? Can we omit the agent?*

5. Rewrite Your Draft

Students should consider their partners' comments from the peer review and rewrite as necessary. Encourage students to proofread their work again before turning it in.

10 Passive Sentences (Part 2)

Overview

This chapter covers complex passive forms: future passive (e.g., *A cure will be/is going to be found.*), present perfect passive (e.g., *A cure has been found.*), modal passive (e.g., *A cure must be found.*), phrasal modal passive (e.g., *A cure has got to be found.*). The passive voice is commonly used in academia to convey an objective and authoritative tone.

Form: The key challenge with these more complex passives is remembering the multiple parts of the various forms of passive verbs with modals and other auxiliaries:

- affirmative verb forms have three parts, including two auxiliaries (e.g., *will* + *be*; *have/has* + *been*; *modal* + *be*; phrasal modal + *be*) + past participle
- questions and negatives with the phrasal modals *have to* and *need to* have four parts, since the additional auxiliary *do* must also be used (e.g., *Do you need to be paid today? I don't need to be paid today.*)

A GRAMMAR IN DISCOURSE

At-Risk Students Can Be Helped, but Not by Budget Cuts . . .

A1: Before You Read

- Point out that in many countries around the world, students dropping out of high school is a problem.
- Have students answer the questions in pairs. Then bring the class together and call on students from different countries to discuss high school dropouts in their society.

- After the discussion, ask *Do you think it is important to finish high school? Why?* Tell students to support their reasons. Write these on the board.

A2: Read

- Ask students to read the letter to the editor to find out what one concerned citizen thinks about the dropout problem.
- Have students make a list on a separate piece of paper of the causes and effects mentioned in Tony Diaz's letter.

Cultural Notes

If students are unfamiliar with at-risk populations, discuss some of the reasons that students become or are classified as at-risk: homelessness, frequent moves, family responsibilities (including working to earn money for the family), poverty, and so on.

A3: After You Read

- Have students do this exercise individually and mark the places in the text where they found the answers.
- Ask them to compare answers with a partner.
- Circulate and note any problematic items. Then go over these with the whole class.
- As a follow-up activity, refer students to the list of causes and effects they wrote up while reading the article. Ask students to identify the effects that happened in the past. Then point out the three rhetorical questions asked in lines 46–51. Ask partners to discuss what the effects might be if each of these actions occurs, both in the short-term and in the long-term. Remind students to focus their discussion on at-risk students.
- Call on students to share ideas and predictions.

The Future, Present Perfect, and Modal Passive

THINK CRITICALLY ABOUT FORM

Method 1
(For students not familiar with the structure)

- **1. IDENTIFY** Write *has ignored* on the board. Elicit that this is a present perfect verb. Ask students how they might form the passive of this verb. Write the correct passive form on the board *(has been ignored)*, and direct students' attention to the underlined verb in the article. Point out the parts of the form: *has/have + been* + past participle.

- Ask students to find five more present perfect passives in the article.

- Call on students to list them. Write them on the board in the column labeled *Present Perfect Passives.*

- **2. IDENTIFY** Repeat the procedure for the circled verb in the article, *will be heard,* by writing *will hear* on the board and eliciting that this is a modal + verb. Explain that *will be heard* is the future passive and that the parts of the form are *will + be* + past participle.

- Ask students to find and call out two more future passive verbs. Write them on the board in the column labeled *Future Passive.*

- Elicit that the future passive can also be formed with *be going to* instead of *will*. Elicit the three parts of the *be going to* passive *(be going to + be* + past participle).

- **3. ANALYZE** Ask students to tell you the three parts of the verb form *cannot be allowed* in the example sentence. Explain that this is the modal passive and that the parts of the form are modal + *be* + past participle.

Method 2
(For students familiar with the structure)

- First, divide the board into three columns labeled *Modal Passive, Future Passive,* and *Present Perfect Passive.*

- **1. IDENTIFY** Have students find examples of present perfect passives. Call on one student to write them on the board. Then have a student write the three parts of the present perfect passive under the column heading (*has/have + been* + past participle).

- **2. IDENTIFY** Have students find examples of future passives, and call on one student to write these on the board. Elicit the three parts of future passives (*will + be* + past participle) and write this form under the column heading.

- Elicit the three parts of the *be going to* passive *(be going to + be* + past participle) and write it under the column heading.

- **3. ANALYZE** Ask the class to quickly call out all the modals they can think of before they answer Question 3 *(could, can, should, may, might,* and *must).* If they mention *will,* explain that this modal forms the future passive, not a modal passive. Then tell students to work individually to find modal passives in the article.

- Call on students to tell you the modal passives they found, and write them in the appropriate column on the board. Now ask students to tell you the three parts of the modal passive (modal + *be* + past participle). Write the form under the column head.

FORM CHARTS

- Ask students to close their books.

- On the board write the sentence *TV violence is limited.* Tell students to work in pairs to change this sentence to the future passive with *will* (*TV violence will be limited.*), the present perfect passive (*TV violence has been limited.*), and the modal passive with *must* (*TV violence must be limited.*).

- Tell students to open their books to check their sentences against the charts.

- Then ask them to close their books as you follow the same procedure for questions and short answers. On the board, write *Are the parents blamed? Yes, they are.* Ask students to change the example to a modal passive question and a short answer with the modal *should* (*Should the parents be blamed? Yes, they should.*), the future passive with *will* (*Will the parents be blamed? No, they won't.*), and the present perfect passive (*Have the parents been blamed? Yes, they have.*).

- Erase the board.

- Have students read the explanations of the future, present perfect, and modal passives and phrasal modal passives on page 215.
- To check their comprehension, write this sentence on the board: *Children will be harmed if programs are cut.*
- Then write the following list of forms on the board. Tell students to change the above sentence to these forms:

  future passive with *be going to*
  (*Children are going to be harmed if programs are cut.*)

  passive *Yes/No* question with *be going to*
  (*Are children going to be harmed if programs are cut?*)

  negative phrasal modal passive with *have to*:
  (*Children don't have to be harmed if programs are cut.*)

  passive *Yes/No* question with *have to*:
  (*Do children have to be harmed if programs are cut?*)

- Bring the class together and call on students to write the answers on the board. Answer any remaining questions. Make sure that students use *do* with the negative and question forms of the phrasal modal *have to*.

C MEANING AND USE 1

The Role of the Agent

THINK CRITICALLY ABOUT MEANING AND USE

- **1. IDENTIFY** Put students into pairs. Have them underline the agent in each sentence and then discuss Question 2.
- **2. ANALYZE** Ask which agents give important or unexpected information (1b and 2a).
- Ask students which agents seem unnecessary (In 1a and 2b, the agent is unnecessary because including it does not provide any new or important information).

MEANING AND USE NOTES

- Ask students to close their books. Write the sentences from Note 1A on the board. Read them out loud and ask why the agent is

mentioned in two sentences (in the first one, the agent is surprising; in the second one, the agent is unexpected), and why it isn't mentioned in the other two sentences (in both, the agent is obvious).

- Ask students to open their books to read Notes 1A and 1B. Have them check their answers by reading the explanations.
- For Note 1C, read the two sentences and ask students which one is vague or incomplete (*Washington, D.C. was designed.*) and which one is specific and complete (*Washington, D.C. was designed by Pierre L'Enfant.*).

D MEANING AND USE 2

The Passive in Academic and Public Discourse

THINK CRITICALLY ABOUT MEANING AND USE

- **1. GENERATE** Give students a few minutes to change the example sentences from passive to active. Call on several students to read their answers out loud (a, *We use sulfur dioxide to produce sulfuric acid.* b, *As a special benefit to on-line customers, we will ship orders free of charge.* c, *You must insure your vehicle. You must present proof of insurance.*).
- **2. EVALUATE** Students should notice that in all cases, the passive sentences sound more formal and objective and express more authority.
- **3. PREDICT** The following are possible contexts for the passive sentences: a, a chemistry book; b, an Internet retailer; c, information from the Department of Motor Vehicles.

MEANING AND USE NOTES

- Ask students to close their books.
- Remind them that the passive is commonly used in less personal, more formal, or authoritative situations.
- Divide students into small groups. Give them a few minutes to list as many contexts as they can in which the passive might be used and write an example for each one.

- Elicit contexts and examples from all the groups and list the contexts on the board.
- Ask students to open their books and read the Notes, comparing the list on the board with the contexts in the book.

Informally Speaking: Using Passives with *Get* (p. 224)

- Choose two students to read the text in the speech bubbles. Then tell the class you will play the recording and that they should listen to how the underlined form in the cartoon is different from what they hear. If needed, play the recording more than once.
- Have students point out the differences. (The cartoon reads *I'm going to be promoted.* The form on the recording is *I'm going to get promoted.*) Explain that the form on the recording is considered more informal English. Point out that the form in the cartoon is standard English and students should use this form when writing and speaking, although they may hear native speakers using the informal form.

WRITING

THINK CRITICALLY ABOUT MEANING AND USE

- Have students do A individually. Then, in small groups, have them compare answers and discuss any differences.
- Have them stay in groups and do B.
- As a class, review any difficult items from A. Then elicit answers to B:

  1.–2. PREDICT (Sentence 7, because it's the kind of statement that you would hear being announced at an airport, just before a flight; Sentence 3, because expressions with "get" [i.e., "got robbed"] are typical of informal speech.)

WRITE

The purpose of this activity is to give students practice in using future, present perfect, modal, and other passive forms by writing a letter to the editor about how education could be improved in your country.

1. Brainstorm

As a class, start a brainstorm on the board about the state of education in your country. Ask students to name several aspects of education that could be improved and write their ideas on the board. For example, students might suggest outreach to at-risk students, support for students with learning disabilities, and helping students gain the real-life skills they need to succeed after high school graduation. Ask students to discuss what improvements have been made in recent years about these and other problems, and write their ideas on the board. Have students work individually to add to the brainstorming notes about how education could be improved.

2. Write a First Draft

Before students begin writing, make sure they have read the checklist in the Edit section. Also have them look at the example on page 228. Remind students to use the best points from their brainstorming notes to write their letter to the editor.

3. Edit

Direct students to read and complete the self-assessment checklist on page 228. Ask for a show of hands for how many students gave all or mostly *yes* answers. If desired, ask students to comment on some of the errors they found.

4. Peer Review

Pair students and direct them to read each other's work. Ask students to answer the questions in the checklist and discuss them. Give students suggestions of helpful feedback: e.g., *The verb* got *is a bit informal for a letter to the editor. Can you suggest a different verb that is more formal? / Can we omit the agent in this sentence? Does the agent tell us anything important?*

5. Rewrite Your Draft

Students should consider their partners' comments from the peer review and rewrite as necessary. Encourage students to proofread their work again before turning it in.

11 Contrasting Gerunds and Infinitives

Overview

One of the difficulties students face with gerunds and infinitives is that there are few set rules to follow and a lot of memorization. Students may need help finding ways to remember which verbs can be followed only by gerunds (e.g., *finish, enjoy*) and which only by infinitives (e.g., *agree, plan*), and which by both (e.g., *like, stop*). Point out that for the latter category, a sentence with a gerund and the same sentence with an infinitive may not have the same meaning (e.g., *I stopped eating.* vs. *I stopped to eat.*).

Form: Make sure students understand that a gerund is not a verb. It is the *-ing* form of the verb which is used as a noun—as a subject or an object of a sentence (e.g., *Skating is fun. I like skating.*).

A GRAMMAR IN DISCOURSE

Become a Less Aggressive Driver

A1: Before You Read

- Tell students that traffic congestion is a terrible problem in many cities in the United States. Ask if traffic congestion is a problem in their countries. Have students share their experiences driving in their countries and compare it with driving in the United States.

- Ask students to think of the last time they were delayed while driving in heavy traffic, and to visualize the experience.

- Write these questions on the board and tell students to think about them for a few minutes: *How are you feeling? Do you feel relaxed or tense? What are you saying to yourself? How do you feel about the other drivers around you? Are you driving differently than you do usually?* Focus students' attention on the stressful nature of

driving in heavy traffic. Then, in pairs, have students discuss the questions.

- Bring the class together and call on students for comments about the stressful nature of driving in heavy traffic.

- Tell the class they are going to read an excerpt about stress, written by a psychologist. Ask students to predict what a psychologist might say about the dangers of driving in stressful situations (e.g., people become careless and can cause accidents, stress is bad for one's health, etc.). Write these on the board to refer to during the After You Read activity.

A2: Read

- Tell students they will read the book excerpt to find out what psychologist Richard Carlson has suggested for aggressive drivers.

- Divide students into small groups. Explain that half the groups will read and make a list of the characteristics of an aggressive driver, while the other half will read and make a list of the characteristics of a calm driver. Explain that the characteristics may not be stated directly, but can be inferred from the reading.

- Make two columns on the board, one labeled *Characteristics of Aggressive Drivers* and the other labeled *Characteristics of Calm Drivers.*

- Call on members from each group to write items from their list on the board.

Cultural Notes

There is much concern about the causes and effects of stress around the world. As a result, stress is a popular topic of self-help books, magazine articles, and television shows. Many people think that stress is the result of social pressures to work hard, to achieve success, and particularly for women, to balance family life with a career.

A3: After You Read

- Have students to do this exercise individually and mark the places in the excerpt where they found their answers.

- Ask them to compare answers with a partner.

- Circulate and note any problematic items. Then go over these with the whole class.

- Direct students' attention to the predictions on the board that they made before reading the excerpt. As a class, check if these predictions were correct.

- As a follow-up activity, write these questions on the board: *What are the sources of stress in your life? Do you think stress really has a great impact on your ability to do things such as drive?* Encourage students to support their opinions with examples. Finally, ask *Do you think sources of stress are the same across cultures, or are they more specific to individuals, regardless of culture?*

Trouble Spots

Students sometimes confuse the *-ing* in the gerund form (e.g., *Swimming is fun.*) with the *-ing* in the continuous form (e.g., *She is swimming.*). This may cause problems when students see a stative verb (such as *know* or *have*) and, remembering that stative verbs do not typically occur in the continuous, hesitate to use a gerund. To avoid this confusion, point out that any verb can be used as a gerund, giving a few examples of stative verbs in the gerund form (e.g., *Knowing how to relax is important for your health. Having a job makes me very tired.*).

B) FORM 1

Gerunds and Infinitives

THINK CRITICALLY ABOUT FORM

Method 1
(For students not familiar with the structure)

- **1. IDENTIFY** As a precursor, write the sentence *Driving is fun* on the board. Elicit the subject of the sentence *(Driving)*. Elicit that *Driving* is a gerund that functions as the subject of the sentence.

- Direct students to the circled example in the excerpt *(driving in traffic)*.

- Ask students to find another gerund in the text that is the subject of a sentence *(Second, driving aggressively is extremely stressful.)*. Write it on the board in a column labeled *Gerunds*. Make sure students include the whole gerund phrase if appropriate.

- **2. IDENTIFY** As a precursor, write this sentence on the board: *I enjoy driving*. Elicit the verb of the sentence *(enjoy)*. Point out that *driving* is not part of a verb here but that it is a gerund, the *-ing* form of the verb used as a noun. It is the object of *enjoy*.

- Direct students' attention to the underlined example in the article *(saving no time at all)*. Elicit the form of the gerund (verb + *-ing*).

- Ask students to find and tell you one more example of a gerund following a verb in the article *(begin using your time)*. Write this on the board in the column labeled *Gerunds*.

- **3. RECOGNIZE** Ask students to tell you what the infinitive form of a verb is *(to + base form of the verb)*. Elicit some examples. Direct their attention to the last paragraph of the excerpt to find the infinitive that directly follows a verb *(try to relax)*. Write this on the board in a column labeled *Infinitives*.

- **4. EVALUATE** Elicit the infinitive in the example sentence *(to speed)*. Elicit the subject of the sentence *(It)*.

Method 2
(For students familiar with the structure)

- Have students work in pairs to answer the questions.

- Give students a few minutes to refer to the charts to check their answers and review the structures.

- Call on students to go over the exercise. Discuss any disagreements and have students make any necessary corrections.

FORM CHARTS

- Have students read the charts and bulleted notes.

- Choose a few verbs from each of the categories in the charts and bulleted notes and write them on the board.

- Ask students to write sentences using each verb and either a gerund or an infinitive.
- Put students into pairs to check their sentences. Refer them to the charts for assistance.
- Call on students to share their sentences and elicit or offer feedback as necessary.
- Then write the following sentences on the board:

  Learning a foreign language takes a lot of time.
  Doing homework regularly pays because you'll get higher grades.

- Have students rewrite these sentences beginning with the pronoun *It*. Ask two students to write their answers on the board.

  It takes a lot of time to learn a foreign language.
  It pays to do homework regularly because you'll get higher grades.

- Discuss any problems and answer any questions. Refer students to Appendices 8 and 9 for more information on gerunds and infinitives.

Vocabulary Notes: Short Answers to Questions with Infinitives (p. 236)

- Write the verbs *hope, expect, plan,* and *want* on the board.
- Put students into pairs. Ask each student to write one information question beginning with *What* and one *Yes/No* question for their partner. They should use two of the verbs on the board + an infinitive (e.g., *Do you hope to get a degree from an American university? What do you want to do once you have finished this course?*).
- Have the pairs answer each other's questions using short answers (*Yes, I hope to. Enter my degree program.*).
- Circulate, checking that students are including or omitting *to* as appropriate.

C MEANING AND USE 1

Verbs Used with Infinitives and Gerunds

THINK CRITICALLY ABOUT MEANING AND USE

- Ask the class to identify the infinitive and gerund in each pair of sentences.

- **EVALUATE** Ask the students to note the differences in meaning between each pair of sentences. They should see that in the first pair of sentences, there is a clear difference in meaning. With the infinitive, the verb indicates that a purpose or future action will follow, whereas with the gerund, the verb indicates that the action is completed. In the second pair, however, the meaning is the same with both the gerund and the infinitive.
- For additional clarification of the difference in meaning of sentence pair 1, direct students' attention to the sentences that provide a context (*It's so inexpensive.* vs. *It's so expensive.*).

MEANING AND USE NOTES

- Divide students into groups and assign one of the Notes to each group.
- Tell each group to read the Note and prepare to teach the information to the class. Each group should paraphrase the information and write a few original example sentences that clearly illustrate the meaning and use. Encourage the groups presenting Notes 3 and 4 to add information about each sentence's context to make the meanings clearer.
- Circulate as the groups work, helping as necessary.
- As the groups present, ask the rest of the class if the example sentences are correct. If not, work together to improve them.

D FORM 2

More About Gerunds and Infinitives

THINK CRITICALLY ABOUT FORM

Before you begin the exercise, write the following terms on the board and elicit examples:

  verb phrase (e.g., *am tired, waste time*)
  phrasal verb (e.g., *run away, look out*)
  preposition (e.g., *under, in*)
  adjective (e.g., *tired, old*)

- **1. ANALYZE** Make sure that students understand that the gerund can be more than just verb + *ing*. It can be a gerund phrase as shown in examples a, b, and c. Have them do the task individually and then check their answers in pairs.

- Go over the answers as a group. Make sure that students correctly identify the verb phrase, phrasal verb, and preposition. In b, the gerund follows a verb phrase ending in a noun (*probably spend a lot of time*); in c, the gerund follows a phrasal verb (*end up*); in a, the gerund follows a preposition (*of*).

- **2. DIFFERENTIATE** Have students find the underlined phrase containing an infinitive (d) and then identify what part of speech it follows (an adjective, *anxious*).

FORM CHARTS

- Give students time to read the Notes and ask questions.

- To check their comprehension, write the following sentences on the board and ask if they are correct:

    *I'm not accustomed to listen to different accents of English. (Incorrect—*accustomed to* is a *be* + adjective + preposition combination followed by a gerund.)

    Kim is afraid of walking home alone at night, and Rika is also afraid to walk home alone. (Correct—Point out the difference between *be* + adjective + preposition followed by a gerund vs. an adjective followed by an infinitive.)

- Refer students to Appendices 8 and 9 in the Student Book for more examples. Help students memorize different infinitive and gerund forms by giving quizzes and holding competitions in class.

E MEANING AND USE 2

Interpreting Gerunds and Infinitives

THINK CRITICALLY ABOUT MEANING AND USE

- **1.–2. ANALYZE** Have students work in pairs to answer the questions (1. In 1a, Jane is driving and in 1b Tom is driving; 2. In 2a, Sam might come early and in 2b, Susan might come early).

- Give students a few minutes to refer to the

Notes to check their answers.

- Call on students to read the questions and answers aloud. Discuss any disagreements and have students make any necessary corrections.

MEANING AND USE NOTES

- Divide students into small groups and assign one of the Notes to each group.

- Tell each group to read the Note and prepare to teach the information to the class. Each group should paraphrase the information and write two example sentences that clearly illustrate the meaning and use.

- Circulate as the groups work, helping as necessary.

- As the groups present, ask the rest of the class if the example sentences are correct. If not, work together to improve them.

WRITING

THINK CRITICALLY ABOUT MEANING AND USE

- Have students do A individually. Then, in small groups, have them compare answers and discuss any differences.

- Have them stay in groups and do B.

- As a class, review any difficult items from A. Then elicit answers to B:

    1. PREDICT (In the original sentence, we understand that the speaker did not take out the garbage because he forgot that he was supposed to do it. In the revised sentence, the speaker suggests that he had no recollection of having taken out the garbage. It's also not clear whether or not the garbage was actually taken out [perhaps it was, and perhaps it wasn't.] More context is needed to clarify the situation.)

    2. PREDICT (In the original sentence, the female stopped what she was doing [for example, working, walking] so that she could eat lunch. The meaning of the revised sentence depends on the greater context, which we aren't given. One possibility is that the female had been eating her lunch and then something happened [for example, the phone rang, someone walked in unexpectedly], which caused her to stop eating. A second possibility is that she decided to not eat lunch for a period of time [i.e., She stopped eating lunch, and only ate breakfast and dinner over a period of time.].)

WRITE

The purpose of this activity is to give students practice in using gerunds and infinitives by writing a persuasive essay about managing stress.

1. Brainstorm

As a class, start a brainstorm on the board about stress in your students' lives. Ask them to name several things that cause stress for them, and write their ideas on the board. For example, students might experience stress because of schoolwork, family obligations, work situations, or having too many things to do. Ask students to discuss some of the reasons stress can be harmful. List one or two of their ideas, e.g., health consequences or less enjoyment of life. Then have them share a few things they usually do to combat stress, such as exercising or talking with a friend. Have students work individually to add to the brainstorming notes about stress and to choose the ideas they want to write about. Remind them that they'll want to pick the ideas that will be the most persuasive for their audience.

2. Write a First Draft

Before students begin writing, make sure they have read the checklist in the Edit section. Also have them look at the example on page 252. Remind students to use the best points from their brainstorming notes to write their persuasive essay.

3. Edit

Direct students to read and complete the self-assessment checklist on page 252. Ask for a show of hands for how many students gave all or mostly *yes* answers. If desired, ask students to comment on some of the errors they found.

DO I ...	YES
use gerunds and gerund phrases as subjects and objects, and after prepositions or common verb phrases?	☐
use the correct gerund or infinitive form after specific verbs?	☐
use at least one example of a sentence with *It . . +* infinitive?	☐
make suggestions with imperatives + appropriate gerunds or infinitives?	☐

4. Peer Review

Pair students and direct them to read each other's work. Ask students to answer the questions in the checklist and discuss them. Give students suggestions of helpful feedback: e.g., *Should you use an infinitive or a gerund after the verb* agree? / *Could you change this sentence so it begins with a gerund as the subject?*

5. Rewrite Your Draft

Students should consider their partners' comments from the peer review and rewrite as necessary. Encourage students to proofread their work again before turning it in.

12 Indefinite and Definite Articles; Review of Nouns

Overview

The English article system has numerous rules and exceptions, making it one of the most difficult grammar areas for students to master. This chapter reviews count and noncount nouns and presents the various rules for definite and indefinite articles. Help students understand that articles must be used for singular count nouns: indefinite if the noun is not specific and definite if it is specific (e.g., *I read a book.* vs. *I read the book you recommended.*).

Form: Students may be familiar only with the articles *a/an,* and *the.* Point out that for plural count nouns the *Ø* article (no article) or *some* can be used (e.g., *I had cherries/some cherries for lunch.*) and for noncount nouns *the, some,* or *Ø* article can be used (e.g., *I drank the milk/some milk. Milk is good for you.*).

A GRAMMAR IN DISCOURSE

Chicken Soup, Always Chicken Soup

A1: Before You Read

- Before students start reading, check their comprehension of the key word *remedy.* On the board, write: *My remedy for a cold is tea.* Have them guess the meaning of the word (something that helps treat an illness).

- Divide students into groups. Tell them to discuss the questions and encourage them to share any remedies they have discovered on their own.

A2: Read

- Before students read, ask if any of them are familiar with the basic principles of scientific research. If no one is, explain that in order to prove (or disprove) a theory or idea, researchers often conduct experiments by testing their theory on subjects (participants in an experiment) under different conditions.

- Ask students to read the excerpt and note how a medical doctor was able to prove that old-fashioned chicken soup has medicinal properties.

- Put students into pairs to discuss their answers.

- Call on several students to state the main points of the study (see lines 52–67). Write them on the board.

Cultural Notes

Chicken soup isn't the only natural cure for the sniffles. Some other foods that are used include ginseng and cinnamon (Korea), onion and turmeric (Iran), and scallions and garlic (Mexico).

A3: After You Read

- Ask students to do this exercise individually and note the places in the article where they found their answers.

- Ask them to compare answers with a partner.

- Circulate and note any problematic items. Then go over these with the whole class.

- As a follow-up activity, ask students to make a list of the natural or herbal medicines that are popular in their countries. The list should also include the conditions treated by the medicines.

- Divide students into small groups to compare their lists.

- Call on several students to share items from their list. Write these on the board.

Indefinite and Definite Articles; Review of Nouns

THINK CRITICALLY ABOUT FORM

Method 1
(For students not familiar with the structure)

- **1. IDENTIFY** Give students a few minutes to find the nouns.

- **2. RECOGNIZE** Have students tell you the nouns that only have adjectives before them *(early medical literature)*.

- Have students tell you the nouns that only have articles before them *(the drugs, the soup)*.

- Finally elicit the nouns that have both adjectives and articles before them *(a certain chemical, a common drug)*.

- **3. RECOGNIZE** Have students name the nouns that do not have adjectives before them *(centuries, Chicken)*.

- **4. LABEL** Make two columns on the board labeled *Singular* and *Plural*. Elicit and list the singular nouns *(literature, Chicken, chemical, soup, drug)* and plural nouns *(centuries, drugs)*.

Method 2
(For students familiar with the structure)

- Have students work in pairs to answer the questions.

- Give students a few minutes to refer to the charts to check their answers and review the structures.

- Call on students to go over the exercise. Discuss any disagreements and have students make any necessary corrections.

FORM CHARTS

- Give students a few minutes to read the charts and ask questions if necessary.

- Divide the class into four groups and assign each group one of the four sections of the bulleted notes. Have each group read over the information and prepare to present it to the class with examples.

- Circulate as the students work and offer assistance as necessary.

- To review, elicit the answers to these questions: *What articles can we put in front of a singular count noun?* (*a*, *an*, and *the*); *What articles can we put in front of a plural count noun?* (*the*, Ø, or *some/any*); and *What articles can we put in front of a noncount noun?* (*the*, Ø, or *some/any*).

- Check students' comprehension of *some* vs. *any* by writing the following sentences on the board and asking if they are correct or incorrect. If incorrect, have students tell why.

    Sally doesn't want any rice with her meal. (Correct.)

    *We're going to do any homework this weekend. (Incorrect—use *any* for negative statements with noncount nouns; use *some* in affirmative statements.)

The Indefinite Article

THINK CRITICALLY ABOUT MEANING AND USE

- **1.–2. ANALYZE AND DIFFERENTIATE** Put students into pairs to study the sentences and discuss the questions.

- Call on several pairs to share their answers (1. 1a; 2. 2b refers to a small quantity of the underlined noun, 2a classifies the underlined noun). Ask students to explain how they arrived at their answers.

- Ask the pairs to create a context or situation in which each sentence might be heard.

MEANING AND USE NOTES

- Help students understand that the choice of article is determined by the extent to which the speaker and listener share the same information. If they do not share the information, the noun is not specific and an indefinite article is used. If they do share information, the noun is specific and the definite article is used.

- Ask students to silently read the Notes.

- For Note 1A, reinforce students' understanding of the indefinite article by having them create additional sentences. Give each student a verb/

noun pair, such as *read/book, went/restaurant, visited/friend,* and ask them, *What did you do last night? (I read a book. I went to a restaurant, I visited a friend.).*

- For Note 1C, have partners take turns choosing an object in the room and making two statements and two questions using the word's singular and plural forms (e.g., *I see a pencil. I see some pencils. Do you see a pencil? Do you see any pencils?*).

- For Note 2, put students into pairs and have them interview each other about the occupations of their family and friends. For example, *What does your mother/father/sister/brother do? My mother is an artist. My father is a truck driver.*

D) MEANING AND USE 2

The Definite Article

THINK CRITICALLY ABOUT MEANING AND USE

- **1.–3. ANALYZE** Put students into pairs to read and discuss the sentences and questions.

- Go over the activity as a class. For each question, call on a different pair to answer the question and explain what information in the sentence helped them to arrive at the answer (1. b, because the word *sweater* is mentioned twice; 2. a, because the sentence says *the mayor* and *the news,* so it is clear that the speaker and the listener live in the same city; 3. c, because the listener can obviously see the salt being referred to).

MEANING AND USE NOTES

- Read the introduction to the first Note out loud.

- Divide the class into small groups and assign one of the Notes to each group.

- Tell each group to read their Note and prepare to teach the explanation to the class. Each group should paraphrase the explanation and write two new example sentences that clearly illustrate the meaning and use.

- Circulate as the groups work, helping as necessary.

- As the groups present, ask the rest of the class if the example sentences are correct. If not, work together to improve them.

Vocabulary Notes: *Another* vs. *The Other* (p. 268)

- Have students read the Notes.

- Point out that a way to remember that *another* is indefinite is to look at the beginning of the word; it begins with *an,* which is an indefinite article.

- Check students' comprehension of the Notes by writing these sentences on the board and asking students to complete them using *another* or *the other.*

  I speak two languages. One is English, and . . . (the other . . .)

  Two students have read this book; one liked it, but . . . (the other . . .)

  Someone stole my book, so I had to buy . . . (another . . .)

  There are so many countries I'd like to visit. One is Australia and . . . (another is . . .)

Beyond the Sentence: Connecting Information (p. 269)

This section is intended to give students practice with the meaning and use of grammar as it functions naturally in extended discourse such as paragraphs and conversations.

- Ask students to read the explanation and the paragraph once for general meaning.

- Elicit the main idea of the paragraph. (A family got a kitten, and the boy loved it so much that, at first, he checked on it every night.)

- Ask students to circle the indefinite articles (*a* kitten) and underline the definite articles in the paragraph (*my* son, *the* kitten, *his* own room, *her* nights, *her* little house).

- Tell students to think about why these articles were used in these sentences.

- Call on students to share their answers.

- Then point out to students the bolded pronouns in the paragraph. Remind them that pronouns also help make sentences clear and connect ideas in a paragraph or conversation.

Article Use with Generic Nouns

THINK CRITICALLY ABOUT MEANING AND USE

Before you start the exercise, you may want to do the following task to review the concept of a class of nouns.

- Write the following lists of nouns on the board and have students name the class for each list. Write the class above each list.

Chinese	apple	penguin
Spanish	peach	eagle
Farsi	plum	parrot
French	banana	ostrich
Greek	orange	hawk

(The classification for column 1 is *languages*, column 2 is *fruit*, and column 3 is *birds*.)

- 1.–2. ANALYZE Once students understand the concept of a class of nouns, put them into pairs and ask them to examine the sentences in their books and answer the questions.

- Call on individual students to tell you which underlined nouns refer to a whole class or group of nouns (1b, 2a, 3b, and 4a). Then ask other students to identify the underlined nouns that refer to a specific noun or nouns (1a, 2b, 3a, and 4b).

MEANING AND USE NOTES

- Read Note 1 out loud. Explain that this Note introduces the other Notes in the section.

- Give students time to read Notes 2, 3, and 4. Answer any questions or clarify meaning as needed.

- Divide students into small groups. Give each group a different singular count noun. Ask them to write three sentences that use the noun generically: one with no article, one with an indefinite article, and one with the definite article. Tell students to provide a context if necessary to clarify the use of the articles. Possible singular count nouns:

  <u>cell phone</u> (e.g., *Cell phones are popular with teenagers. A cell phone is not as reliable as a standard phone. The cell phone is a useful*

invention for business people.)
  <u>family</u> (e.g., *Families like to spend the holidays together. A family consists of a person's closest relatives. The family is important to a well-functioning society.*)
  <u>airplane</u>
  <u>computer</u>
  <u>microwave</u>

- As the groups work, circulate and help as necessary.

- Call one student from each group to write the group's sentences on the board. Ask the class to comment on accuracy of form and on correct meaning and use.

Beyond the Sentence: Indefinite Generic Nouns in Discourse (p. 274)

This section is intended to give students practice with the meaning and use of grammar as it functions naturally in extended discourse such as paragraphs and conversations.

- Ask students to read the explanation and the paragraph for the main idea.

- Elicit the generic noun that the paragraph is about *(an onion/onions)*. Reinforce the idea that despite repeated use, *onion* does not become definite because it is generic.

- Ask students where they would expect to see a paragraph like this one (in a magazine or book). Point out that this style of writing or speaking is considered more formal.

WRITING

THINK CRITICALLY ABOUT MEANING AND USE

- Have students do A individually. Then, in small groups, have them compare answers and discuss any differences.

- Have them stay in groups and do B.

- As a class, review any difficult items from A. Then elicit answers to B:

  1. ANALYZE (We can assume that the listener has knowledge of the apartment from a previous conversation with the speaker.)

2. PREDICT (The speaker would have said: "Snakes frighten that little girl.")

WRITE

The purpose of this activity is to give students practice in using count, noncount, and generic nouns with definite, indefinite, and no articles by writing part of a pamphlet about healthy eating.

1. Brainstorm

As a class, start a brainstorm on the board about healthy and unhealthy foods. Ask them to name several unhealthy foods, such as candy, potato chips, and fast food, and write their ideas on the board. Have students tell how they feel or what can happen after they eat such foods (e.g., they feel sick to their stomach, they gain weight). Then elicit and list some healthy foods, such as vegetables, nuts, and fruits. Ask students to tell how they feel or what happens when they eat these foods (e.g., they have a lot of energy, they have good test results at the doctor's office).

Ask students if they know of health benefits that specific foods may have, such as olive oil being heart-healthy and carrots helping eyesight. Have students work individually to add to the brainstorming notes about food and to choose the ideas they want to write about. Remind them that they'll want to include facts because they're writing an informative pamphlet.

2. Write a First Draft

Before students begin writing, make sure they have read the checklist in the Edit section. Also have them look at the example on page 278. Remind students to use the best points from their brainstorming notes to write their pamphlet.

3. Edit

Direct students to read and complete the self-assessment checklist on page 278. Ask for a show of hands for how many students gave all or mostly *yes* answers. If desired, ask students to comment on some of the errors they found.

DO I...	YES
use indefinite articles (*a/an, some/any*) for nonspecific nouns?	☐
use no article (Ø) for nonspecific plural count nouns and noncount nouns?	☐
use the definite article *the* with specific nouns?	☐
use plural count nouns and noncount nouns without articles to make generic statements ?	☐

4. Peer Review

Pair students and direct them to read each other's work. Ask students to answer the questions in the checklist and discuss them. Give students suggestions of helpful feedback: e.g. *Is this a count or a noncount noun? Should you use* a *or* some *with it? / One of the words in this sentence needs an article. Can you tell me which one?*

5. Rewrite Your Draft

Students should consider their partners' comments from the peer review and rewrite as necessary. Encourage students to proofread their work again before turning it in.

13 Relative Clauses with Subject Relative Pronouns

Overview

Relative clauses are dependent clauses that modify nouns. This chapter focuses exclusively on relative clauses with subject relative pronouns. There are two types of relative clauses: restrictive and nonrestrictive. A restrictive relative clause is used to distinguish one noun from another (e.g., *The company that produces women's hair products is going bankrupt.*). A nonrestrictive relative clause is used to provide extra information about a noun (e.g., *The company's products, which are made from 100 percent organic materials, are very expensive.*).

Form: Typical errors students make with relative clauses are incorrectly placing the clause in the sentence (e.g., **Mr. Berry lives in San Francisco, who is my English teacher.* Incorrect) and not knowing which relative pronoun to use (e.g., **Mr. Berry, that is my English teacher, lives in San Francisco.* Incorrect).

A) GRAMMAR IN DISCOURSE

Office Outfits That Work

A1: Before You Read

- Give students time to discuss the questions in their books in pairs. Call on several students to share their answers.

- Ask the class how they would dress for an interview. Would their clothing choices be more formal, the same, or less formal than what they usually wear? Have them justify their answers.

A2: Read

- Before students start reading, divide the board into two columns: *formal business wear* and *"business casual."* Ask students to guess what clothing is suitable for each category. Write their guesses on the board.

- Have students read the article to learn what advice is given to each person.

A3: After You Read

- Before students begin the activity, have them compare their predictions on the board with information in the first part of the article. Then ask: *Does the writer advise the male to wear "business casual"?* (No. A formal suit is advised.)

- Have students do the exercise individually and mark the places in the text where they found the answers.

- Ask them to compare answers with a partner.

- Circulate and note any difficult or problematic items. Then go over these with the whole class.

- As a follow-up activity, write these questions on the board: *Would you prefer to dress casually or formally for work? Would you rather do so all of the time or some of the time? What are the advantages and disadvantages of dressing up and dressing down? Is formal dress more important for certain professions? Why do you think so?*

- Divide students into small groups to discuss the questions.

- Call on a member of each group to summarize the group's position for the class.

- Take a quick poll to find out how students prefer to dress for work.

B) FORM

Relative Clauses with Subject Relative Pronouns

THINK CRITICALLY ABOUT FORM

Method 1
(For students not familiar with the structure)

- **1. IDENTIFY** Have students look at the three underlined relative clauses in the article. Then have them underline nine more.

- Call on several students to write each sentence on the board and underline the relative clause. Check that the commas have been copied correctly.

- **2. RECOGNIZE** Have a new group of students come to the board to circle the subject relative pronoun (*who, which,* or *that*) in each relative clause and the noun or noun phrase it refers to.

- **3. LABEL** Have students look at the underlined examples in the book and tell you which one is nonrestrictive (the third example). Then ask a student to come to the board and find two more examples of sentences with nonrestrictive clauses. Tell the student to write *NR* next to those examples. Remind the class that nonrestrictive relative clauses are separated from the noun they modify with commas.

Method 2
(For students familiar with the structure)

- Have students work in pairs to answer the questions.

- Give students a few minutes to refer to the charts to check their answers and review the structures.

- Call on students to go over the exercise. Discuss any disagreements and have students make any necessary corrections.

FORM CHARTS

- Give students time to read the charts and the bulleted notes and ask questions.

- Write the following sentences on the board and have students copy them in their notebooks:

  Belinda knows a woman . . .

  I have a friend . . .

  He likes eating food . . .

  We saw a movie . . .

- Tell students to add a relative clause to each sentence.

- When they are finished, call on a few students to write their completed sentences on the board.

- Check students' comprehension of the bulleted notes by having them look at the sentences on the board and identify the subject of each

relative clause. Make sure students understand that the verb in the relative clause agrees with the noun in the main clause.

- Ask students if they added restrictive or nonrestrictive relative clauses. If necessary, refer students to the bulleted notes to go over the difference between the two.

- For more practice, write the following sentences on the board. Explain that each sentence has a relative clause error. Give students time to read the sentences and discuss them in pairs. Call on individual students to explain the errors.

  *I like movies that they are exciting. (Incorrect—the pronoun *they* should not be used after the subject relative pronoun *that.*)

  *I saw three students who is in my class. (Incorrect—the verb in the relative clause, *is,* should be plural to agree with the noun in the main clause, *three students.*)

  *San Francisco, that is in California, is my favorite city. (Incorrect—*that* is used only in restrictive relative clauses. *Which* is the relative pronoun that must be used here.)

C MEANING AND USE 1

Identifying Nouns with Restrictive Relative Clauses

THINK CRITICALLY ABOUT MEANING AND USE

- **1.–2. ANALYZE** Have students work in pairs to answer the questions (1. 1b; 2. 2b).

- Give students a few minutes to read the Notes to check their answers.

- Then call on students to read the questions and answers out loud. Elicit corrections.

MEANING AND USE NOTES

- First, ask students to explain the meaning of *restrict*. Students might use gestures to illustrate the definition (limiting or making something smaller).

- For Note 1A, read the information out loud and ask students to explain the difference in meaning between the two pairs of sentences. (In the sentence without a relative clause, it is not clear which girl and boy are B's children. The sentence with the relative clauses provides clear information identifying B's boy and girl.)

- Divide students into small groups and assign them Notes 1B or 1C. Tell each group to read and discuss the Note and example sentences. Then have them write two original example sentences, one with and one without a relative clause.

- Circulate as the groups work, helping as necessary.

- Ask a student from each group to write the group's sentences on the board. The class should decide which sentences are more descriptive: those with or without relative clauses. Leave the sentences on the board.

- Give students time to read Note 2. Check for comprehension and discuss as necessary.

- If any of the student sentences on the board have a subject relative pronoun + *be*, ask students to come to the board and reduce the restrictive clauses. If none of the clauses can be reduced, write the following examples on the board for students to reduce:

    The man who is standing on the corner is my brother. (The man standing on the corner is my brother.)

    The movie that is at the Lido this week is great. (The movie at the Lido this week is great.)

Beyond the Sentence: Combining Sentences with Relative Clauses (p. 293)

This section is intended to give your students practice with the meaning and use of grammar as it functions naturally in extended discourse such as paragraphs and conversations.

- Tell students to close their books. Read the two paragraphs out loud and have students tell you which one is smoother and less repetitious (paragraph 2). Then ask them why. (It uses relative clauses.)

- Tell students to open their books and read the two paragraphs silently. Ask them to note the number of sentences in each paragraph. Elicit which has fewer (paragraph 2). Ask students to circle each noun in paragraph 1 that is replaced with a relative clause in paragraph 2.

D MEANING AND USE 2

Adding Extra Information with Nonrestrictive Relative Clauses

THINK CRITICALLY ABOUT MEANING AND USE

- **1.–2. ANALYZE** Have students work in pairs to answer the questions (1. a, necessary information; b, not essential information; 2. b).

- Give students a few minutes to read the Notes to check their answers.

- Then call on students to read the questions and answers out loud. Discuss any disagreements and have students make any necessary corrections.

MEANING AND USE NOTES

- Have students read the information in Note 1A to check if they understand the difference between the two types of relative clauses in the Think Critically About Meaning and Use exercise above.

- Tell students to read Note 1B silently. Then write this sentence on the board to elicit if it is possible to use a restrictive relative clause with a proper noun or a unique noun: *My father who lives in Germany called me last week.* (No, it is not possible. This sentence is incorrect because proper nouns and unique nouns are already restricted. An exception is the case where there is more than one proper or unique noun, e.g., *I went to the Manhattan that is in Kansas, not the one that is in New York.*)

- Have students practice writing nonrestrictive relative clauses with proper nouns by writing sentences about the cities they live in, come from, and would like to visit.

- Give a few models on the board first:

    I come from New York, which is the city that never sleeps.

    I would like to visit Venice, Italy, which has river canals.

- Have students share their answers in small groups. Then ask a few volunteers to write their sentences on the board. Elicit and offer feedback as necessary.

- Have students read Note 2. It reminds students that restrictive relative clauses allow us to distinguish one noun from another, while nonrestrictive relative clauses simply add extra information about a noun. Write this sentence on the board and ask if it is restrictive or nonrestrictive: *My mother, who is a teacher, lives in Kansas.* (nonrestrictive). Then ask why it cannot be rewritten as a restrictive relative clause. (We have only one mother, so we do not need to distinguish which mother we are referring to.)

- For Note 3, write the first example sentence (*I spoke to Pedro, who is the boss.*) on the board, and explain that this form can be reduced by omitting the relative pronoun + *be*. Cross out these words in the example sentence.

- To check students' understanding, write these sentences on the board and elicit the reduced forms from the class.

   I phoned Alex, who is my friend. (I phoned Alex, my friend.)

   Teresa, who was lying in the sun, felt sleepy. (Teresa, lying in the sun, felt sleepy).

WRITING

THINK CRITICALLY ABOUT MEANING AND USE

- Have students do A individually. Then, in small groups, have them compare answers and discuss any differences.

- Have them stay in groups and do B.

- As a class, review any difficult items from A. Then elicit answers to B:

   1. EVALUATE (From sentence 1 ["The woman who works for my mother …], the direct article *the* allows us to infer that only one woman works for the speaker's mother. In the sentence "A woman who works for my mother … ," it's impossible to say for sure how many women are on the mother's staff without more context.)

   2. PREDICT (If we change the sentence to "I took the umbrella that was in the car," it is no longer possible to say for sure that choice is

true: all we know for sure is that the speaker is referring to the umbrella in the car. Perhaps the speaker has other umbrellas [e.g., at home or at his or her office,] but this is not clear from the context. Choice b ["The umbrella was in the car"] remains True.)

WRITE

The purpose of this activity is to give students practice in using relative pronouns with subject relative pronouns by writing a "for and against" essay.

1. Brainstorm

As a class, start a brainstorm on the board about school uniforms. Ask students to give one or two reasons for and against the idea. For example, students might be for uniforms because it creates a sense of community. Students might be opposed because they don't like the look of the uniforms. Have students work individually to add to the brainstorming notes.

2. Write a First Draft

Before students begin writing, make sure they have read the checklist in the Edit section. Remind students to use the best points from their brainstorming notes to write their essay.

3. Edit

Direct students to read and complete the self-assessment checklist on page 300. Ask for a show of hands for how many students gave all or mostly *yes* answers.

4. Peer Review

Pair students and direct them to read each other's work. Ask students to answer the questions in the checklist and discuss them. Give students suggestions of helpful feedback: e.g., *Can you combine these sentences using a relative clause? How?*

5. Rewrite Your Draft

Students should consider their partners' comments from the peer review and rewrite as necessary. Encourage students to proofread their work again before turning it in.

14 Relative Clauses with Object Relative Pronouns

Overview

Whereas relative clauses with subject relative pronouns differ in form from those with object relative pronouns, their meanings and uses are similar. Relative clauses with object relative pronouns can be restrictive, used to distinguish one noun from another (e.g., *I helped the kind man who I met at the bus stop.*), and nonrestrictive, used to provide extra information about a noun (e.g., *The blue house on our block, which I pass every day, has been robbed.*).

Form: One key difference in form between subject and object relative pronouns is that object relative pronouns are followed by a subject + verb (e.g., *I read the essay that <u>Roberta</u> <u>wrote</u>.*), and subject relative pronouns are followed by a verb (e.g., *Roberta, who <u>is</u> a good writer, won a scholarship.*).

A GRAMMAR IN DISCOURSE

The New Face of a Role Model

A1: Before You Read

- Ask students if they enjoy playing or watching soccer. Ask if they saw or remember the 1999 Women's World Cup. Then ask if anyone remembers who won the championship and who some of the stars were. Ask if anyone recognizes the name Mia Hamm and explain that the class is going to read an article about her.

- Before students look at the article, elicit the meaning of *role model* by giving students a few example sentences and asking them to guess the meaning of the term. (*A lot of kids want to grow up and be like Michael Jordan; he is a role model to them. My daughter's role model is our doctor. She wants to be just like her when she grows up.*)

- Put students into pairs to discuss the questions in the book.

- Call on several students to share their opinions about the qualities of a good role model. Write these on the board to refer to during the After You Read activity.

A2: Read

- Tell students they will read about soccer star Mia Hamm to find out what she thinks about being a role model.

- Do the reading in two parts. First ask students to silently read the section before the interview and prepare a one-minute oral summary. Tell them to jot down notes as they read.

- Put students into pairs to present their summaries to each other.

- Have students read the interview section of the article silently to themselves. Then have them read the interview out loud in pairs, with one partner reading the interviewer's part and the other reading Mia Hamm's part.

Cultural Notes

This article introduces students to an important element of America's battle with discrimination: the relatively recent enactment of laws providing girls with equal access to school sports. This issue may come as a surprise to many students, who may come from countries where women never engage in sports, or conversely, countries where no law has ever been necessary because women and men have always been treated equally in sports.

A3: After You Read

- Have students do this exercise individually and mark the places in the text where they found the answers.

- Ask them to compare answers with a partner.

- Circulate and note any problematic items. Then go over these with the whole class.

- As a follow-up activity, put students into pairs and have them compare the information on the board from the Before You Read activity about good role-model qualities with the information in the article about Mia Hamm. On the board write: *Do you think Mia Hamm is a good role model? Why or why not?*

- Call on students to share their answers.

B) FORM 1

Relative Clauses with Object Relative Pronouns

THINK CRITICALLY ABOUT FORM

Method 1
(For students not familiar with the structure)

- **1. IDENTIFY** Elicit the relative pronouns that students have been working with (*who, that,* and *which*).

- Write the first sentence from the first paragraph of the article on the board (*The Women's World Cup, which the media called the biggest female sporting event in history, arrived for the first time in the United States in 1999.*). Underline the relative clause as in the book.

- Elicit the object relative pronoun of the clause *(which).* Circle it on the board.

- Elicit the noun or noun phrase it modifies (*The Women's World Cup*). Circle it on the board.

- Ask students to examine each relative clause with an object relative pronoun and mark it in the same way in their books.

- **2. EVALUATE** Direct students' attention to the subtitle of the article. Write it on the board (*In women's soccer, girls finally get the role model they deserve: Mia Hamm.*).

- Elicit the relative clause (*they deserve*). Elicit the noun it modifies (*role model*).

- Ask students what the object relative pronoun is. (There is none.) Explain that the relative pronoun is implied. Insert the pronoun *that* or *who* into the sentence on the board. Remind students that one of these pronouns must be

used because *role model* refers to a person. The pronoun *which* cannot be used, because it refers to things.

- Give students time to insert a pronoun into the other relative clauses that are missing one in the rest of the article.

- Circulate, helping students to choose a pronoun based on the noun it modifies. Several answers are possible.

Method 2
(For students familiar with the structure)

- Have students work in pairs to answer the questions.

- Give students a few minutes to refer to the charts to check their answers.

- Call on students to go over the exercise. Discuss any disagreements and have students make any necessary corrections.

FORM CHARTS

- Tell students to read the example sentences in the charts and then the bulleted notes. Ask them to tell you which relative pronouns can be used with each kind of relative clause, restrictive and nonrestrictive. (In restrictive clauses, *who, whom,* and *that* are used for people; *which* and *that* are used for things. In nonrestrictive clauses, *who* and *whom* are used for people; *which* is used for things.)

- Students may need more practice identifying object relative pronouns. Write the following sentences on the board. Have students identify the relative clause and the relative pronoun and tell you whether the relative pronoun is the subject or object of the clause.

   The movie <u>that you told me about</u> was terrible. (The relative pronoun, *that*, is the object of the relative clause.)

   My friend <u>who works at the university</u> is coming for dinner. (The relative pronoun, *who*, is the subject of the relative clause.)

   The fish <u>that we had last night</u> was delicious. (The relative pronoun, *that*, is the object of the relative clause.)

   New York, <u>which we visited last year</u>, is my favorite city. (The relative pronoun, *which*, is the object of the relative clause.)

- If necessary, tell students that the easiest way to determine whether a relative pronoun is an object relative pronoun is to see if a noun or pronoun directly follows the relative pronoun. If so, that noun or pronoun is the subject of the relative clause and the relative pronoun is the object of the clause. (For example, *We looked at the photos that we had bought.* In the relative clause *that we had bought*, the subject is *we* and the object is the relative pronoun *that.*)

- Follow up by asking students in which sentences on the board we can omit the relative pronoun (Sentences 1 and 3). To explain Sentence 2, point out that we cannot delete the subject relative pronoun because the verb in the clause is *work* (and not *be* + participle or *be* + prepositional phrase). For Sentence 4, point out that object relative pronouns cannot be omitted when the relative clause is nonrestrictive.

Vocabulary Notes: Object Relative Pronouns (p. 307)

- Give students time to read the Notes.

- Divide students into small groups and ask them to write two informal sentences using an object relative clause with *who.* Tell them to think of a situation in which these sentences would be appropriate (talking to a friend, writing a personal letter, etc.).

- Ask students to write two formal sentences using *whom.* Tell them to think of a situation in which these sentences would be appropriate (talking to a professor, writing a business letter, etc.).

- Call on several students to share their answers. Write them on the board.

- Ask another student to come to the board to delete the relative pronouns where possible.

the relative clause in each one. (In 1a, the relative clause is *that costs $200.* In 1b, the relative clause is *you wanted*—there is an omitted object relative pronoun. In 2a, the relative clause is *who was only 16.* In 2b, the relative clause is *who I know.*)

- Elicit a possible relative pronoun for the one omitted in sentence 1b (*that* or *which*).

- Have students answer the questions in pairs. Then call on individual students to explain their answers. (The noun referred to in both 1a and 1b is *coat*; the noun referred to in 2a and 2b is *Megan Quann.*)

- **2. EVALUATE** Elicit that sentences 1a and 1b contain restrictive relative clauses, which help to identify the noun, and that sentences 2a and 2b contain nonrestrictive relative clauses, which provide extra information about the noun but are not needed to identify it.

MEANING AND USE NOTES

- Have students close their books. Write several example sentences from the Notes on the board and ask students to explain the purpose of each relative clause (to identify the noun in restrictive clauses; to add extra information in nonrestrictive clauses).

- Ask students to open their books and read Note 1B silently. Then have them work in pairs to write two new sentences using a relative clause with an object relative pronoun. One sentence should introduce a person using an indefinite article. The second sentence should talk about a definite noun (e.g., *A man I know sells cars. That's the student who I met on the bus.*).

- Call on several students to read their sentences to the class. Offer feedback as necessary.

C MEANING AND USE 1

Identifying Nouns and Adding Extra Information

THINK CRITICALLY ABOUT MEANING AND USE

- **1. IDENTIFY** Read each sentence in the Student Book out loud. Ask students to identify

D FORM 2

Object Relative Pronouns with Prepositions

THINK CRITICALLY ABOUT FORM

Method 1
(For students not familiar with the structure)

- Do a quick review of prepositions. Write this sentence on the board: *I put the apple on the table.* Underline the word *on*, and ask students to name the part of speech (preposition). Tell students to name other prepositions. Write them on the board.

- Have students read the sentences in the exercise and ask if they have the same meaning (yes).

- **1. IDENTIFY** Then have students work individually to identify the object relative pronouns and prepositions. (In sentence a, the object relative pronoun is *that* and the preposition is *about*. In sentence b, *about* is the preposition and *which* is the object relative pronoun.)

- **2. COMPARE AND CONTRAST** Write the sentences on the board. Give students a minute to examine the prepositions. Then ask a student to come to the board to label the words in the relative clauses (object relative pronoun + subject + verb + preposition for sentence a; preposition + object relative pronoun + subject + verb for sentence b). Offer feedback as necessary.

- Elicit from students that the relative pronoun *that* in sentence a can be replaced by *which* or omitted altogether. In sentence b, only the relative pronoun *which* can be used.

Method 2
(For students familiar with the structure)

- Have students work in pairs to answer the questions.

- Give students a few minutes to refer to the charts to check their answers and review the structures.

- Call on students to go over the exercise. Discuss any disagreements and have students make any necessary corrections.

FORM CHARTS

- Ask students to read the charts and bulleted notes silently.

- Put students into pairs and have them write four new sentences with relative clauses, two ending in prepositions and two beginning with prepositions.

- Circulate as students work and offer feedback.

- Call on pairs to write their sentences on the board. Elicit corrections from the class.

E MEANING AND USE 2

Reducing Relative Clauses

THINK CRITICALLY ABOUT MEANING AND USE

- Ask students if the three sentences in their book express the same idea (yes).

- **ANALYZE** Then give them a few minutes to think about and answer the question. (Sentence b sounds the most formal.)

- Give students a few minutes to refer to the Notes to check their answers.

- Discuss any problems as a class and have students make any necessary corrections.

MEANING AND USE NOTES

- By this point, students should know that it is possible to omit the relative pronoun as well as write a relative clause with the preposition at the end (e.g., *Give the names of two professors you have taken courses with.*). However, they may not know which of these options to choose when speaking or writing. Have students read the Notes.

- Then write the following sentences on the board:
  1. a. *Have you finished the work about which you were talking?*
     b. *Have you finished the work you were talking about?*
  2. a. *He attended the lecture in which he was interested.*
     b. *He attended the lecture he was interested in.*
  3. a. *The least expensive thing I saw that you would like is a silver ring.*
     b. *The least expensive thing that I saw that you would like is a silver ring.*

- For the first pair of sentences, ask *Where does the preposition move to when we omit the relative pronoun?* (To the end of the sentence as in 1b.)

- For the second pair of sentences, ask *Which sentence is more formal?* (2a) Why? (The preposition is before the relative pronoun.)

- For the third pair of sentences, ask *What is the difference between these sentences?* (In sentence a the first object relative pronoun is omitted.)

Vocabulary Notes: *When* and *Where* in Relative Clauses (p. 320)

- Give students time to read the Notes.

- Divide them into small groups and ask them to write two sentences using *when* and *where* as replacements for prepositions and object relative pronouns. Tell them they can write about a school where they studied English before (e.g., *The school where I studied English in my country was . . .*) and a time when they did something interesting (e.g., *The summer when I traveled through Europe was . . .*).

- Call on several groups to share their sentences. Write them on the board and elicit corrections as necessary.

WRITING

THINK CRITICALLY ABOUT MEANING AND USE

- Have students do A individually. Then, in small groups, have them compare answers and discuss any differences.

- Have them stay in groups and do B.

- As a class, review any difficult items from A. Then elicit answers to B:

    1. IDENTIFY (Sentences 2, 6, 8)

    2. GENERATE (2. The man with whom my sister works has a sailboat; 6. Ms. Wang wrote the book about which I heard on a radio show; 8. Charlotte, for whom I once worked, took over the company.)

WRITE

The purpose of this activity is to give students practice in using relative clauses with object and subject relative pronouns by writing a report about women's sports in your country.

1. Brainstorm

As a class, start a brainstorm on the board about the status of women's sports. Ask students to give a few examples of sports that are popular with women, such as basketball and volleyball. Ask students to offer ideas about training for girls. For example, students might tell about clubs, teams, or physical education

classes for girls of different ages in their countries. Have students name some well-known female athletes, such as Germany's Maria Riesch (Olympic gold medalist skier) and tennis duo Venus and Serena Williams. Have students work individually to add to the brainstorming notes on women's sports.

2. Write a First Draft

Before students begin writing, make sure they have read the checklist in the Edit section. Also have them look at the example on page 324. Remind students to use the best points from their brainstorming notes to write their report.

3. Edit

Direct students to read and complete the self-assessment checklist on page 324. Ask for a show of hands for how many students gave all or mostly *yes* answers. If desired, ask students to comment on some of the errors they found.

DO I...	YES
use headings to help readers see how the information is organized?	☐
use relative clauses to connect ideas and combine sentences?	☐
use correct relative pronouns?	☐
use at least one object relative pronoun with a preposition?	☐
use appropriate verb forms to reflect past, present, and future time?	☐

4. Peer Review

Pair students and direct them to read each other's work. Ask students to answer the questions in the checklist and discuss them. Give students suggestions of helpful feedback: e.g., *Your subject is a person in this sentence. Is it correct to use the word* which *for the object relative pronoun? / How can we make this sentence more formal, so that it sounds better in a report?*

5. Rewrite Your Draft

Students should consider their partners' comments from the peer review and rewrite as necessary. Encourage students to proofread their work again before turning it in.

15 Real Conditionals, Unreal Conditionals, and Wishes

Overview

This chapter introduces real and unreal conditionals, and wishes. The real conditional is used for events that could potentially happen (e.g., *If I study for this test, I will pass it.*), or to express a fact (e.g., *If you heat ice, it melts.*). The unreal conditional is used for imaginary situations (e.g., *If I had a million dollars, I would quit my job.*). Similar to the unreal conditional, the verb *wish* is used to express a desire for an unreal situation (e.g., *I wish I had a million dollars.*).

Form: Students are often confused by the past tense form in unreal conditionals (e.g., *If she knew how to sew, she would save a lot of money.*), which does not indicate past time, but indicates that the situation is not real at the present time (in the above example, she does not know how to sew).

A GRAMMAR IN DISCOURSE

Reflections on Life

A1: Before You Read

- Ask students to make a list of three to five wishes they have. Give them some examples to encourage diverse responses (e.g., *live in a different time period, be president, be rich*). Tell them they do not need to write in complete sentences.

- Put students in pairs to compare their lists and discuss the questions.

A2: Read

- For students who have not heard of the various writers, explain that Sir Walter Alexander Raleigh (not to be confused with the explorer Sir Walter Raleigh) was a British essayist and critic who lived in the late 1800s/early 1900s. Jane Seymour

is a British actress who has appeared in American films and television. Nadine Stair was an American woman who was eighty-five years old when she wrote this poem (which is often incorrectly attributed to Jorge Luis Borges, the Latin American poet). Elicit the meaning of *anonymous*. Ask *Is it a name?* (*Anonymous* means *not named or identified*. This word is used when the name of a writer is unknown.)

- Ask students to follow along in their books as you read the Chinese proverb.

- Elicit the main idea and write it on the board. (Peace in the world depends on the relationships between the individual, the family, and the nation.)

- Divide students into three groups and assign one of the three remaining passages to each group. Ask the groups to read their passage and summarize the writer's outlook. Have a member of each group write the summary on the board.

- Tell students to silently read the summaries on the board and decide which is closest to his or her personal outlook on life and why.

- Have students discuss their opinions in groups.

- Call on several students to report the opinions from their group.

A3: After You Read

- Ask students to do this exercise individually and mark the places in the text where they found their answers.

- Have them compare answers with a partner.

- Circulate and note any difficult or problematic items. Then go over these with the whole class.

- As a follow-up, write these questions on the board for the students to discuss in groups: *Is there anything in your life that you regret doing or not doing? Do you know anyone who regrets doing or not doing something?*

- Some students may be reluctant to speak about themselves or those close to them in this way. If so, do not pressure them. Tell them to simply invent someone to speak about.

- Put students into pairs to discuss their answers.

- Then call on a few students to share their answers.

Real Conditionals, Unreal Conditionals, and Wishes

THINK CRITICALLY ABOUT FORM

Method 1:

(For students not familiar with the structure)

Before you start the Think Critically About Form activity, you may want to do the following exercise with your students to review the terms *clause* (*dependent* and *independent*) and the verb *wish*.

- Write this sentence on the board: *If I had a kitten, I would be very happy.*

- Ask students if they can identify which part of the sentence is a clause (there are two clauses: *If I had a kitten* and *I would be very happy*). If necessary, confirm that students know what exactly a clause is (a group of words that has a subject and verb). Note the subject and verb in each of the above clauses (*I had* and *I would be*).

- Ask the students these questions to test their knowledge: *Which of the two clauses in the above sentence can stand alone and make sense?* (*I would be very happy*); *What is the name of this type of clause?* (independent, not dependent on another clause); *Can the other clause stand alone and make sense?* (No, it leaves you waiting for more information.); *What is the name of this type of clause?* (dependent, it depends on another clause). Explain that a clause starting with *if* is a dependent clause and needs a main clause to accompany it.

- Finally write the sentence *I wish I had a kitten.* Ask students what the sentence means (I would like a kitten very much, but I don't have one.).

- **1. IDENTIFY** Have a student read out the underlined example of an *if* clause in the Chinese Proverb, and write the complete sentence on the board (*If there is light in the soul, there will be beauty in the person.*).

- Have students give you another example of the real conditional with the simple present in the *if* clause (*If there is beauty in the person . . .*). Write the complete sentence under the other one on the board and label this column *Real Conditionals*.

- Ask students to call out the other two examples (*If there is harmony. . .* and *If there is order. . .*) and ask two students to write these in the same column.

- **2. RECOGNIZE** Have students find the sentences with the simple past in the *if* clause in selections 2 and 3 (selection 2: *if I had it to do over again* and *if I had my life to live over*; selection 3: *if it were over tomorrow*). Call on two students to write the complete sentences on the board in another column. Label this column *Unreal Conditionals*.

- Ask one student to come to the board and underline the verbs in the *if* clauses of both types of conditional sentences and explain to the class which tense is used in each type (present in real conditionals, past in unreal conditionals).

- Have another student come to the board to underline and describe to the class the verb forms in the main clause for both real and unreal conditional sentences (*will* + verb in real, *would* + verb in unreal). Point out that the conditionals in selection 1 are future real conditionals.

- **3. RECOGNIZE** Tell students to underline all the verbs that follow *wish* in the Sir Walter Alexander Raleigh passage. Explain that in sentences with *wish*, the simple past is used in the *that* clause. If necessary, clarify that *that* is left out of the sentences, but it is implied.

- Leave the sentences from Think Critically About Form on the board to refer to when introducing the Form Notes.

Method 2
(For students familiar with the structure)

- Have students work in pairs to answer the questions.

- Give students a few minutes to refer to the charts to check their answers and review the structures.

- Call on students to go over the exercise. Discuss any disagreements and have students make any necessary corrections.

FORM CHARTS

- Divide students into groups. Tell them to read the charts and mark any new verb forms in the main clauses that are not in the sentences on the board. (*Be going to* and *may* can be used in addition to *will* in the real conditional main clause. *Could* and *might* can be used in addition to *would* in the unreal conditional main clause.)

- Tell students to skim the bulleted notes and write three examples each of the real and unreal conditional using the new verb forms. Circulate and offer feedback as necessary.

- Have the students read the chart *Wishes About the Present and Future*. Tell them to mark the verb forms in sentences with *wish* that are not on the board (negative, past continuous, would, could).

- As students mark the new forms for unreal conditionals and wish sentences, point out that in these types of sentences, *be* changes to *were* with all subjects.

Informally Speaking: Using *Was* (p. 334)

- Choose two students to read the text in the speech bubbles. Then tell the class you will play the recording and that they should listen to how the underlined form in the cartoon is different from what they hear. If needed, play the recording more than once.

- Have students point out the differences. (The cartoon reads *I wish I were taller.* On the recording the form is *I wish I was taller.* The cartoon reads *If it were earlier*, whereas on the recording the form is *If it was earlier.*) Explain that the form on the cassette is considered more informal English. Point out that the form

in the cartoon is standard English and students should use this form when writing and speaking, although they may hear native speakers using the informal form.

C MEANING AND USE 1

Real Conditionals

THINK CRITICALLY ABOUT MEANING AND USE

- **EVALUATE** Have students work in pairs to answer the questions (b, a promise; a, a statement of fact; d, a warning; and c, an instruction).

- Give students a few minutes to refer to the Notes to check their answers.

- Call on students to read the sentences and give their answers. Discuss any disagreements and have students make any necessary corrections.

MEANING AND USE NOTES

- Read the explanation in Note 1 and ask students to identify first the *if* clause and then the main clause in the example. Then ask them what meaning is expressed in the main clause (a possible result), and what meaning is expressed in the *if* clause (a possible condition).

- Divide students into groups of three and assign one of the remaining Notes to each group. Have each group read the Note and prepare to present it to the class with a couple new example sentences.

- Circulate among the groups and check that they are on the right track. Make any necessary corrections.

- Have each group present their Note and share the new example sentences on the board.

- Check the form and meaning of each sentence as a class and answer any questions.

Vocabulary Notes: *If* and *Unless* (p. 339)

- Write the following sentence on the board: *Unless you study, you will fail the test.* Tell students to identify the dependent and independent clause (dependent: *unless you study*; independent: *you will fail the test*).

- Then ask students to think of another way to say the same thing. If they don't know, hint to start the sentence with *If* (*If you don't study, you will fail the test.*). If students forget to change the affirmative verb to negative in the dependent clause, point out that the sentence does not make sense: *If you study, you will fail the test.* Explain that *unless* has the same meaning as the negative *if* clause.

- Give students time to read the Notes and ask questions.

- To check students' comprehension, write the following sentences on the board and ask students to rewrite them using *unless.*

  You won't pass the exam if you don't study. (You won't pass the exam unless you study.)

  If she doesn't get a scholarship, she won't be able to go to college. (Unless she gets a scholarship, she won't be able to go to college.)

  The airlines won't sell you a ticket if you don't have a visa. (The airlines won't sell you a ticket unless you have a visa.)

- Have a student come to the board to write the answers. Answer any outstanding questions.

D MEANING AND USE 2

Unreal Conditionals

THINK CRITICALLY ABOUT MEANING AND USE

- **1.–2. ANALYZE AND DIFFERENTIATE** Have students work in pairs to answer the questions (1. 1a is more likely to happen and 1b is probably imaginary; 2. 2b is more direct and 2a is more indirect).

- Give students a few minutes to refer to the Notes to check their answers.

- Call on students to read the questions and answers out loud. Discuss any disagreements and have students make necessary corrections.

MEANING AND USE NOTES

- Give students time to read Notes 1A, 1B, and 1C and ask questions. Write a few *if* clauses on the board that are not true for the students

(e.g., *If I were a native speaker of English . . .; If I were an Olympic gold medalist . . .*).

- Ask students to complete the sentences with their own ideas and write them in their notebooks.

- Call on several students to share their answers.

- Tell students to close their books and listen carefully as you read the two sample sentences from Note 2. Ask students to tell you which sentence seems more direct (the sentence with a modal) and which seems more indirect (the sentence with an unreal conditional). Have students open their books to check their responses.

- Finally, tell students to read the conversations in Note 3 in pairs, switching parts after each one. When they finish, ask them to write their own dialogue in which they practice using conditionals to ask permission. Write some interesting topics on the board to make the activity more lively, e.g., asking permission to use the family car, to go to the movies, to go on a trip with a friend..

Beyond the Sentence: Omitting *If* Clauses (p. 343)

This section is intended to give your students practice with the meaning and use of grammar as it functions naturally in extended discourse such as paragraphs and conversations.

- Give students a minute to read the explanation and the example paragraph.

- Elicit the omitted *if* clause for each sentence (*If I were the boss, . . .*).

- Refer students to the passage "If I Had My Life to Live Over" on page 328 in their books. Explain that this is another example of omitting *if* clauses. Elicit that each sentence is a result of the condition *If I Had My Life to Live Over.*

E MEANING AND USE 3

Wishes

THINK CRITICALLY ABOUT MEANING AND USE

- As a precursor, explain that we can make wishes for different time frames (present, future, and past) and for different purposes (to express desire, disappointment, complaints, regret).

- **1.–2. ANALYZE** Have students work in groups to answer the questions (1. 1b is present and 1a is future; 2. 2a is a complaint and 2b is a regret).

- Give students a few minutes to refer to the Notes to check their answers.

- Then call on students to read the questions and answers out loud. Discuss any disagreements.

MEANING AND USE NOTES

- Set up a jigsaw activity for the Notes. Divide students into three groups, and assign one Note to each group.

- Tell each group to read the Note and write a paraphrase of the explanation. Ask students to write a new example sentence that expresses the meaning and use of this grammar point. Give groups about ten minutes to prepare this information.

- Divide students into new groups so that there is at least one member from each of the four original groups. Each member of the new group will explain his or her information and example sentence to the others.

- Circulate as the groups work, helping them with any problems.

WRITING

THINK CRITICALLY ABOUT MEANING AND USE

- Have students do A individually. Then, in small groups, have them compare answers and discuss any differences.

- Have them stay in groups and do B.

- As a class, review any difficult items from A. Then elicit answers to B:

    1. GENERATE (*If only it would stop raining; I wish it would stop raining; If only we could leave; I wish we could leave.*)

    2. SYNTHESIZE (*If I had a choice, I wouldn't take the exam.*)

WRITE

The purpose of this activity is to give students practice in using real and unreal conditionals by writing a public service announcement about home safety.

1. Brainstorm

As a class, start a brainstorm on the board about safety in the home. Ask students to list some common injuries or accidents that happen in the home, such as falls or kitchen fires. Have students give one or two examples of safety devices in the home. For example, they might name a fire extinguisher or a list of emergency phone numbers posted in a prominent place. Have individuals add their own ideas about home safety to the brainstorming notes.

2. Write a First Draft

Before students begin writing, make sure they have read the checklist in the Edit section. Also have them look at the example on page 350. Remind students to use the best points from their brainstorming notes to write their announcement.

3. Edit

Direct students to read and complete the self-assessment checklist on page 350. Ask for a show of hands for how many students gave all or mostly *yes* answers. If desired, ask students to comment on some of the errors they found.

4. Peer Review

Pair students and direct them to read each other's work. Ask students to answer the questions in the checklist and discuss them. Give students suggestions of helpful feedback: e.g. *Is this sentence a wish or a fact? / Let's use the word* unless *in this sentence. How can we rewrite it?*

5. Rewrite Your Draft

Students should consider their partners' comments from the peer review and rewrite as necessary. Encourage students to proofread their work again before turning it in.

16 Past Unreal Conditionals and Past Wishes

Overview

The past unreal conditional is used for imaginary situations that did not take place in the past (e.g., *If Li had studied hard, she would have passed the test.*). The reality is that Li did not study hard and as a result did not pass her test. The verb *wish* can be used similarly to express a desire for an unreal past situation (e.g., *Li wishes she had studied harder.*). Another way to express past wishes is with the construction *if only* (e.g., *If only Li had studied harder.*).

Form: In the *if* clause, the past perfect is used to indicate the situation was unreal in the past. In the result clause, *would have, could have,* or *might have* indicate the result was unreal in the past.

A GRAMMAR IN DISCOURSE

The Ifs of History

A1: Before You Read

This is a longer and more complex text than the previous ones, so allow plenty of time for students to read it.

- To introduce the concept of *what if?*, give students five minutes to answer the questions in the book.

- Put students in pairs and have them share what they wrote with a partner.

- Explain that the article discusses several important historical events, some of which they may not know.

- Write the names Adolf Hitler, Cleopatra, Franklin Delano Roosevelt, and Vincent van Gogh on the board. Point out that these are historical figures, and ask students if they know who any of them are. If so, call on these students to give some information about the

historical figure. Describe the figures that the students are unfamiliar with. *(Adolf Hitler was the fascist leader of Nazi Germany during World War II. Cleopatra was an Egyptian queen famous for her beauty, who lived about 2000 years ago. Franklin Delano Roosevelt was President of the United States during World War II, and he is credited with pulling the United States out of its worst economic depression. Vincent van Gogh was a Dutch painter who is as famous for his insanity as he is for his artistry. He once cut off his ear.)*

A2: Read

- Before students read, give them some examples of ifs from your own life, perhaps describe what would have happened to you if you hadn't experienced whatever it was that inspired you to become a teacher. Explain that the article explores some possible alternatives to actual historical events.

- The first three paragraphs of the article introduce the main idea. Tell students to read them and write one sentence that expresses the main idea. (The article encourages us to imagine how history would have turned out if certain events had happened differently.)

- Call on several students to read their sentences out loud.

- Divide students into four groups, one for each historical personality described in the article. Each group will be responsible for reading, understanding, discussing, and summarizing the "if" described in the paragraph.

- When they are finished, one group member will present the information to the class. The other students will listen and ask questions. The four personalities are Franklin Roosevelt (paragraph 2), Adolf Hitler (paragraph 4),

Cleopatra (paragraph 5), and Vincent van Gogh (paragraph 6).

- After they finish, ask students if they agree with the writer's ideas. Make sure they explain why or why not.

A3: After You Read

- Have students to do this exercise individually and mark the places in the text where they found the answers.
- Ask them to compare answers with a partner.
- Circulate and note any difficult or problematic items. Then go over these with the whole class.
- As a follow-up activity, ask students to think of a major event in the history of their countries that affected the lives of many people (e.g., the election of a president, the birth or death of a member of a royal family, a currency crisis, etc.).
- Put students into pairs to discuss their answers. If possible, pair students from the same country so they both have knowledge of the event.

B FORM

Past Unreal Conditionals and Past Wishes

THINK CRITICALLY ABOUT FORM

Method 1
(For students not familiar with the structure)

- **1. IDENTIFY** Direct students' attention to the first underlined past unreal conditional sentence. Ask *How many clauses are in this sentence?* (two); *What are they?* (the *if* clause and the main clause).
- Ask students to find and note three more examples of past unreal conditional sentences. Call on several students to tell you the sentences. Write them on the board.
- **2. RECOGNIZE** Elicit the verb form used in the *if* clause (past perfect) and the one used in the main clause (*would have* + past participle). Some students may say that the present perfect

is used in the main clause, but point out that this is not accurate.

Method 2
(For students familiar with the structure)

- Have students work in pairs to answer the questions.
- Give students a few minutes to refer to the charts to check their answers.
- Call on students to go over the exercise. Discuss any disagreements and have students make any necessary corrections.

FORM CHARTS

- Tell students to read the *Past Unreal Conditionals* charts to see all the possible modals for the main clause (*would, could,* and *might*) Then ask them to compare these with the modals in the main clauses of the sentences from the Think Critically About Form activity.
- Ask students to write three of the sentences from the exercise in their notebooks and change *would* in the main clause to *could* or *might* (*What might have happened if there had been no Franklin Delano Roosevelt?*).
- Have students read the bulleted notes. Then check their comprehension by writing the following sentences on the board and asking students to identify and explain the errors.

    I would have come to the party, if you had invited me. (Incorrect—there should be no comma if main clause is first.)

    If she called me, I'd have come to the meeting. (Incorrect—the past perfect must be used in the *if* clause.)

    If he had been on time, he would have missed his train? (Incorrect—questions are formed with the main clause in question word order: *would he have missed his train?*)

- Tell students to read the *Past Wishes* chart, then elicit a few examples of things students wish they had done last year, e.g., studied harder, moved to a new apartment, saved money, etc. Write these prompts on the board.
- Call on various students to create complete sentences from the prompts on the board (e.g., *I wish (that) I had studied harder.*).

Informally Speaking: Reduced Forms of Past Conditionals (p. 357)

- Choose two students to read the text in the speech bubbles. Then tell the class you will play the recording and that they should listen to how the underlined form in the cartoon is different from what they hear. If needed, play the recording more than once.

- Have students point out the differences. (The cartoon reads *Well, I would have shown him the mistake. I sure wouldn't have paid the extra money.* On the recording this is pronounced *Well, I "woulda" shown him the mistake. I sure "wouldn't-uv" paid the extra money.*) Explain that the form on the recording is considered more informal English. Point out that the form in the cartoon is standard English and students should use this form when writing and speaking, although they may hear native speakers using the informal form.

C MEANING AND USE 1

Past Unreal Conditionals

THINK CRITICALLY ABOUT MEANING AND USE

- **1.–2. EVALUATE** Have students work in pairs to answer the questions (1. a; 2. b).

- Give students a few minutes to refer to the Notes to check their answers.

- Call on students to read the questions and answers out loud. Discuss any disagreements and have students make any necessary corrections.

MEANING AND USE NOTES

- Have students read the information in Note 1A. Call on one student to create another sample sentence by asking *If you had been the boss, what would you have done?*

- Elicit the modals that can be used in the result clause of a past unreal conditional sentence *(would, could, might)*. Write these on the board. Ask *Which of these modals indicates the most certainty? (would).*

- Give students time to read Note 1B and ask questions. Elicit the full form of the contraction *(had had)* and point out to students that although this may look unusual, this is the correct form.

- Direct students' attention to the example sentences in Note 2. Ask if the sentences have the same or a different meaning (the same). Elicit which is a more direct way of giving the advice (the sentence with *should*). Point out that giving advice with an unreal conditional is perceived as more polite or indirect. Give students time to read Note 2 and ask questions.

- Ask students to read Note 3 and answer any questions. Have them to write a pair of sentences with the same meaning: one past unreal conditional, and the other a true sentence with *but*. Write an example on the board for the class first (e.g., *I would have called you if I hadn't lost your number. I would have called you, but I lost your number.*).

- Call on several students to write their sentences on the board.

D MEANING AND USE 2

Past Wishes

THINK CRITICALLY ABOUT MEANING AND USE

- **1.–2. ANALYZE** Have students work in pairs to answer the questions (1. 1a and 2a are about present situations, 1b and 2b are about past situations; 2. 2a and 2b express stronger feelings).

- Give students a few minute to refer to the Notes to check their answers.

- Call on students to read the questions and answers out loud. Discuss any disagreements and have students make any necessary corrections.

MEANING AND USE NOTES

- Tell students to read Note 1. Have students give an additional example by asking, *How was dinner yesterday?* (It was great! I wish you could have eaten with us.)

- Tell students to read the information in Note 2. Call on one or two students to read the examples out loud and try to show regret or dissatisfaction in their voices. Model such a tone for them if necessary.

- Follow the same procedure with tone for the *if only* sentences in Note 3.

- Have students read the Note and create two more sentences using *if only*. Call on students to share their sentences and go over them as a class. Encourage students to experiment with tone as they read the sentences.

- Point out that *if only* is used to express strong feelings of regret. Explain that this language is slightly more formal and common in written English.

WRITING

THINK CRITICALLY ABOUT MEANING AND USE

- Have students do A individually. Then, in small groups, have them compare answers and discuss any differences.

- Have them stay in groups and do B.

- As a class, review any difficult items from A. Then elicit answers to B:

  1. GENERATE (Answers will vary. Some examples are: 2. If I'd taken a vacation, I wouldn't have been here when the boss had to fire 50% of our staff; If I'd taken a vacation, I could have joined my friends on their cruise in the Caribbean; If I'd taken a vacation, I might not have been so tired all last month.)

  2. GENERATE (Answers will vary. Some examples are: 4. If I hadn't followed his advice, my boss probably wouldn't have had a reason to fire me; If I hadn't followed his advice, I wouldn't have lost so much money and I could have bought a new car; If I hadn't followed his advice, I might not have gotten into trouble; 8. If we'd been told about the delay, we would not have set out for the airport at 6 A.M.; If we'd been told about the delay, we could have changed our plans; If we'd been told about the delay, we might not have had an accident while we were rushing to get to the airport.)

WRITE

The purpose of this activity is to give students practice in using past unreal conditionals and wishes by writing an email to a professor.

1. Brainstorm

As a class, start a brainstorm on the board about some of the problems you might have while researching history. For example, you might need information from a museum that was closed on the day you visited. Have students suggest one or two things they might have done differently, such as calling the museum for information on opening hours. After several ideas have been listed in the brainstorm, have individuals write some of their own ideas and decide what they want to write about.

2. Write a First Draft

Before students begin writing, make sure they have read the checklist in the Edit section. Remind students to use the best points from their brainstorming notes to write their email. Point out that since they are asking the professor for a favor (an extension), they must be able to show that they deserve one.

3. Edit

Direct students to read and complete the self-assessment checklist on page 368. Ask for a show of hands for how many students gave all or mostly *yes* answers.

4. Peer Review

Pair students and direct them to read each other's work. Ask students to answer the questions in the checklist and discuss them. Give students suggestions of helpful feedback: e.g., *You've used* might *in this sentence to show a possible result. How can we make this clause show stronger probability? How about using the word* would? / *Can you change a sentence to an "if only" sentence in this paragraph? Which one would show the strongest regret?*

5. Rewrite Your Draft

Students should consider their partners' comments from the peer review and rewrite as necessary. Encourage students to proofread their work again before turning it in.

17 Noun Clauses

Overview

Noun clauses are dependent clauses that can occur in the same place as a noun or noun phrase in a sentence. There are three types of noun clauses: *Wh- Clauses* (e.g., *I don't know where she is.*), *If/Whether Clauses* (e.g., *I wonder whether it stopped raining.*), and *That Clauses* (e.g., *I think that you are smart.*).

Form: Students may confuse the form of noun clauses with question forms, and this can explain word order error such as, *I don't know what time is it*. Remind students that just as nouns and noun phrases can function as objects in a sentence, so can noun clauses (e.g., *I don't understand the question* [noun]. *I don't understand what you just asked me* [noun clause].). Stress that nouns and noun clauses are used the same way.

A GRAMMAR IN DISCOURSE

Career Currents

A1: Before You Read

- Divide students into small groups to discuss the first question. Their answers may vary according to their cultural background.

- Ask a volunteer from each group to come to the board and write one way to find a job that was discussed by their group.

- When all groups have contributed to the list, read it out loud. Elicit other ways to find a job. Add these to the list. Ask the class to rank the top three ways to find a job. Write the appropriate number (1–3) beside each of these.

- Tell students to discuss the other two questions in their groups.

- Take a class vote to find out how many students would quit their job before finding a better one. Ask students who have different opinions to share their reasons.

Cultural Notes

Many students may not know that it is not uncommon for Americans to hold several jobs in several kinds of careers before retiring. Point out that this is a fairly recent trend. In fact, in previous generations, people would rarely leave a good job and would often have the same job for their entire career. This may come as a surprise to students who come from more traditional backgrounds, such as Japan, where it is customary to keep one job for a very long time.

A2: Read

- Before students begin reading, elicit some of the benefits of looking for a job even if you have a job (make sure students understand that you mean *looking for* a job and not *changing* jobs). Make a list of their ideas on the board.

- Tell students to read the article to find out some of the benefits of looking for a new job.

- As a class, check the list on the board. Add any new benefits mentioned in the article.

A3: After You Read

- Ask students to do this exercise individually and then compare their answers in pairs.

- Go over any difficult or problematic items.

- As a follow-up activity, ask students to consider their own job search experiences. Write these questions on the board for students to discuss in pairs: *How did you search for a job? prepare a résumé? prepare for an interview?* If students have never looked for a job, ask them to think about a friend's or family member's job search experience.

- Divide students into small groups to discuss their experiences.

- Ask the groups to devise the most effective job- search plan based on the group members' experiences.
- Call on several groups to share their plans.

Noun Clauses

THINK CRITICALLY ABOUT FORM

Method 1:
(For students not familiar with the structure)

- **1. IDENTIFY** Have students work individually to find three examples of each type of clause in the article and then compare their answers with a partner.
- Explain that *how* is grouped with *wh-* words (*who, what, why, where, when*) even though it does not begin with *wh.*
- **2. ANALYZE** Call on several students to write the examples of the different types of clauses they found on the board. Make sure there is at least one example of each type of clause. Tell students to circle the subject and verb. Have them write *S* above the subject and *V* above the verb. *S* followed by *V* is statement word order. Point out to students that statement word order is used in all the clauses.

Method 2
(For students familiar with the structure)

- Have students work in pairs to answer the questions.
- Give students a few minutes to refer to the charts to check their answers and review the structures.
- Call on students to go over the exercise. Discuss any disagreements and have students make any necessary corrections.

FORM CHARTS

- Tell students to label the subjects and verbs of the noun clauses in the charts with *S* and *V* and compare this with the labeling they did in Think Critically About Form. (Again, this will reveal statement word order.)

- Ask students to read the bulleted notes. Tell them to underline the subjects and verbs in the examples of noun clauses in the Notes.
- Explain the concept of embedded questions. These are questions that appear within a statement (e.g., *He asked who she is.*) or a question (e.g., *Do you know if he is here?*).
- Check students' comprehension of embedded questions by writing these sentences with word order errors on the board and calling on students to correct them. Underline the embedded question in each example.

  *Do you know <u>when did she leave?</u> (Incorrect— Do you know when she left?)

  *I wonder <u>where did the sun go?</u> (Incorrect— I wonder where the sun went.)

  *I don't know <u>if is she here today.</u> (Incorrect— I don't know if she is here today.)

- For the second and third sentence, explain that these are not questions and should not be punctuated with question marks. Write the correct forms on the board and then analyze them together. Point out that the incorrect sentences use question word order instead of statement word order.

Wh- and If/Whether Clauses

THINK CRITICALLY ABOUT MEANING AND USE

- **1.–2. IDENTIFY AND EVALUATE** Have students work in pairs to answer the questions.
- Give students a few minutes to refer to the Notes to check their answers (1. *decide, know,* and *wonder* express mental activities; 2. 2b).
- Then call on students to read the questions and answers out loud. Discuss any disagreements and have students make any necessary corrections.

MEANING AND USE NOTES

- Put students into pairs. Tell them to read the Notes and examine the examples in Notes 1A, 1B, and 1C. Have them write new sentences using some of the verbs from 1B, the expressions from 1C, and a *wh-* word or *that* clause (e.g., *I decided where to go. She figured out that he was lying.*).

- Ask one person from each pair to read one of the sentences to the class. Offer feedback as necessary.

- Give students a few minutes to read Note 2 and ask questions. Ask the same pairs to choose two of the verbs and phrases, and write sentences with *wh-* or *if/whether* clauses.

- Have one person from each pair read one of these sentences. Offer feedback as necessary.

- Tell students to read the explanation and examples in Notes 3A and 3B. Then give them a new *wh-* question: *Where is the nearest pay phone?* to change into an indirect question (*I was wondering where the nearest pay phone is.*).

- Repeat the procedure with a new *Yes/No* question: *Is the subway on this block?* Have students change it into an indirect question (*Do you know if the subway is on this block?*).

Vocabulary Notes: *If* and *Whether* (p. 382)

- Give students a few minutes to read the Notes and example sentences.

- Point out that although *whether* is considered more formal, it is not actually informal or impolite to use *if*. *If* is used even more often than *whether*.

D) MEANING AND USE 2

That Clauses

THINK CRITICALLY ABOUT MEANING AND USE

- **1.–2. ANALYZE** Ask students to silently read the two pairs of sentences and tell you which pair has the same meaning (2a and 2b).

- Write 2a and 2b sentences on the board and ask a student to come up and underline the noun clauses. Ask another student to come up and circle the verb in each noun clause and tell you the form of the verbs (2a, *was*, simple past; 2b, *is*, simple present).

- Repeat the procedure for the first pair of sentences. (The meaning is different. In 1a,

the verb is *left,* simple past. In 1b the verb is *'s leaving,* present continuous.)

- Ask students to explain why the meaning is different in pair 1 but the same in pair 2. If necessary, direct students to the particular verbs. (In sentence 1a, the past tense means that the action in the noun clause is in the past and complete; in sentence 1b, the present continuous means that the action is in progress or will happen soon. In the second pair, the verbs in the noun clause express a fact that is always true. For example, after someone has visited another country, she might describe it two ways: *Italy* was *beautiful. Italy* is *beautiful.* She may have felt that way when she was there, but the information is still true now.)

MEANING AND USE NOTES

- Tell students to silently read the explanations and examples in Notes 1A, 1B, and 1C.

- Divide students into pairs and ask them to choose two of the mental activity verbs to use in new sentences with *that* clauses.

- Ask several groups to share their sentences. Offer feedback as necessary.

- For Note 2A, have students write three new sentences using the same verb and format: present + present; present + past; present + future.

- For Notes 2B, 2C, and 2D, read the explanations and examples in each box out loud. Tell students to work in their pairs again. For each Note, give the pair a few minutes to create a new sentence using the same main verb as in the example sentence (e.g., *thought, knew*).

- Ask a few students to write their sentences on the board for each Note. Tell the other students to check the verb use in each and correct any errors.

Trouble Spots

The use of both the present tense and the past tense to talk about generalizations is often confusing to students who have been taught only to use a past form to talk about something that happened in the past. The key here is to emphasize that the rule for generalizations applies only to events and actions that are factual or general truths. For example, we can say, *Columbus believed that the world* is *round*. We can also say, *Columbus believed that the world was round*.

WRITING

THINK CRITICALLY ABOUT MEANING AND USE

- Have students do A individually. Then, in small groups, have them compare answers and discuss any differences.
- Have them stay in groups and do B.
- As a class, review any difficult items from A. Then elicit answers to B:

  1.–2. GENERATE AND SYNTHESIZE
  (Answers will vary. Some examples are: 1. Mary left/has left; 7. He was sorry that he left/had left early; We supposed they had won, but we didn't know for sure.)

WRITE

The purpose of this activity is to give students practice in using noun clauses and mental activity verbs by writing an FAQ page for a travel website.

1. Brainstorm

As a class, start a brainstorm on the board about some of the things that a traveler might want to know when visiting a foreign country. For example, students might say that a traveler would want to know how to book a room in advance or whether there were going to be any festivals happening in the near future. Have students suggest one or two popular attractions to visit from their country as well, such as museums or palaces. After sufficient discussion, have individuals write further ideas about tourism in their own country.

2. Write a First Draft

Before students begin writing, make sure they have read the checklist in the Edit section. Also have them look at the example on page 390. Remind students to use the best points from their brainstorming notes to write their FAQ page.

3. Edit

Direct students to read and complete the self-assessment checklist on page 390. Ask for a show of hands for how many students gave all or mostly *yes* answers. If desired, ask students to comment on some of the errors they found.

DO I…	YES
add a paragraph at the beginning to introduce the FAQs?	☐
use a range of mental activity and other verbs that are usually followed by noun clauses?	☐
use at least one example of a *wh-* clause, an *if/whether* clause, and a *that* clause?	☐
take care to use statement word order in indirect questions?	☐

4. Peer Review

Pair students and direct them to read each other's work. Ask students to answer the questions in the checklist and discuss them. Give students suggestions of helpful feedback: e.g., *Is the word order in this sentence correct? Which words should you switch to form an indirect question? / What else could you say in the first paragraph to introduce your country to the audience?*

5. Rewrite Your Draft

Students should consider their partners' comments from the peer review and rewrite as necessary. Encourage students to proofread their work again before turning it in.

18 Reported Speech

Overview

Reported speech is used to recount what someone has said or written, but from the point of view of the reporter rather than the original speaker or writer (e.g., *My mother said, "You can't go to the movies."* becomes *My mother said that I can't go to the movies.*).

Form: Reported speech has a reporting verb in the main clause (e.g., *say, tell, ask*) followed by a noun clause (e.g., *She said <u>that I am early</u>.*) or an infinitive (e.g., *Joseph asked us <u>to help</u> him.*). Reported speech often differs from quoted speech in tense, pronouns, and adverbs. Emphasize that tense choice plays an important role. Note this sentence: *I want to go home.* In reported speech it can change to these three forms: *He said that he wanted to home. He said that he wants to go home. He says that he wants to go home.*

A) GRAMMAR IN DISCOURSE

Doctor-Patient Relationship in Critical Condition

A1: Before You Read

- This article focuses on the attitudes of doctors and patients. Involve students in the topic by asking them what kind of relationship patients and doctors have in their countries. For example, are visits formal or informal? Long or short? Do doctors and patients work together to develop a plan for health care, or does the doctor dictate the plan?

- Then put students into groups and write these questions on the board for them to discuss concerning their last doctor's appointment. *How long did you have to wait to get an appointment? How long did you wait in the waiting room before seeing the doctor? How well did the doctor communicate with you? Did you like him or her?* Some students may not feel comfortable talking about their experiences at the doctor's. Don't pressure them.

- Once students have discussed these questions, have them work individually to make a list of the qualities of a good doctor. Call on several students to share one of the qualities from their list. Write these on the board.

- Ask students to make a list of the negative qualities of some doctors they have seen or heard about. Call on several students to share one of the qualities, and write them on the board.

Cultural Notes

The issue of doctor-patient communication may be unfamiliar to many students. They may come from countries where patients are assigned doctors and there are few choices for health care. Point out that in many countries, people can choose their doctor and may change doctors if they become dissatisfied. Also, explain that the issue of doctor-patient communication and other issues related to patient care are widely discussed in the United States.

A2: Read

- Have students read the article to find out what happens when doctors and patients don't communicate well.

- Set up a jigsaw activity. Divide students into small groups and assign each group a section from the article.

- Have each group write a one- or two-sentence summary of the information in the assigned section.

- Form new groups, making sure that there is at least one member representing each section. Each member will summarize his or her section for the others.

A3: After You Read

- Have students to do this exercise individually and note the places in the article where they found their answers.
- Ask them to compare answers with a partner.
- Circulate and note any difficult or problematic items. Then go over these with the whole class.
- As a follow-up activity, ask students to compare their experiences seeing a doctor in their native country with seeing a doctor in another country, if they have done so. Ask which experience was more positive and why. Tell them to focus on the cultural aspects of health care in both countries. If students have not yet visited a doctor in another country, ask them what they would expect such a visit to be like.
- Call on several students to share their experiences.

B) FORM

Reported Speech

THINK CRITICALLY ABOUT FORM

Method 1
(For students not familiar with the structure)

- For a quick review of reported speech, tell one student this sentence: *You can go home early today.* Then elicit from the class what you just told the student *(You told him that he can go home early. You said that he can go home early.).* Write the responses on the board.
- **1. IDENTIFY** Have students look at the underlined examples of reported speech clauses and then circle the reporting verbs related to each example *(were asked, were asked, reported, ask).*
- **2. CATEGORIZE** Have students identify which underlined clause is a *wh-* clause *(what health problem they had discussed with each patient)*, a *that* clause *(that they had such problems)*, an *if/whether* clause *(if they understand)*, and an infinitive clause *(to fill out a detailed questionnaire).* Have students check their answers with a partner.

- **3. RECOGNIZE** Have students find other examples of reported speech in the third paragraph and circle the reporting verbs. Bring the class together to check the answers and go over any questions.

Method 2
(For students familiar with the structure)

- Have students work in pairs to answer the questions.
- Give students a few minutes to refer to the charts to check their answers and review the structures.
- Call on students to go over the exercise. Discuss any disagreements and have students make any necessary corrections.

FORM CHARTS

- Have students work individually to find the basic differences between quoted speech and reported speech in the charts.
- Tell students to read the *Overview* notes to check their understanding of the basic differences in form. For example, *Yes/No* questions change to *if/whether* clauses (e.g., *Do you like Mexican food? She asked me if I like Mexican food.*), imperatives change to infinitives (e.g., *Don't go. He told me not to go.*).
- Ask students to silently read the information in the *Present Tense Reporting* chart.
- Ask a student to tell you the rule for present tense reporting. (The tense in the *that* clause does not change if the reporting verb is in the present tense.)
- Have students read the examples in the *Past Tense Reporting* chart and the bulleted notes. Ask *What happens to present tense verbs?* (They change to past tense.); *What happens to present continuous verbs?* (They change to past continuous.); *What happens to future with* be going to *verbs?* (They change to *was going to.*); *What happens to the modals* can, may, *and* have to? (They change to *could, might,* and *had to.*).
- Ask students what they notice about the form of the modals *should, ought to,* and *could* in past reported speech. (There is no change.)
- Have students test each other in pairs. The first student should read the quoted speech in the

book and the second student, with the book closed, should say the sentence in reported speech in the past tense, beginning with *I said*. When they finish, have students switch roles.

Trouble Spots

The verbs *say* and *tell* have a similar meaning and are widely used in reported speech. However, there is an important difference in form: *tell* is followed by a noun object and *say* is not (e.g., *Our teacher said that we would have a test on reporting verbs.* vs. *Our teacher told us that we would have a test on reporting verbs.*). Students often attempt to use these two verbs interchangeably, which explains why they produce such errors as *She said me to turn left at the corner.* (Incorrect.) Remind students that *say* isn't followed by a noun object and *tell* is. Ask students to write similar sentence pairs using *say* and *tell* so they can see the form difference (e.g., *She said that we should wait for her. She told us that we should wait for her.*).

Vocabulary Notes: *Tell, Say,* and *Ask* (p. 397)

- Give students a few minutes to read the Notes and example sentences.

- Check students' comprehension by asking *Which verbs are used to report statements?* (*tell* and *say*); *Which verb is used to report questions?* (*ask*); *Which verbs are used to report imperatives?* (*tell, say, ask*); *Which verb is not followed by a noun or a pronoun?* (*say*); *Which verb is followed by a noun or pronoun?* (*tell*).

- Point out that *ask* can be followed by a noun or pronoun, but it does not have to be.

C MEANING AND USE

Reported Speech

THINK CRITICALLY ABOUT MEANING AND USE

- 1.–2. ANALYZE Have students work in pairs to answer the questions (1. a and c; 2. b).

- Give students a few minutes to refer to the Notes to check their answers.

- Then call on students to read the questions and answers out loud. Discuss any disagreements and have students make any necessary corrections.

MEANING AND USE NOTES

- Ask students to silently read the explanations in Notes 1 and 2. Explain that it is often necessary to change to the past tense in reported speech, but that this is not always true.

- Divide students into three groups and assign Notes 3A, 3B, 3C, to the groups. Explain that each group will teach the class about one of the reasons for not shifting the tense in a reported sentence. Have them read the explanations and the examples and then create a short dialogue, which two group members will perform for the class.

- Circulate as the groups work, helping with any difficulties.

- Begin each presentation by asking one student to explain in his or her own words the reason for not changing the tense (e.g., the event has just taken place or it is a generalization).

- Ask students to give the context of the conversation before performing the dialogue (e.g., *This is a telephone conversation between a store clerk and a customer at home. The customer on the phone is reporting the information to his wife.* Student A: *We close at 8:00 P.M.* Student B: *He said that they close at 8:00 P.M.*).

- Tell students to silently read the information and example sentences in Notes 4 and 5. Then write this sentence on the board: *I like my new job.* Ask students to change this to reported speech with *He stated that . . .* (*he likes his new job.*).

- To focus on adverb changes (e.g., *here, there*), write this sentence on the board: *I'll wait for you here until you come.* Ask students to change it to reported speech (*He said he'd wait for me there until I come.*).

Vocabulary Notes: More Reporting Verbs (p. 402)

- Give students time to read the Notes and examples.

- Clarify any unfamiliar verbs, though it may be difficult to clearly express all the nuances between them.

- Write this sentence on the board: *He took the wallet.*

- Ask students to use three of the verbs from the Notes to report the sentence. If they choose a verb such as *inform*, which requires an object pronoun, they can use *me* (e.g., *He informed me that he'd taken the wallet.*).

- Ask several students to read their sentences and give a context for each.

Vocabulary Notes: Reporting Verbs Used for Advising (p. 404)

This information is useful but rather complex, so cover it only after you feel your students have had enough practice using the easier reporting verbs and reported speech in this chapter.

- On the board, write sentences with some of the verbs from this Note:

  The teacher asked that we eat our lunch outside.

  The law requires that we drive slowly near a school.

  Many parents insist that their children behave well in public.

  The police officer demanded that we stop the car.

  Experts suggest that people get eight hours of sleep.

  My friend recommended that I talk to a doctor.

  Scientists advise that everyone stay out of the sun.

  We propose that we have homework only on the weekend.

- Read each sentence out loud, ask students to identify the reporting verb, and if necessary, elicit the meaning of the verb.

- Ask students to look at all the sentences and tell you what they notice about the form of the verb in the *that* clause. (It is always in the base form, even when the main verb is in the past tense [*They demanded that we* listen *to them.*] or third-person singular [*The woman insists that her daughter* visit *her more often.*].) This may be hard for students to understand or remember, so give them time and examples to practice it.

THINK CRITICALLY ABOUT MEANING AND USE

- Have students do A individually. Then, in small groups, have them compare answers and discuss any differences.

- Have them stay in groups and do B.

- As a class, review any difficult items from A. Then elicit answers to B:

  1. COMPARE AND CONTRAST (The sentence "I said I'd seen her" is a generalized statement where sentence 4 is specific to one person; to change each back to quoted speech, you would write "I said, 'I'd seen her,'" or "I said, 'I'll see Marie.'")

  2. COMPARE AND CONTRAST (Sentence 6 implies that the conversation is referring to the current time period; the sentence listed here implies the speakers are referring to a time period in the past. To change each back to quoted speech you would write, "Amelia asked, 'Have you been sick?'" or 'Were you sick?'")

WRITE

The purpose of this activity is to give students practice in using reported speech by writing an email to a Customer Service department expressing a complaint.

1. Brainstorm

As a class, start a brainstorm on the board about some common problems that people have with products or services. For example, a product might be defective, missing a piece, or not work as advertised. Services might be provided by rude or inexperienced employees who do a poor job. Ask students to suggest possible solutions or actions that can be taken to fix such problems, such as replacing a defective product or receiving a refund for poor service. Have individuals make further notes about problems with products or services and then choose what they want to write about.

2. Write a First Draft

Before students begin writing, make sure they have read the checklist in the Edit section. Also

have them look at the example on page 409.
Remind students to use the best points from
their brainstorming notes to write their email.

3. Edit

Direct students to read and complete the self-
assessment checklist on page 409. Ask for a
show of hands for how many students gave all
or mostly *yes* answers. If desired, ask students
to comment on some of the errors they found.

DO I...	YES
organize my ideas into paragraphs?	☐
use reported speech to relate what was said?	☐
make needed changes in tense, pronouns, and adverbs in reported speech?	☐
use a range of reporting verbs, each followed by the correct structure?	☐

4. Peer Review

Pair students and direct them to read each
other's work. Ask students to answer the
questions in the checklist and discuss them.
Give students suggestions of helpful feedback:
e.g., *What verb tense should you use in the clause
of this sentence? / Is there a different reporting
verb you could use in this sentence to add
variety? Will the verb require an object pronoun,
like* me *or* us?

5. Rewrite Your Draft

Students should consider their partners'
comments from the peer review and rewrite as
necessary. Encourage students to proofread
their work again before turning it in.

Student Book Audioscript

 **CHAPTER 1**

A2 (p. 4)

Please refer to the magazine article in the Student Book.

B1: Listening for Form (p. 8)

1. Are you eating enough?
2. Are you getting enough sleep?
3. Do you have many new friends?
4. Are your friends studying English, too?
5. Do you have a lot of homework?
6. Do your classes meet every day?
7. Does your roommate speak Korean?
8. Is it raining there today?

Informally Speaking (p. 11)

F1: You feeling OK?
F2: No. I have a headache. You have any aspirin?

B5: Understanding Informal Speech (p. 11)

1. Feeling tired in the morning? Maybe you need a new mattress. Stop in at Sleep World for the answer to all your dreams.
2. Need a vacation? We have great deals at Star Travel. Call us today!
3. Having car problems again? Call Smith Auto Works. We're the best in town!
4. Doing it yourself? Let us help you at Stone Hardware. We have all the tools you need.
5. Have any old clothes in your closets? Donate them to the Youth Center Rummage Sale. Clean out your closets and help our kids at the same time.
6. Like to shop late? Then Norton's is for you. We're the only grocery store in town open twenty-four hours every day!
7. Working too hard? We have great weekend getaways. Call Travel Time for the best deals on many fares.
8. Need a house sitter? Well, look no further. We'll clean your house for you and watch it while you're away.

C1: Listening for Meaning and Use (p. 14)

1. What are you doing?
2. That story is unbelievable. Are you kidding?
3. What do you do?
4. What happens at the end of the movie?
5. Do you drink coffee at night?
6. What does "nap" mean?
7. Is Amir talking on the phone again?
8. Are you working hard these days?

D1: Listening for Meaning and Use (p. 19)

1. Jennifer feels sick today. Her throat itches and she has a fever.
2. Mr. Silva walks to work. He stops for coffee on the way. He carries his briefcase in one hand and his coffee in the other—and he tries not to spill it.
3. Dinner costs a lot at Joe's Restaurant, but it includes four courses. Lunch is cheaper. There are always at least two specials. Everything tastes fresh, and it smells so good.
4. A: Do you hear music?
   B: Yes, I think the radio is on.

5. Ms. Wilson's kindergarten class is behaving strangely today. Two children are running around the room, one boy is crying, and two others are yelling very loudly.
6. A: I can't see that sign. I'm nearsighted, and I don't have my glasses.
   B: Well, I don't see very well without my glasses either, but I'm farsighted. I need my glasses for things that are close.

Informally Speaking (p. 22)

M1: Do you like the movie?
M2: I'm loving it!
M1: You're kidding! I'm just hating it!

D6: Understanding Informal Speech (p. 22)

1. I'm liking my apartment more and more each day!
2. I'm hating this new television show!
3. We're just loving the beautiful weather!
4. She's really disliking this trip!
5. I'm loving this movie!
6. I'm really liking my new job!

CHAPTER 2

A2 (p. 28)

Please refer to the book excerpt in the Student Book.

B1: Listening for Form (p. 32)

Where were you when the lights went out this morning? That's the question everyone is asking today. Early this morning, a construction crew was working on Thirty-third Street while people across the city were going to work. At 8:29 A.M., a simple mistake by the construction crew caused a blackout that cut off power to almost a million people.

The blackout forced airports to send incoming flights elsewhere. But according to one report, a jet liner was landing just when the power in the control tower failed. After the jet lost contact with the tower, the pilot landed the plane himself with no problems.

The mayor declared a state of emergency. Fortunately, no major accidents or injuries occurred, and the power returned after six hours and twenty minutes, at 2:49 this afternoon.

C1: Listening for Meaning and Use (p. 37)

1. The professor was writing a book of poetry. He was looking for an editor to help him. When he met an experienced editor at a conference, he hired her immediately.
2. Sam was eating dinner when he heard the terrible news on the radio. He finished his dinner quickly and left.
3. I called Roger, but he couldn't talk to me. He was painting his kitchen. It took him all day, but it came out great.
4. Jill was baking a cake for father's surprise birthday celebration. When he suddenly walked into the kitchen, she didn't know what to say.
5. Jane was writing a letter in the library yesterday. She seemed so sad when she mailed it on her way out.

D1: Listening for Meaning and Use (p. 43)

1. When I went home, I opened the mail.
2. After I played tennis, I took a shower.
3. The phone rang while I was fixing the bathroom sink.

4. She came home before it started to rain.
5. While I was waiting for John, I saw Erica.
6. The water ran out when I opened the drain.
7. After I called the operator, she connected me with Bogotá.
8. When I shouted, she turned around.

🎧 CHAPTER 3

A2 (p. 50)

Please refer to the newspaper article in the Student Book.

B1: Listening for Form (p. 54)

1. Don't worry about me. I'll call you as soon as I get home.
2. It's not going to rain this afternoon. Look at the sky.
3. The movie starts in five minutes. You still have time to get a snack.
4. We'll be cruising at an altitude of thirty thousand feet. We expect a smooth flight, so sit back and relax.
5. We're leaving early tomorrow morning. Can you take out the garbage when you get up?
6. They're going to send a lot of work to us tomorrow. Let's get ready for it.
7. I can't come on Saturday. John will be arriving at noon, and I have to pick him up.
8. Are you going skiing this weekend? I'd like to join you.

C1: Listening for Meaning and Use (p. 59)

1. I invited Jill to see our apartment.
2. The door is stuck!
3. Oh, no! The oven's broken.
4. I'm sorry I didn't finish the report today.
5. No one can come to the phone right now. Please leave your name and number.
6. The fax machine is out of paper.
7. Excuse me. My car just broke down.
8. Just imagine, next week at this time . . .

D1: Listening for Meaning and Use (p. 63)

1. Look. It's going to rain.
   Look. It's raining.
2. We're going to celebrate my aunt's fortieth birthday next week.
   We're celebrating my aunt's fortieth birthday next week.
3. I think our team is going to win the tournament.
   I think our team is winning the tournament.
4. I go to sleep early.
   I'm going to sleep early.
5. I'm going to take a trip this summer with the money I've saved.
   I'm taking a trip this summer with the money I've saved.
6. We're leaving before dawn. All the plans are made.
   We leave before dawn. All the plans are made.

E1: Listening for Meaning and Use (p. 67)

1. Nina, look out!
2. This recorded announcement will not be repeated. Please hold.
3. Bob, I can't answer the phone. My hands are covered with paint.
4. Why are you turning off the TV?

5. Would someone please help me with the dishes?
6. Let's hurry up. The sky is dark, and I hear some thunder.
7. Can I have a drink of water?
8. What are your summer plans?

🎧 CHAPTER 4

A2 (p. 78)

Please refer to the magazine article in the Student Book.

B1: Listening for Form (p. 81)

1. He's won the race.
2. They called their senator.
3. Who's read the book over there?
4. Where's the team playing this week?
5. She's worried about her father.
6. Who's gone fishing?
7. You've bought all of the equipment already.
8. We looked up his telephone number.

Informally Speaking (p. 84)

F1: Seen any good movies lately?
F2: Yes, as a matter of fact. Last night I saw that new Japanese movie.

B5: Understanding Informal Speech (p. 84)

1. Heard any good jokes lately?
2. You taken your vacation yet?
3. Been to the beach yet this summer?
4. Eaten at that new restaurant yet?
5. She left yet?
6. You seen my keys?
7. You done any programming?
8. He called you lately?

C1: Listening for Meaning and Use (p. 86)

1. How many times have you seen that movie?
2. Have you ever won a prize?
3. Has the number twenty-nine bus come yet?
4. Have you been to Tokyo?
5. Have you finished the assignment yet?
6. What have you done so far?

D1: Listening for Meaning and Use, A (p. 89)

1. Have you noticed a change in students' attitudes lately?
2. The captain has turned off the seat belt sign.
3. We've known each other for such a long time. We're almost like sisters.
4. People have studied the universe since ancient times.
5. We have a late-breaking news report. The governor has just declared a state of emergency.
6. I hear the mail carrier. I think the mail has arrived.

D1: Listening for Meaning and Use, B (p. 90)

1. Mary came to class at 10 A.M. She's been in class for one hour.
   What time is it?
2. It's 5 P.M. and the repairman still hasn't called. Our printer broke this morning.
   How long has the printer been broken?
3. Jennifer arrived exactly on time for her two o'clock

appointment with the doctor. She's been in the waiting room for an hour and a half.
What time is it now?
4. It's midnight. The baby has had a fever since 9 P.M. and her temperature still hasn't gone down at all. It's time to call the doctor.
How long has the baby had the fever?

E1: Listening for Meaning and Use (p. 94)

1. I lived there for a year. I really miss that place.
2. We've worked with him for six months. We're getting along so well.
3. He's kept the secret all week. I know he'll never tell anyone.
4. She studied physics for two years. Then she changed her major.
5. I've had a parrot for a long time. I'm very fond of it.
6. I owned a car for years. I sold it when I moved.
7. They worked there for three years. Then they were laid off.
8. I've played the piano for years. It relaxes me.

 CHAPTER 5

A2 (p. 102)

Please refer to the book review in the Student Book.

B1: Listening for Form (p. 105)

1. What's happening this week?
2. Jack has been visiting his grandparents.
3. It's been raining all day.
4. They're living in Florida.
5. He's been sleeping on the sofa.
6. She's been exercising at the gym.

Informally Speaking (p. 108)

M1: You been going to the study sessions?
M2: No. I been writing my English paper all week. It's due tomorrow.

B5: Understanding Informal Speech (p. 108)

1. What'cha been doing all day?
2. I been visiting my friend.
3. You been feeling OK?
4. No, I been having some problems with my back.
5. You been exercising at all?
6. I been walking a lot.

C1: Listening for Meaning and Use (p. 110)

1. A: I've been reading the latest John Grisham novel. I can't put it down.
   B: Really? I've been thinking about reading it.
2. A: I haven't been feeling well for a few months.
   B: Really? I was sick for a few months too.
3. A: So what have you been doing lately, Helen?
   B: I've been volunteering at the hospital. I enjoy it so much.
   A: I volunteered at the hospital for a while. I found it very rewarding.

4. A: How are your children, Max?
   B: They're good, thanks. What about yours?
   A: Terrific. I just visited them in Chicago.
   B: Really. I've been going to Chicago for medical treatments this year.
5. A: So, Helen, have you seen Eddie?
   B: No. I've been trying to call him for days, but his phone has been busy from morning until night.
   A: I know. He's always online. I was trying for a while, too, but I gave up.
6. A: So what else is new, Max?
   B: I've been learning to play chess. I love it.
   A: Oh, I love chess, but I haven't been playing at all since I moved here. Maybe I should start again.

D1: Listening for Meaning and Use (p. 114)

1. I've been painting my office all morning.
2. He's already taken a shower.
3. They've been giving free samples in the supermarket since yesterday.
4. We've known each other for only two months.
5. My sister has interviewed at that company.
6. The manager has been waiting for you. Hurry up!
7. I've lived here since last year.
8. We've just seen that movie.

 CHAPTER 6

A2 (p. 122)

Please refer to the book excerpt in the Student Book.

B1: Listening for Form (p. 126)

In 1928, Amelia Earhart became the first woman to fly across the Atlantic. Ten years before, she'd been working as a nurse's aide when she visited an airfield near Toronto. She made up her mind that she wanted to fly an airplane right then. After her trans-Atlantic flight, Ms. Earhart became an instant heroine, although she really hadn't flown the plane. Her two male companions hadn't let her touch any of the controls. But the world didn't care. Charles Lindbergh had crossed the Atlantic a year earlier, and many aviators had been trying to repeat his successful flight since then. Sadly, fourteen pilots, including three women, had died since Lindbergh's triumph. Because Ms. Earhart had been embarrassed about her role in her first trans-Atlantic flight, she seemed more determined than ever to fly across the Atlantic alone. And that's exactly what happened in 1932 when she finally flew over the Atlantic by herself.

Informally Speaking (p. 129)

F1: Did you see Dana and Maria at the library last night?
F2: Dana'd already left by the time I got there, but I saw Maria.

B6: Understanding Informal Speech (p. 129)

1. She'd never been alone in the woods before.
2. Her family'd gone camping when she was young.
3. Her father'd taught her the skills she needed.
4. No one'd prepared her for this experience, though.
5. Why'd she signed up for this program?
6. Who'd she been trying to impress?

C1: Listening for Meaning and Use (p. 132)

1. The patient's condition had improved by the time the doctor came.
2. By the time the plane landed, we had gotten to the airport.
3. I entered the building before I took off my hat.
4. The emergency crew arrived after the building had collapsed.
5. I saw Betty before she heard the news.
6. He became vice president after he had worked hard.
7. After I called my mother, I spoke to my sister.
8. Even though she'd hurt her wrist, she went to work.

D1: Listening for Meaning and Use (p. 137)

1. I had just picked up the phone when the doorbell rang.
2. He was a good writer, but he'd written a boring book.
3. We'd been eating dinner before we heard the news.
4. I'd waited at home until she called.
5. I didn't want to read the book because I'd seen the movie.
6. I wasn't surprised by the traffic because I'd been listening to the traffic report.
7. We took the class because many people had recommended it.
8. She'd left town by the time I tried to contact her.

 ## CHAPTER 7

A2 (p. 146)

Please refer to the online post in the Student Book.

B1: Listening for Form (p. 150)

The Abominable Snowman of the Himalayas and the Loch Ness Monster of Scotland are two creatures that may or may not be real—that depends on your beliefs. If you ask someone about them, they may respond, "That can't be true," or they might respond, "That must be true." Over the years, it has been difficult to separate fact from fiction as stories about these creatures continue.

Could it be true that an apelike creature with long hair lives high in the Himalayas? Could the large footprints found there belong to such a creature? While many scientists say this has to be a myth, others claim that there may be some kind of creature out there. But no one knows for sure.

In Scotland, could there really be a mysterious water monster with a long neck and a large body like a brontosaurus? Many claim that there's got to be some truth to this story that's been around since the fifteenth century. Just ask the two million tourists who visit the area each year, hoping to see the monster.

C1: Listening for Meaning and Use (p. 155)

1. The cat could be in the yard, or she might be under the porch.
2. It's 10:30. He must be on his way home.
3. The trip could take two days—maybe three.
4. He can't be getting an A. He failed two tests.
5. She must be so tired. She stayed up all night.
6. Your car should be ready. They said to pick it up at two.
7. The cake ought to be ready now. The oven timer just rang.
8. He might not be working right now, or maybe he is. Who knows?

D1: Listening for Meaning and Use (p. 162)

1. It might rain next week. Let's make a different plan, just in case.
2. The plane should arrive on time since it left on time.
3. The package will arrive tomorrow. I sent it by express mail.
4. There could be a storm tomorrow so let's be prepared.
5. The car shouldn't give us any more problems. It's been repaired.
6. In a few years, they won't be selling that type of computer.
7. In twenty years, we might be using robots to do housework. Who knows?
8. She ought to be here any minute. She left an hour ago.

 ## CHAPTER 8

A2 (p. 168)

Please refer to the magazine article in the Student Book.

B1: Listening for Form (p. 172)

Most scientists now agree that an asteroid collision or a similar event must have been responsible for starting the mass extinction of dinosaurs and other animals about 65 million years ago. But there is still disagreement about another wave of extinction that occurred more recently, just 13,000 years ago. That's when great woolly mammoths, mastodons, saber-tooth tigers, and other large animals known as megafauna died off in northern Eurasia and the Americas.

What could have caused the disappearance of these great beasts? Some say that human colonizers from Siberia may have done the damage over a period of a thousand years. But others disagree. In their opinion, a relatively small group of hunters couldn't have killed off so many animals across three whole continents. As one researcher told me, "We should have found evidence of such overhunting, but we haven't. So humans can't have been the cause."

Others think it might have been climate change. Scientists know that there was a cold snap that led to a partial return to Ice Age conditions between 12,900 and 11,500 years ago, and some believe that this may have put stress on the megafauna. Again, for the theory to be true, they ought to have found proof, but so far they haven't.

The most recent theory is that a major cosmic catastrophe such as an airburst or impact from a comet could have caused the extinctions. Evidence to support this may have already been found in soil samples at more than 50 sites across North America, and glacier scientists think they might have found signs in the Greenland ice sheet as well.

Informally Speaking (p. 175)

F1: This traffic is terrible! We should-uv stayed in the office!
F2: Yeah. We could-uv left after rush hour.

B5: Understanding Informal Speech (p. 175)

F: I'm sorry I'm late. I should-uv called you. Then you could-uv met me downtown.
M: That might not-a worked anyway. I didn't get out of work until six. And then there must-a been fifty people waiting for the elevator. It took me ten minutes to get out of the building.

F: So where's Linda? She should-uv been here by now. She must-uv forgotten.
M: I doubt that. She could-a gotten stuck in traffic, or she might-a left work late, too. Let's sit down over there and wait for her.

C1: Listening for Meaning and Use (p. 177)

1. Neanderthals may have built shelters for safety.
2. They couldn't have sewn their clothing.
3. They can't have lived in Africa.
4. They have to have had a language.
5. They may not have had a complex language.
6. Cold weather might have driven them into Asia.
7. They could have died because of disease or change in climate.
8. They couldn't have been relatives of modern humans.

D1: Listening for Meaning and Use (p. 182)

1. All the students were supposed to apply for the scholarship, but John didn't.
2. John had the opportunity to leave early, but he stayed.
3. It was a good idea to ask the teacher for help, but John didn't do it.
4. John's school required him to take two English courses.
5. John was allowed to register late.
6. John promised to call his parents yesterday, but then he forgot to do it.
7. John had two job opportunities: one at a bank and one at a department store. He chose the department store.
8. I was sorry that I didn't call John last night.

CHAPTER 9

A2 (p. 192)

Please refer to the textbook excerpt in the Student Book.

B1: Listening for Form (p. 195)

1. Last year some research was being done on smiling across cultures.
2. I was asked to join the study after it began.
3. A number of questions were being studied at the same time.
4. For example, is the general meaning of a smile always understood?
5. Why is the mouth covered in some cultures?
6. Is it true that smiles are reserved for friends and family in some cultures?
7. The results of this research were reported at a psychology conference.
8. The results are also being published in a popular psychology magazine.

C1: Listening for Meaning and Use (p. 199)

1. Twenty-five students were asked to participate in a research study.
2. Each student took a test.
3. The test was designed to measure cultural attitudes.
4. The instructions were given by a graduate student.
5. Several sentences were read aloud.
6. The students were looking at some pictures at the same time.
7. The students matched the sentences with the pictures.

8. The results were reported by the professor on his website.

D1: Listening for Meaning and Use (p. 203)

1. Visitors are asked not to park in front of the building.
2. French is spoken in Quebec.
3. We called Julie at the hospital yesterday. She was permitted to speak to us briefly.
4. Several people were injured by a falling tree.
5. The book was written in 1966.
6. Your assistance is appreciated.

CHAPTER 10

A2 (p. 212)

Please refer to the letter to the editor in the Student Book.

B1: Listening for Form (p. 215)

1. What can be done to help students at risk?
2. Some students drop out of high school because of real-life events, such as an illness or death in the family.
3. Should some of the blame be put on teachers and parents?
4. According to experts, students can be helped if their problems are diagnosed early.
5. Should special tutoring programs be established for at-risk students?
6. Educators have been worrying about the problem for quite some time.
7. Has the government been ignoring the problem?
8. Will the dropout rate be reduced if new programs are set up?

C1: Listening for Meaning and Use (p. 219)

1. Have you ever been blamed by someone for something that you didn't do?
2. I was punished by my fifth-grade teacher for someone else's bad behavior.
3. Later that year, I was sent for by the principal. I was so scared!
4. I was chosen by the school to represent my school at a student conference.
5. I was allowed by the school to miss classes for a whole day.
6. At the conference, we were given lunch by the conference organizers.
7. I wrote an article about the conference. It was published by the publisher in my local newspaper.
8. Not long after, I was interviewed by another newspaper in the next town.

D1: Listening for Meaning and Use (p. 222)

1. Tonight we bring to you the following question: Could the latest teachers' strike have been prevented? Our panel is a group of parents, teachers, and government officials who have all been personally affected by the current strike.
2. I'd like to summarize what has been covered so far. First, it is generally assumed that mental processes are accompanied by changes in the brain. Similarly, it is assumed that changes in the brain accompany the encoding, storage, and retrieval of information. In other words, memory is a mental process that is accompanied

by changes in the brain.

3. It was a great weekend. The most experienced managers were sent to the new facility in Phoenix, Arizona. We were required to spend two weeks training newcomers, after participating in several workshops on interpersonal relations.

4. Tonight's performance has been canceled due to the weather. Tickets will be refunded at the ticket office, beginning on Monday, January second. Refunds can also be arranged by mail. For further information about mail refunds, press two. Thank you.

5. They're not gonna accept this unless you bring another form of identification with you. Look, it says right here that two forms of identification are required. Take a look at the list of acceptable documents that's given in the manual on page forty-three.

6. A look at the future, brought to you by the United Fabric Guild. In a few years, clothing will be made of antibacterial fabrics. Odors will be eliminated, which means that deodorant will no longer be needed. Also, more industrial materials like Kevlar, Teflon, and Tyvek will be used to make durable, cutting-edge clothing.

7. Remember, computer programming is a field that is constantly changing. In the early days, programming languages like FORTRAN and COBOL were used. Today, those have been replaced by programs like Java, C, and Visual Basics. Ten years from now, still others will have been adopted. As a professional programmer, you will be expected to keep up with changes in the field.

8. Several aftershocks were again felt this afternoon by survivors of the latest earthquake to hit the area. No major damage has been reported, although unconfirmed reports of gas leaks in outlying areas are being investigated as we speak.

Informally Speaking (p. 224)

F: Guess what? I'm going to get promoted to district manager.
M: Congratulations!

D3: Understanding Informal Speech (p. 224)

1. Do you think you'll get sent to the convention in Hawaii?
2. I might get promoted soon.
3. John may get transferred to the Boston office.
4. He got accepted by Harvard Business School.
5. The manager got caught breaking the rules.
6. He could get fired.
7. Steve finally got rewarded for all of his extra work.
8. He got nominated for a special award yesterday.

🎧 CHAPTER 11

A2 (p. 230)

Please refer to the book excerpt in the Student Book.

B1: Listening for Form (p. 234)

1. I try to relax when I drive.
2. Experts recommend learning simple breathing exercises.
3. Breathing a certain way can calm your mind almost immediately.
4. Most of us don't allow ourselves to breathe deeply and release tension.

5. If you can't seem to relax, simple breathing exercises can help enormously.
6. Anytime you feel stress, remember to breathe in, breathe out, and relax.

C1: Listening for Meaning and Use (p. 240)

1. I stopped helping John.
2. I didn't remember to put gas in the tank.
3. I tried to take fish oil.
4. I regret to tell you that she left.
5. I stopped to buy the newspaper.
6. I'll never forget meeting the President.

D1: Listening for Form (p. 245)

A: You should consider taking a vacation. You could spend some time relaxing.
B: I can't. I'm busy working on a project that's due soon. My boss has told me to finish it as quickly as possible.
A: I know. That's the point. Aren't you sick of working?
B: Well, instead of taking a long vacation, I might be interested in going away for a weekend. But I'd have trouble leaving before noon on Saturday. I save Saturday morning for catching up on my office email.
A: Didn't you promise to relax more?

E1: Listening for Meaning and Use (p. 248)

1. The doctor advised my friend not to work so hard.
2. I asked the doctor to recommend some exercises.
3. She had us call a health club.
4. They didn't mind us calling in the evening.
5. We arranged to speak to the manager.
6. My brother invited us to come over.
7. The roads were wet. I worried about my friend's driving in the rain.
8. Before we left, the manager made us leave a deposit.

🎧 CHAPTER 12

A2 (p. 256)

Please refer to the book excerpt in the Student Book.

B1: Listening for Form (p. 260)

Although the common cold is generally not serious, it causes people to be absent from work and go to the doctor more often than other illnesses. The majority of colds come from contact with surfaces that people touch frequently. People transmit the cold viruses on these surfaces to their eyes, noses, and mouths. Once the symptoms appear, there are many treatments for relieving the discomfort. Whatever a person does, unfortunately, a cold will probably still last from six to ten days.

C1: Listening for Meaning and Use (p. 263)

1. I drank orange juice with my breakfast this morning.
2. Apples are supposed to be very healthy.
3. I need a new doctor. Mine has retired.
4. I have a friend who works for Dr. Garcia. I'll ask her if she recommends him.
5. Please have some soup. I made it myself. It'll help your cold.
6. I made an appointment with Dr. Garcia after I spoke to your friend. I'm going tomorrow at three.

7. I'd like to find a book about herbal medicine. Do you know of any?
8. I took cough medicine last night before I went to bed. It didn't help.

D1: Listening for Meaning and Use (p. 267)

1. The salesman showed me a beautiful blue shirt and a plaid tie.
2. My neighbor's daughter was selling candy to make money for her school trip.
3. We'd like to invite a writer to come and speak to our creative writing class.
4. I went to a wedding yesterday.
5. What are they fixing on your car?
6. Is that new CD on the top shelf?
7. Please hold on for a minute.
8. I sent them a check last week, but they didn't receive it.

E1: Listening for Meaning and Use (p. 273)

1. I threw out the carrot. It was rotten.
2. Almonds are a high-fat food that is actually good for the heart.
3. The National Cancer Institute is carrying out research on the effects of garlic for preventing and treating cancer.
4. I cooked food that was good for her cold. I made chicken soup with garlic and pepper in it.
5. The onion has many health benefits, according to the latest research.
6. I had a cold for only a few days this time. I was lucky.
7. My doctor thinks people don't need to take vitamins if they eat properly.
8. A headache can last for a few minutes, hours, or days.

🎧 CHAPTER 13

A2 (p. 280)

Please refer to the newspaper article in the Student Book.

B1: Listening for Form (p. 284)

1. I like to wear clothes that express my individuality.
2. The dress code, which is very casual, is being eliminated.
3. I was talking to Ms. Chang, who is the manager.
4. In some banks and law firms, the dress code is still very conservative.
5. Barker Bank, which has a strict dress code, seems out of date.
6. We used to wear clothes that were more formal.
7. At some companies, the men don't have to wear ties anymore.
8. Everyone likes my boss, who dresses very casually.

C1: Listening for Meaning and Use (p. 289)

1. Which one is your boss?
2. What do you think about the dress code?
3. Which computer isn't working?
4. Who's on the phone?
5. Who's going to lunch with you?
6. Who is Juan's neighbor?
7. Which books are yours?
8. What did they say you should wear?

D1: Listening for Meaning and Use (p. 295)

1. My sister, who lives in New York, has two children. She calls me on Saturdays.
2. Have you met her brother who works at the bank? He's not as tall as the younger one.
3. Give me the sheet of paper which has the list of names. It's next to those other papers.
4. The man who is talking is my boss. Do you know the men who are sitting with him?
5. She showed me her necklace, which had beautiful stones. She got it for her birthday.
6. Her grandmother, who lived until eighty, was a teacher.

🎧 CHAPTER 14

A2 (p. 302)

Please refer to the magazine article in the Student Book.

B1: Listening for Form (p. 306)

1. The team that played didn't do very well.
2. The equipment which broke is expensive to repair.
3. Did you hear about the team that we beat?
4. We didn't know about the rules they changed.
5. I didn't meet the player they called.
6. The man who called wanted to join the team.

C1: Listening for Meaning and Use (p. 310)

1. A woman I know has become a professional hockey player.
2. She started out on a local boys' hockey team, which she quit to join a girls' team.
3. She had a wonderful coach, who her parents adored too.
4. Two women who I knew in high school became professional athletes.
5. My high school, which didn't have a lot of money, actually had a sports program for girls.
6. Well, the sports they offered girls in my high school weren't that interesting.

D1: Listening for Form (p. 315)

1. Do you know the woman he's married to?
2. The man who he spoke to helped quite a bit.
3. Let's look at the book I brought in.
4. Did you meet the people he works with?
5. Did you see the doctor? I was waiting for her.

E1: Listening for Meaning and Use (p. 318)

1. Q: Didja download the songs I told you about?
   A: No, not yet.
2. This lecture will explore two issues about which you've already read a great deal, and one more with which you may be unfamiliar.
3. Ladies and gentlemen, there is someone in this room whom we would all like to thank. Let's have a round of applause for Robin Strauss, who has worked tirelessly for the last six years.
4. Scotty, please pick up the magazine you were just looking at.
5. The court has the list of the witnesses whom you will call. Be advised that . . .
6. After you beat the eggs, pour them into the bowl you mixed the dry ingredients in.

CHAPTER 15

A2 (p. 328)

Please refer to the selections in the Student Book.

B1: Listening for Form (p. 332)

1. I wish we could spend more time together.
2. If we lived in the same city, our phone bills would be less.
3. If you finish your term paper by Wednesday, take an early train on Thursday.
4. If you don't take classes this summer, we'll spend all our time together.
5. Don't you wish we attended the same university?
6. If our summer plans don't work out, it doesn't matter.
7. I'd be upset if cousin Teresa didn't want to visit us during spring break.
8. If we decide to travel this summer, where do you want to go?

Informally Speaking (p. 334)

F1: I need a jacket, but nothing fits me. I wish I was taller.
F2: If it was earlier, we could go to another store. Let's do that tomorrow.

B6: Understanding Informal Speech (p. 334)

1. If I wasn't so tired, I'd go out for a cup of coffee with you.
2. What would you do if it was too late to take the bus?
3. I wish my boss wasn't so unfriendly.
4. If he was ready, we could leave now.
5. She'd tell you if she was mad at you.
6. Don't you wish he was going with us?

C1: Listening for Meaning and Use (p. 337)

1. You have reached A and H Healthcare. If you want to speak to a representative, press one.
2. If I am elected, I'll lower taxes and spend more money on education.
3. If a holiday falls on a Thursday, the company usually closes for the weekend.
4. It's 3 A.M. If you don't turn down the music, I'm going to complain to the police.
5. I'll help you this morning if you help me this afternoon.
6. If it snows hard, you should get a ride with Lauren.
7. Generally, the mall is crowded if it's raining.
8. Call me if the flight gets delayed.

D1: Listening for Meaning and Use (p. 341)

1. Would you mind if I came late?
2. What'll you do if the bus arrives late?
3. Would you quit your job if your boss didn't treat you well?
4. If you could have dinner with a famous person, who would you choose?
5. Will you be home later if I call?
6. Would it be OK if I used your phone?

E1: Listening for Meaning and Use (p. 345)

1. I wish I didn't have a cold. I'd go to the lecture tonight.
2. I wish this book had pictures. It would be so much easier to follow.
3. If only I had free time, I'd volunteer at the hospital.
4. I wish I didn't have a car. It's so much trouble.

5. I wish he'd get a safety lock for that window.
6. I wish there weren't a limit for carry-on luggage on planes. Then I could take more bags.
7. If only I didn't have a credit card, then I couldn't spend so much money.
8. I wish you would get rid of your guitar.

 CHAPTER 16

A2 (p. 352)

Please refer to the magazine article in the Student Book.

B1: Listening for Form (p. 355)

1. A: Do you agree with what I did?
   B: Not really. If it had been me, I wouldn't have interrupted him.
2. A: Would you do anything differently next time?
   B: If I had another chance, I'd prepare more for the interview.
3. A: If it had been you, would you have come so late?
   B: No, I wouldn't have.
4. A: What do you think about the introductory course?
   B: If I had listened to my roommate, I wouldn't have taken it.
5. A: Have you ever thought about moving?
   B: Yes, if I'd had my way, we would have moved to Seattle.
6. A: You didn't call.
   B: I know. I would have called if it hadn't been so late.

Informally Speaking (p. 357)

F: The waiter overcharged me for lunch today, but I didn't say anything.
F: Well, I woulda shown him the mistake. I sure wouldn't-uv paid the extra money.

B4: Understanding Informal Speech (p. 357)

1. Would you-uv chosen a different career if you hadn't married so young?
2. If I had studied, I might-uv done much better on the quiz.
3. We wouldn't-a been so late if the car had been working.
4. If I hadn't been careful, I could-a had an accident.
5. I would-uv been late if I'd missed the bus.
6. If I hadn't scored, we wouldn't-uv won the game.

C1: Listening for Meaning and Use (p. 360)

1. What would have happened if John F. Kennedy hadn't been shot?
2. Would he have ended the Vietnam War sooner?
3. Would he still be in politics?
4. Would the sixties have been different?
5. Would the students still have rebelled?
6. Would the world be a safer place right now?
7. Would your country be any different?
8. Would there have been a nuclear war?

D1: Listening for Meaning and Use (p. 364)

1. I wish I'd read about World War II before I saw the movie.
2. If only I'd been home when the phone rang.
3. If only she'd been elected to the council, then she'd be able to represent us.

4. I wish you had called at the end of your exam.
5. We would've flown home but we couldn't get reservations.
6. If only the tree hadn't fallen on the driveway as I was leaving.
7. Don't you wish you had taken a day off last week instead of today?
8. I wish I had stayed, but I had a headache.

🎧 CHAPTER 17

A2 (p. 372)

Please refer to the website article from the Student Book.

B1: Listening for Form (p. 375)

1. Find out what opportunities are out there.
2. If possible, find out who your boss would be.
3. Decide if you would work weekends or not.
4. Demonstrate how you will achieve the company's goals.
5. Figure out whether you want to work for a big or small company.
6. Don't assume that you'll find work immediately.
7. Decide what you want.
8. Consider whether or not you would work part-time.

C1: Listening for Meaning and Use (p. 380)

1. Do you know what time the show starts?
2. I was wondering why John's not taking the job.
3. Do you know what office she works in?
4. Our meeting's been postponed.
5. Please tell me if you got the raise.
6. Do you know whether the mail has come?
7. Can you tell me what time the meeting is?
8. Could you tell me what the most important advice for a job hunter is?

D1: Listening for Meaning and Use (p. 386)

1. Linda is going to meet us tonight.
2. Someone's at the door.
3. He regrets that he left the meeting.
4. I've decided I'm going to buy more insurance.
5. He admitted he was wrong.
6. I thought she was sleeping when I called.

🎧 CHAPTER 18

A2 (p. 392)

Please refer to the magazine article in the Student Book.

B1: Listening for Form (p. 396)

1. I asked Scott what he wanted for his birthday, and he said that he didn't know.
2. I asked if he wanted some books.
3. I said I'd call him back on Monday.
4. He asked if I could call him back on Tuesday instead.
5. I asked him what he was doing on Monday night.
6. He said that he couldn't tell me yet.
7. I asked him if everything was OK.
8. He told me not to worry.

C1: Listening for Meaning and Use (p. 401)

1. He asked me if he needed a prescription.
2. I told you that she has a headache.
3. She said she'll call when she gets the results.
4. He asked when the results would come.
5. She said they would come tomorrow.
6. She told me that I'd missed my last appointment.
7. I informed them that my ankle was sprained.
8. He said they'd call back that day.

Student Book Answer Key

CHAPTER 1

A3: After You Read (p. 5)

2. T   3. F   4. F   5. T   6. F

Think Critically About Form (p. 6)

1. Simple Present

line 1: 's	line 46: say
line 1: is	line 46: 're
line 9: does	line 46: interferes
line 12: 's	line 48: misses
line 17: helps	line 49: says
line 19: are	line 50: are
line 21: contains	line 51: 're
line 24: have	line 52: 're
line 31: predicts	line 54: is
line 38: needs	line 55: leads
line 41: is	line 56: doesn't stop
line 42: get	line 58: found

Present Continuous

line 2: ('re) plowing	line 27: are springing
line 4: 're fighting	line 34: is getting
line 5: are zooming	line 35: is aging
line 6: is beginning	line 36: are not getting
line 11: are beginning	line 58: 're napping
line 13: are sleeping	line 60: are trying
line 14: (are) working	line 62: 're putting
line 16: are warming up	line 62: ('re) pretending
line 19: are providing	

2. Simple Present Negative Statements
line 12: 's not
line 52: 're not
line 54: is not
line 56: doesn't stop

Present Continuous Negative Statements
line 36: are not getting

To make a negative statement in the simple present with forms of *be,* the form to use is *BE + not.* With other verbs, the form to use is *do/does + not +* verb. To make a negative statement in the present continuous, the form to use is *BE + not +* verb + *-ing.*

3. a. Does the average adult sleep six hours a night?
   b. Are Americans sleeping less?

In sentence a (simple present), you have to add *do/does* before the subject and change the main verb to its base form. In sentence b (present continuous), you have to invert the subject and *be* (auxiliary verb).

B1: Listening for Form (p. 8)

2. c
3. b
4. c
5. a
6. c
7. a
8. b

B2: Working on Verb Forms (p. 9)

	BASE FORM	SIMPLE PRESENT	PRESENT CONTINUOUS
2.	open	open / opens	opening
3.	fix	fix / fixes	fixing
4.	stop	stop / stops	stopping
5.	wake	wake / wakes	waking
6.	say	say / says	saying
7.	rest	rest / rests	resting
8.	dry	dry / dries	drying

B3: Working on Present Continuous Statements and Questions (p. 9)

Conversation 1
2. I'm wearing shoes.

Conversation 2
1. Are you buying a soda?
2. I'm not getting anything.
3. What are you doing?
4. I'm trying to get back my money.

Conversation 3
1. What are you doing?
2. I'm looking for a pencil.
3. Why are you making such a mess?

B4: Working on Simple Present Statements and Questions (p. 10)

A. 2. Earth doesn't revolve around the moon. It revolves around the sun.
3. Palm trees don't grow in cold climates. They grow in warm climates.
4. Bees don't live in ponds. They live in hives.
5. The sun doesn't rise in the north. It rises in the east.
6. Penguins don't live in the desert. They live in the Antarctic.
7. Flowers don't bloom in the winter. They bloom in the summer.
8. Spiders don't have six legs. They have eight legs.

B. Answers will vary. Some examples are:
2. A: What does Earth revolve around?
   B: Earth revolves around the sun.
   A: Does Earth revolve around the moon?
   B: No, it doesn't. It revolves around the sun.
3. A: Where do palm trees grow?
   B: Palm trees grow in warm climates.
   A: Do palm trees grow in warm climates?
   B: Yes, they do.
4. A: Where do bees live?
   B: Bees live in hives.
   A: Do bees live in ponds?
   B: No, they don't. Bees live in hives.
5. A: Where does the sun rise?
   B: The sun rises in the east.
   A: Does the sun rise in the east?
   B: Yes, it does.
6. A: Where do penguins live?
   B: Penguins live in the Antarctic.
   A: Do penguins live in the desert?
   B: No, they don't. They live in the Antarctic.

7. A: When do flowers bloom?
   B: Flowers bloom in the summer.
   A: Do flowers bloom in the summer?
   B: Yes, they do.
8. A: How many legs do spiders have?
   B: They have eight legs.
   A: Do spiders have six legs?
   B: No, they don't. They have eight legs.

B5: Understanding Informal Speech (p. 11)

2. Do you need
3. Are you having
4. Are you doing
5. Do you have
6. Do you like
7. Are you working
8. Do you need

Think Critically About Meaning and Use (p. 12)

1. b   2. a

C1: Listening for Meaning and Use (p. 14)

2. c   4. c   6. b   8. c
3. c   5. a   7. b

C2: Contrasting Activities in Progress with Routine Activities (p. 14)

Answers will vary. Some examples are:
A. A woman and her son are sitting on a bench.
   The boy is listening to music.
   His mother is reading a book and is wearing a baseball cap.
   Two teenage girls are sitting on the ground on a blanket.
   They are talking.
   One girl is holding a drink in her hand.
   A man is playing with his son.
   He is throwing a ball to his son.
   The boy is catching the ball.
   Some young men are playing volleyball.
B. Answers will vary.

C3: Describing Activities in the Extended Present (p. 15)

Answers will vary.

C4: Contrasting Permanent and Temporary Situations (p. 15)

2. f   3. e   4. a   5. b   6. d

C5: Expressing Complaints (p. 16)

Answers will vary.

C6: Introducing a Topic with the Simple Present (p. 16)

A. Answers will vary.
B. Answers will vary.

Think Critically About Meaning and Use (p. 17)

1. b, d   2. a, c, e

D1: Listening for Meaning and Use (p. 19)

	STATE OR CONDITION	ACTIVITY
2.		✓
3.	✓	
4.	✓	
5.		✓
6.	✓	

D2: Making Critical Remarks with Stative Verbs (p. 19)

Answers will vary. Some examples are:
2. I don't like it. It smells awful.
3. I don't like it. The fabric feels cheap.
4. I'm not sure. They seem small.
5. I don't like it. It sounds terrible.
6. I don't think so. It is expensive.

D3: Choosing the Simple Present or the Present Continuous (p. 20)

Conversation 1
2. Is it
3. depends on
4. guess
5. 's
6. 'm having

Conversation 2
1. hope
2. 'm not interrupting
3. need
4. seems
5. smell

Conversation 3
1. do you dream
2. don't dream
3. has
4. don't remember

Conversation 4
1. are you doing
2. am smelling
3. think
4. does it smell
5. seems

D4: Describing Physical Sensations (p. 21)

Answers will vary. Some examples are:
2. B: My head aches. OR My head is aching.
3. B: My eye burns. OR My eye is burning.
4. B: My ankle hurts. OR My ankle is hurting.
5. B: My stomach feels bad. OR My stomach is feeling bad.
6. B: My arm itches. OR My arm is itching.

D5: Describing Behavior (p. 21)

A. The birds are sick.
   The birds are purple.
   The flowers are purple.
   The children are quiet.
   The children are sick.
   The children are rude.
   The children are being quiet.
   The children are being rude.
B. Answers will vary. Some examples are:
   2. She often helps her friends and family.
   3. It is usually very stingy.
   4. Usually, they are very noisy.
   5. He yells at his employees for no reason.
   6. Usually, he is very understanding.
   7. Usually, she says hello.

D6: Understanding Informal Speech (p. 22)

2. I hate
3. We just love
4. She really dislikes
5. I love
6. I really like

D7: Writing Descriptions (p. 23)

Answers will vary.

Think Critically About Meaning and Use (p. 24)

1. a. No	b. It's not clear	c. Probably not
2. a. No	b. Yes	c. No
3. a. It's not clear	b. Probably not	c. It's not clear
4. a. No	b. No	c. It's not clear
5. a. No	b. Yes	c. No
6. a. No	b. No	c. Probably

Edit (p. 25)

It's mid-afternoon at a busy law firm in Washington, D.C.
The telephones ~~is~~ *are* ringing, voice mail ~~piles~~ *is piling* up, and faxes are
arriving. But what many of the lawyers ~~are~~ *are* doing? They ~~take~~ *are taking*
naps at their desks! As more and more busy professionals
~~works~~ *work* from morning until night, many are ~~sleep~~ *sleeping* in their offices
for just 15 or 20 minutes during the afternoon. And they are not
embarrassed about it at all. It ~~becomes~~ *is becoming* a new trend, according
to a recent survey on napping.

Some people ~~sleeps~~ *sleep* in their chairs, while some ~~are~~
~~preferring~~ *prefer* the floor or couches. Everyone agrees that a little
nap ~~help~~ *helps* them get through their very long workday. Meanwhile,
many experts are asking "What ~~means~~ *does* this *mean* new trend?" It's
simple, according to the most experienced nappers. They are
~~do~~ *doing* what people in other cultures and climates do every day.
And they are pleased that napping finally ~~gets~~ *is getting* more common in
the workplace.

CHAPTER 2

A3: After You Read (p. 29)

2. c   3. b   4. b   5. a   6. b

Think Critically About Form (p. 30)

1. **Regular Simple Past**

line 10: lifted	line 45: occurred
line 12: asked	line 55: faded
line 14: replied	line 57: disappeared
line 20: glanced	line 58: continued
line 20: stared	line 64: seemed
line 22: realized	line 64: rushed
line 31: seemed	line 65: swirled
line 39: impressed	line 66: slammed
line 40: clattered	line 67: leaped
line 41: scattered	

Irregular Simple Past

line 4: were	line 33: was
line 6: saw	line 34: was
line 7: was	line 38: came
line 8: grew	line 40: was
line 11: rang	line 43: were
line 12: did see	line 45: were
line 15: said	line 46: were
line 18: felt	line 51: felt
line 21: thought	line 52: ran
line 21: saw	line 53: got
line 22: was	line 54: saw
line 23: was	line 57: went
line 28: did	line 61: rang
line 32: was	line 69: found

2. **Singular Past Continuous**

line 17: was standing	line 54: was scraping
line 37: was making	line 60: was talking

Plural Past Continuous

line 26: were sitting	line 47: were enjoying
line 27: were doing	line 49: were enjoying
line 28: were gossiping	line 50: were playing
line 30: were talking	line 51: (were) laughing

3. **Before Main Clause**
   line 30: while they were talking
   line 38: When the jolt came
   line 50: While they were playing and laughing
   line 53: When they got there
   line 66: Before the watertight door slammed down

   After Main Clause
   line 5: when Fleet suddenly saw something directly ahead
   line 21: before he realized it was an iceberg
   line 44: when the strange vibration occurred
   line 61: when the warning bell rang

B1: Listening for Form (p. 32)

2. went	9. failed
3. was working	10. lost
4. were going	11. landed
5. caused	12. declared
6. cut off	13. occurred
7. forced	14. returned
8. was landing	

B2: Building Simple Past and Past Continuous Sentences (p. 33)

When did you go online yesterday?
What did you do when the bell rang?
What were you studying this morning?
Did you buy a computer?
Did you go online yesterday?
Who paid cash?
What happened last night?
You paid cash.

B3: Identifying Dependent and Independent Clauses (p. 33)

3. Something vibrated inside the ship.
5. The iceberg hit the ship.
6. Some passengers were getting ready for bed.
8. A group was still playing bridge.

B4: Combining Sentences with Time Clauses (p. 34)

2. While he was reading, he was listening to music.
   He was listening to music while he was reading.
   While he was listening to music, he was reading.
   He was reading while he was listening to music.
3. After he studied hard, he went to law school.
   After he went to law school, he studied hard.
   He studied hard after he went to law school.
   He went to law school after he studied hard.
4. Before she fell asleep, the doorbell rang.
   The doorbell rang before she fell asleep.
   Before the doorbell rang, she fell asleep.
   She fell asleep before the doorbell rang.
5. When the fire started, we were sleeping.
   We were sleeping when the fire started.
   When we were sleeping, the fire started.
   The fire started when we were sleeping.
6. Before the TV show started, they went to bed.
   They went to bed before the TV show started.
   Before they went to bed, the TV show started.
   The TV show started before they went to bed.
7. While the phone was ringing, they were cooking dinner.
   They were cooking dinner while the phone was ringing.
   While they were cooking dinner, the phone was ringing.
   The phone was ringing while they were cooking dinner.
8. Before the package arrived, she called the post office.
   She called the post office before the package arrived.
   Before she called the post office, the package arrived.
   The package arrived before she called the post office.

B5: Asking and Answering Questions with Time Clauses (p. 34)

Answers will vary.

Think Critically About Meaning and Use (p. 35)

Completed event: 1a and 2a; Unfinished event: 1b and 2b

C1: Listening for Meaning and Use (p. 37)

	ACTIVITY	COMPLETED	MAY CONTINUE
2.	eating dinner	✓	
3.	painting his kitchen	✓	
4.	baking a cake		✓
5.	writing a letter	✓	

C2: Describing Activities in Progress in the Past (p. 37)

Answers will vary. Some examples are:
A woman was talking on a cell phone.
A man was trying to read a book.
A young man was trying to study.
Someone was using a copier.
Two people were using computers.
Someone was looking for a book.
A library employee was shelving books.
A woman was checking out books.
Someone was returning a book.
Someone was asking the reference librarian questions.
A mother was reading to her child.

C3: Contrasting In-Progress and Completed Past Situations (p. 38)

2. were playing
3. were studying
4. was reading
5. was doing
6. heard
7. were telling
8. went
9. stopped
10. heard
11. jumped
12. ran
13. didn't smell
14. didn't see
15. went
16. got

C4: Describing Background Activities (p. 38)

A. Answers will vary. Some examples are:
2. We were cooking dinner.
   My roommate was doing her homework.
3. We were watching television.
   The rain was pouring down.
4. I was using my brother's car.
   I was doing my weekly shopping.
5. I was working on an important report.
   I was doing research on the Internet.
6. Smoke was coming out of the cafeteria.
   The students were taking an exam.

B. Answers will vary.

C5: Describing the Habitual Past (p. 39)

<u>7</u> That all changed a few summers ago after we finished college and got our first jobs.

<u>4</u> In the mornings, my twin brother and I would get up early and go for hikes in the woods.

<u>1</u> My family and I used to spend all our summers at a cottage on a lake.

<u>6</u> We didn't have a TV at the cottage, so we would spend our evenings talking and reading.

<u>8</u> We miss the lake and all the wonderful times we used to have there.

<u>3</u> Our cottage there was like our home away from home, and we loved our life there.

<u>5</u> In the afternoons, we'd meet our friends and go swimming at the lake.

<u>2</u> Every June we would leave our apartment in New York City and head for the lake.

C6: Using the Simple Past in Discourse (p. 40)

A. Answers will vary. Some examples are:
2. When I was five, my parents took me to the circus.
3. Last night, I waited in line for an hour to see a movie, and my feet hurt.

B. Answers will vary.

Think Critically About Meaning and Use (p. 41)

1. c   2. a   3. b

D1: Listening for Meaning and Use (p. 43)

2. a   3. b   4. a   5. a   6. b   7. a   8. a

D2: Using Past Time Clauses (p. 43)

Answers will vary. Some examples are:
After the dam collapsed, a train engineer outside of the town tried to warn people that the flood was coming.
While the train engineer sped down the tracks, he blew his train whistle loudly.
When the water crashed into Johnstown at a very high speed, it destroyed everything in its path.
When the water crashed into Johnstown, it wiped out villages, bridges, and freight trains.

Before the force of the water lifted some houses and knocked them into each other, some people were able to escape to the hills right above Johnstown.
After the Johnstown tragedy, more than 200 photographers came to record the story.

D3: Relating Events with *Before* and *After* (p. 44)

A. Answers will vary. Some examples are:

Situation 2
Before Jim tripped and fell, he was winning the race.
After Jim tripped and fell, he was unable to finish the race.

Situation 3
Before their parents came home, the boys were running around the house.
After their parents came home, they were watching television.

B. Answers will vary.

D4: Understanding Cause and Effect (p. 45)

Answers will vary. Some examples are:
2. a. effect   b. cause
   After they ran out of gas, they had to call for help.
   When they ran out of gas, they had to call for help.
3. a. cause   b. effect
   After the lightning struck, the lights went out.
   When the lightning struck, the lights went out.
4. a. cause   b. effect
   After they painted their house bright pink, their neighbors refused to talk to them.
   When they painted their house bright pink, their neighbors refused to talk to them.
   a. effect   b. cause
   After their neighbors refused to talk to them, they painted their house bright pink.
   When their neighbors refused to talk to them, they painted their house bright pink.
5. a. effect   b. cause
   After his best suit didn't fit anymore, he went on a strict diet.
   When his best suit didn't fit anymore, he went on a strict diet.
   a. cause   b. effect
   After he went on a strict diet, his best suit didn't fit anymore.
   When he went on a strict diet, his best suit didn't fit anymore.
   (In the first situation, he lost weight because his best suit was too small.
   In the second situation, because he lost weight, his best suit was too big for him.)
6. a. effect   b. cause
   After a mosquito bit her, her arm started to itch.
   When a mosquito bit her, her arm started to itch.
7. a. cause   b. effect
   After the doorbell rang, he answered the door.
   When the doorbell rang, he answered the door.
8. a. cause   b. effect
   After she found the lost jewelry, she got a reward.
   When she found the lost jewelry, she got a reward.

D5: Talking About Interrupted Activities (p. 46)

A. 2. while I was going down the stairs, I tripped on a shoe
3. while I was making coffee, I spilled the whole can of coffee on the floor
4. while I was taking a shower, the phone rang
5. when I stepped out of the shower, I slipped on the wet floor
6. While I was trying to explain, he got mad and hung up
7. While I was typing the paper, the computer system went down
8. when I was riding the elevator to class, it got stuck

B. Answers will vary.

Think Critically About Meaning and Use (p. 47)

2. ?   3. T   4. F   5. ?

Edit (p. 47)

2. ~~After~~ *Before* he fell asleep, he was reading a book.
3. ~~Were you having~~ *Did you have* your own car in college?
4. No errors.
5. Oh, no! I ~~was dropping~~ *dropped* my earring. I can't find it.
6. No errors.

CHAPTER 3

A3: After You Read (p. 51)

Circle numbers 4, 6, 7, 9, and 12

Think Critically About Form (p. 52)

1. *am/is/are* + *going to* + verb:
   line 14: is going to increase   line 24: are going to do
   line 23: are going to be   line 40: 're going to see

   will + verb:
   line 12: will become   line 30: will make
   line 20: 'll own   line 33: will continue
   line 26: will spend   line 34: will see
   line 29: will (no longer) exist   line 43: will lead

   will be + verb + *-ing*:
   line 36: will be growing
   line 37: (will be) equipping
   line 38: (will be) generating
2. simple present as future

B1: Listening for Form (p. 54)

2. c   4. c   6. d   8. d
3. a   5. c   7. b

B2: Working on the Future Continuous (p. 55)

Answers will vary. Some examples are:
On Monday evening, he'll be meeting with professor Parker.
On Tuesday, he'll be studying for his history exam.
On Wednesday, he'll be preparing a speech for his debate class.
On Thursday, he'll be cleaning his apartment.

B3: Building Sentences Using Future Forms (p. 55)

I will leave tomorrow.
I'll be leaving soon.
I'm leaving soon.
I leave tomorrow.
Who is going to leave tomorrow?
Who will leave tomorrow?
Who will be leaving soon?
Her family is going to leave tomorrow.
Her family will leave tomorrow.
Her family will be leaving soon.

B4: Asking *When* Questions About the Future (p. 56)

Answers will vary. Some examples are:
2. A: When are you going to get / are you getting / will you be getting a medical checkup?
   B: Next week.
3. A: When are you going to take / are you taking / will you be taking the day off?
   B: Tomorrow.
4. A: When are you going to clean / are you cleaning / will you be cleaning your apartment?
   B: This afternoon.
5. A: When are you going to finish / are you finishing / will you be finishing your work?
   B: Later today.
6. A: When are you going to go / are you going / will you be going out to dinner?
   B: Tomorrow evening.
7. A: When are you going to do / are you doing / will you be doing your laundry?
   B: This Saturday.
8. A: When are you going to shop / are you shopping / will you be shopping for groceries?
   B: Tonight.

B5: Working on the Simple Present as Future (p. 56)

A. Answers will vary. Some examples are:
Fall vacation begins on October 12.
It ends on October 15.
Thanksgiving break starts on November 22.
It lasts until November 25.
Classes end on December 6.
Final exams start on December 13.
They last until December 20.

B. Answers will vary.

B6: Working on Future Time Clauses (p. 57)

Answers will vary. Some examples are:
2. Before I go shopping, I'll call you.
   Before I go shopping, I'm going to call you.
   Before I call you, I'll go shopping.
   Before I call you, I'm going to go shopping.
3. After the mail arrives, I'll eat breakfast.
   After the mail arrives, I'm going to eat breakfast.
   (Illogical: After I eat breakfast, the mail will arrive.
   After I eat breakfast, the mail is going to arrive.)
4. When he reads the newspaper, he'll fall asleep.
   When he reads the newspaper, he's going to fall asleep.
   (Illogical: When he falls asleep, he'll read the newspaper.
   When he falls asleep, he's going to read the newspaper.)
5. Before he sets the table, he'll cook dinner.
   Before he sets the table, he's going to cook dinner.
   Before he cooks dinner, he'll set the table.
   Before he cooks dinner, he's going to set the table.
6. When I go home, I'll clean my house.
   When I go home, I'm going to clean my house.
   (Illogical: When I clean my house, I'll go home.
   When I clean my house, I'm going to go home.)

Think Critically About Meaning and Use (p. 58)

1. 1b describes a plan; 1a expresses a promise.
2. 2a refers to an activity in progress; 2b refers to the beginning of an activity.

C1: Listening for Meaning and Use (p. 59)

2. a	4. a	6. b	8. a
3. a	5. b	7. b	

C2: Expressing Promises, Plans, and Expectations (p. 60)

Answers will vary.

C3: Using Direct and Indirect Requests (p. 60)

A. Answers will vary. Some examples are:
2. A: Will you please drive me to school?
   B: Sure. No problem.
3. A: Will you please lend me your car?
   B: Sorry. I need it tonight.
4. A: Will you please buy me one, too?
   B: Sure. No problem.

B. Answers will vary. Some examples are:
2. A: Will you be driving to school this evening?
   B: Yes. Would you like me to drive you?
   A: Yes. Thank you.
3. A: Will you be using your car later?
   B: Yes, I will.
   A: OK. Never mind.
4. A: Will you be buying concert tickets?
   B: Yes. Would you like me to buy you one, too?
   A: Yes, please.

Think Critically About Meaning and Use (p. 61)

1. a, c   2. b

D1: Listening for Meaning and Use (p. 63)

	SAME	DIFFERENT
2.	✓	
3.		✓
4.		✓
5.	✓	
6.	✓	

D2: Expressing Plans, Scheduled Events, and Predictions (p. 63)

A. Plans or scheduled events:
We're having an exam tomorrow.
We're having an election tomorrow.
We're having a sale tomorrow.
We're going to have a meeting tomorrow.
We're going to have an exam tomorrow.
We're going to have an election tomorrow.
We're going to have a sale tomorrow.
We have a meeting tomorrow.

We have an exam tomorrow.
We have an election tomorrow.
We have a sale tomorrow.
Predictions:
We're having a storm tomorrow.
We're going to have a storm tomorrow.

B. Appropriate:
My new job, It, School, Winter vacation
Illogical:
An explosion, A snowstorm

D3: Discussing Plans and Scheduled Events (p. 64)

A. Answers will vary.

B. Answers will vary.

Think Critically About Meaning and Use (p. 65)

1. 1a. 'll snow
   1b. 's (probably) going to snow
   2a. 'll do
   2b. 'm going to do
2. 2a and 2b
3. 1a and 1b

E1: Listening for Meaning and Use (p. 67)

2. b	4. a	6. b	8. b
3. b	5. a	7. a	

E2: Restating Formal Announcements (p. 68)

Answers will vary. Some examples are:
2. Context: airport announcement
   Restatement: Flight 276 is going to be arriving at Gate 12.
3. Context: sign in subway
   Restatement: On April 1, the fare is going to increase to $1.75.
4. Context: class schedule
   Restatement: Classes are going to resume on January 22.
5. Context: poetry reading
   Restatement: Tonight we are going to begin with a short poem.

E3: Restating Predictions (p. 68)

2. The driver is going to lose control.
3. Computers will cost much less in a few years.
4. The buzzer is going to sound.
5. In a few years, "smart refrigerators" will tell owners when they need milk.
6. The patient's condition is improving. He will be fine.

For numbers 2 and 4, use *be going to* rather than *will* because there is evidence that an event is fairly certain to happen very soon.

E4: Making Quick Decisions and Stating Plans (p. 68)

A. Answers will vary.

B. Answers will vary.

E5: Understanding the Order of Future Events (p. 69)

A. 2. a   3. b   4. b   5. b   6. b

B. Answers will vary.

E6: Verbs Expressing the Future (p. 70)

2. b	4. b	6. a	8. a	10. a
3. a	5. a	7. b	9. a	

E7: Repeating Future Forms in Discourse (p. 71)

Answers will vary.

Think Critically About Meaning and Use (p. 72)

2. I'll be working.
3. I'm going to carry in the packages.
4. I'll answer it.
5. I'll have a bowl of soup.
6. I'm making a cake later.
7. I'm going to cook pasta.
8. I work Monday and Thursday.
9. Maybe I'll do my homework.
10. I did. I'm going to get it.

Edit (p. 73)

One of the most exciting advances in medicine in
                          going to be
the next few years is ~~gonna be~~ the widespread use of

robots in the operating room. Experts predict that
                    will never/are never going to replace
"robot assistants" ~~are never replacing~~ surgeons. Nevertheless,
                          will/are going to
there is no doubt that robots ~~going to~~ revolutionize surgery.
                  will/are going to
In just a few years, robots ^become the standard in certain

types of heart surgery, eye surgery, hip surgery, and brain
            is this
surgery. Why ~~this is~~ going to happen? The answer is simple. No

surgeon will ever be able keep his or her hand as steady as the
                  is ever going to be/will ever be
hand of a robot. No surgeon ~~is ever being~~ able to greatly

magnify a microscopic blood vessel with his or her own eyes.

These are simple and routine tasks for medical robots.

    Some patients are still worried, however. In the words of

one patient before hip surgery, "How do I know the robot
isn't going to/won't   *is going to/will drill*
~~doesn't~~ go crazy? Maybe it ~~drills~~ a hole in my head instead of

my hip!"

    Surgeons are quick to reassure their patients. "That's

impossible," says one optimistic surgeon. "I promise that
isn't going to/won't happen
~~isn't happening.~~ Robots are medical assistants. They'll work
              give
when I ~~am going to give~~ them a command, and they'll stop
      am going to/will
when I ~~will~~ say so. I^be right there the whole time."

Part 1 TEST (pp. 75–76)

1. c	10. a	14. do they usually do
2. c	11. When did the phone	15. I don't drink
3. b	ring?	16. Do you feel
4. a	12. What did they do last	17. knows
5. d	night? / What did	18. b
6. c	they watch last night?	19. a
7. b	13. How many pounds	20. f
8. a	did he lose on that	
9. d	diet?	

CHAPTER 4

A3: After You Read (p. 79)

2. T

3. F

Scientists think that we haven't discovered everything about the human brain.

4. F

Scientists haven't discovered how to move memories from one person to another person.

5. F

Physicists have observed only about 10% of the universe.

6. T

Think Critically About Form (p. 80)

1. line 23: haven't discovered
   line 32: have estimated
   line 34: 've observed
   line 43: hasn't arrived
   line 46: has evolved
   line 51: have reached
   line 56: 've begun

2. The two forms of *have* are *has* and *have*. Use *has* for third-person singular subjects. For first- and second-person subjects, and for third-person plural subjects, use *have*.

3. Regular Verbs
   line 23: haven't discovered
   line 32: have estimated
   line 34: 've observed
   line 43: hasn't arrived
   line 46: has evolved
   line 51: have reached

   Irregular Verbs
   line 56: 've begun
   The past participle of regular verbs is the same as the simple past form (verb +-*ed*). Irregular verbs have special past participle forms.

B1: Listening for Form (p. 81)

2. They called their senator.
3. Who's read the book over there?
4. Where's the team playing this week?
5. She's worried about her father.
6. Who's gone fishing?
7. You've bought all of the equipment already.
8. We looked up his telephone number.

B2: Identifying Past Participles (p. 82)

1. cooked   had
   eaten   heard
   forgotten   sung
   found   written
   gotten
2. appeared   happened
   broken   left
   exploded   rained
   fallen   started
   gone   sunk

3. allowed   driven
   bought   kept
   cut   spent
   destroyed   taken
   drawn   thrown

B3: Building Present Perfect Sentences (p. 82)

I've been sick.
I've forgotten your umbrella.
She hasn't arrived early.
She hasn't been sick.
She hasn't forgotten your umbrella.
She hasn't bought herself anything.
It hasn't snowed a lot.
It hasn't melted quickly.
Have you arrived early?
Have you been sick?
Have you forgotten your umbrella?

B4: Completing Conversations with the Present Perfect (p. 83)

Conversation 1
2. 've heard
3. has begun

Conversation 2
1. has Tom been
2. 's been
3. have known

Conversation 3
1. haven't sent
2. has happened
3. haven't called
4. written

Conversation 4
1. have we done
2. 've made
3. 've done
4. 've swept
5. has bought
6. haven't taken

B5: Understanding Informal Speech (p. 84)

2. Have you taken
3. Have you been
4. Have you eaten
5. Has she left
6. Have you seen
7. Have you done
8. Has he called

Think Critically About Meaning and Use (p. 85)

1. b   2. a

C1: Listening for Meaning and Use (p. 86)

2. a   3. c   4. c   5. c   6. b

C2: Talking About Life Experiences with *Ever* (p. 86)

A. 2. A: Have you ever missed a flight?
        B: Yes, I have. Have you? OR No, I haven't. Have you?
    3. A: Have you ever lost your wallet?
        B: Yes, I have. Have you? OR No, I haven't. Have you?
    4. A: Have you ever run out of gas?
        B: Yes, I have. Have you? OR No, I haven't. Have you?
    5. A: Have you ever told a lie?
        B: Yes, I have. Have you? OR No, I haven't. Have you?
    6. A: Have you ever met a famous person?
        B: Yes, I have. Have you? OR No, I haven't. Have you?
    7. A: Have you ever seen a comet?
        B: Yes, I have. Have you? OR No, I haven't. Have you?
    8. A: Have you ever ridden a motorcycle?
        B: Yes, I have. Have you? OR No, I haven't. Have you?

B. Answers will vary.

C3: Making Up Reminders with Indefinite Past Time (p. 87)

A. Answers will vary. Some examples are:
2. go to bed early, choose an interview suit, set the alarm clock
3. ask the salesperson the price, take it to the mechanic, take it for a test drive
4. pack the sunscreen, buy snacks, bring a beach umbrella

B. Answers will vary.

C. Answers will vary.

C4: Writing About Accomplishments and Progress (p. 87)

A. Answers will vary.

B. Answers will vary.

Think Critically About Meaning and Use (p. 88)

1. c   2. a and b   3. b

D1: Listening for Meaning and Use (p. 89)

A.

	RECENT PAST TIME	CONTINUING TIME UP TO NOW
2.	✓	
3.		✓
4.		✓
5.	✓	
6.	✓	

B. 2. a   3. b   4. b

D2: Talking About Continuing Time up to Now (p. 90)

Answers will vary, but questions will be as follows:
2. How long have you known how to speak English?
3. How long have you had your driver's license?
4. How long have you owned this book?
5. How long have you been a student?
6. How long have you lived in your apartment/house/dorm?
7. How long have you known the students in this class?
8. How long have you owned your car/bicycle?
9. How long have you known how to use a computer?
10. How long have you been in this city?

D3: Reaching Conclusions About Recent Past Time (p. 91)

Answers will vary. Some examples are:
1. Recently, she's become more confident, too.
2. (I think) he has just asked her to marry him.
   He's acted nervous lately.
   Recently, he's become very devoted to his girlfriend.
3. (I think) she has just taken an apple.
   Lately, she's taken many apples from the fruit bowl.
   She's recently learned how to climb on the stepstool.
4. (I think) he has just graduated.
   Lately, he's studied hard to get good grades.
   He recently graduated.

5. (I think) he has just burned his meal.
   He's cooked very few meals lately.
   He's recently learned how to cook.
6. (I think) he has just gone shopping.
   Lately, he's done his shopping on Saturday morning.
   Recently, he's bought extra food for his family.

D4: Writing About Recent Past Events (p. 92)

A. 2. has signed antipollution legislation
3. has saved a child's life
4. has made a rare discovery
5. has received a grant

B. Answers will vary. Some examples are:
2. Technology Stocks Rise
3. MCJ Moves to Texas
4. State Universities Lose Millions
5. Perez Leaves for China and Japan

Think Critically About Meaning and Use (p. 93)

1. In 1a, the speaker still works in Los Angeles, which is indicated by the use of the present perfect verb tense, *'ve worked* and the use of the simple present in *I love my job*. The present perfect can express situations that continue at the present time. In 1b, the speaker no longer works in Los Angeles, which is indicated by the use of the simple past *worked* and *loved*. The simple past can express only situations that are completed and no longer exist.
2. 2a asks about the time of a past event.
   2b does not ask about the time of a past event.

E1: Listening for Meaning and Use (p. 94)

2. a   4. b   6. b   8. a
3. a   5. a   7. b

E2: Choosing the Simple Past or the Present Perfect (p. 95)

2. I bought
3. I moved
4. I've owned
5. I've had
6. It's been
7. Have you called
8. She's worked
9. she graduated

10. I phoned
11. she was
12. Didn't he take
13. he left
14. died
15. He lived
16. They were

E3: Asking for Information (p. 96)

Answers will vary. Some examples are:
3. A: Has the mayor spoken yet?
   B: No, he hasn't. He speaks at twelve.
   A: Did the mayor speak yet?
   B: No, he didn't. He speaks at twelve.
4. A: Has the picnic already started?
   B: Yes, it has. It started at four thirty.
   A: Did the picnic already start?
   B: Yes, it did. It started at four thirty.
5. A: Have the fireworks begun yet?
   B: No, they haven't. They begin in an hour.
   A: Did the fireworks begin yet?
   B: No, they didn't. They begin in an hour.
6. A: Has the three-legged race happened already?
   B: Yes, it has. It happened at two.
   A: Did the three-legged race happen already?
   B: Yes, it did. It happened at two.

7. A: Has the pie-eating contest already ended?
   B: Yes, it has. It ended forty-five minutes ago.
   A: Did the pie-eating contest already end?
   B: Yes, it did. It ended forty-five minutes ago.
8. A: Have The Melodians sung yet?
   B: Yes, they have. They sang an hour ago.
   A: Did The Melodians sing yet?
   B: Yes, they did. They sang an hour ago.
9. A: Has the sing-along taken place already?
   B: No, it hasn't. It takes place at seven thirty.
   A: Did the sing-along take place already?
   B: No, it didn't. It takes place at seven thirty.
10. A: Have the line dancers performed yet?
    B: Yes, they have. They performed at three.
    A: Did the line dancers perform yet?
    B: Yes, they did. They performed at three.

E4: Introducing Topics with the Present Perfect (p. 97)

A. Answers will vary.

B. Answers will vary.

Think Critically About Meaning and Use (p. 98)

2. a. T	4. a. T	6. a. F	8. a. T
b. ?	b. ?	b. T	b. ?
3. a. F	5. a. ?	7. a. F	
b. ?	b. T	b. ?	

Edit (p. 99)

Since 1993, the Hubble Space Telescope has ~~provide~~ *provided* us with extraordinary pictures of the universe. It has shown us new comets and black holes. It ~~is~~ *has* found exploding stars.

Astronomers have been amazed that the Hubble Space Telescope ~~have~~ *has* sent back so many spectacular images. But it hasn't always been this way. The Hubble Space Telescope ~~was~~ *has* actually been in space since 1990. However, for the first three years, there was a problem with the main mirror. The pictures that it sent back to earth were not at all clear. In 1993, two astronauts ~~have~~ fixed the problem. They took a space walk and dropped a special lens over the mirror. Since then, four other servicing missions *have* helped to upgrade the telescope's scientific instruments and operational systems. The last of these ~~has been~~ *was* in May of 2009.

Today the world celebrates Hubble's 20 years in orbit. Its images have delighted and ~~amazing~~ *amazed* people around the world, and its many discoveries have ~~help~~ *helped* to advance our understanding of the universe.

CHAPTER 5

A3: After You Read (p. 103)

2. Ushi
3. chopping wood
4. heart disease
5. Okinawa
6. Power 9

Think Critically About Form (p. 104)

1. line 10: has been chopping and making
   line 12: has been arm-wrestling
   line 16: 's been doing
   line 17: has been farming
   line 19: haven't been working
   line 22: have been living
2. There are two auxiliaries in each example: *have/has* + *been*. The *-ing* ending is added to the main verb. In negative forms, *not* is placed between *have/has* and *been*.
3. The two forms of *have* are *has* and *have*. Use *has* for third-person singular subjects. For first- and second-person subjects, and third-person plural subjects, use *have*.

B1: Listening for Form (p. 105)

2. a	3. b	4. b	5. a	6. a

B2: Completing Conversations with the Present Perfect Continuous (p. 106)

Conversation 1
2. haven't been feeling
3. Have you been getting
4. haven't been sleeping

Conversation 2
1. haven't been going
2. 've been helping
3. 've been packing up
4. 's been taking

Conversation 3
1. has been giving
2. haven't been making
3. has been getting

Conversation 4
1. have you been doing
2. 've been exercising
3. haven't been eating

B3: Unscrambling Questions (p. 107)

A.
2. Who have you been writing to lately?
3. Have you been sleeping well recently?
4. Have you been working hard this semester?
5. Have you been exercising enough lately?
6. What time have you been getting up recently?
7. What have you been doing in the evening?
8. Where have you been eating lunch this semester?

B. Answers will vary.

B4: Writing Your Own Sentences (p. 107)

Answers will vary. Some examples are:
2. I haven't been sleeping.
3. They have been talking.
4. Have you been listening to the teacher?

B5: Understanding Informal Speech (p. 108)

2. I have been visiting
3. Have you been feeling
4. I have been having
5. Have you been exercising
6. I have been walking

Think Critically About Meaning and Use (p. 109)

1. b 2. a 3. c

C1: Listening for Meaning and Use (p. 110)

		MAX	HELEN
2.	Who is no longer sick?	✓	
3.	Who still volunteers at a hospital?		✓
4.	Who has been to Chicago more than once this year?	✓	
5.	Who has tried to call Eddie more recently?		✓
6.	Who is playing chess these days?	✓	

C2: Making Apologies and Excuses (p. 110)

Answers will vary. Some examples are:
2. I'm sorry. I've been waiting for the bus.
3. I'm sorry. I've been working late every night this week.
4. I'm sorry. I've been visiting my friends after school.
5. I'm sorry. I've been thinking about something.
6. I'm sorry. I've been forgetting to help out lately.

C3: Reaching Conclusions (p. 111)

Answers will vary. Some examples are:
There's an open bag of potato chips on the coffee table. Someone has been having a snack.
The computer is on. Someone has been using the computer.
There is a book on the sofa. Someone has been reading.
There is a piece of cake and a glass of milk on the table. Someone has been having a snack.
The bed is unmade. Someone has been sleeping in her bed.
The drawers are open. Someone has been going through her drawers.
The shower is dripping. Someone has been taking a shower.

C4: Writing Advertisements (p. 112)

A. Answers will vary. Some examples are:
2. Have you been trying to exercise more?
3. Have you been looking for an apartment?
4. Have you been planning to get away for a vacation?
B. Answers will vary.

Think Critically About Meaning and Use (p. 113)

1. 2a and 2b
2. 1a and 1b
3. Vera has probably finished the book. In 1a, the activity is continuing up to the present.

D1: Listening for Meaning and Use (p. 114)

	COMPLETED	CONTINUES
2.	✓	
3.		✓
4.		✓
5.	✓	
6.		✓
7.		✓
8.	✓	

D2: Contrasting the Present Perfect and the Present Perfect Continuous (p. 115)

A. 2. have been thinking/have thought
3. have been wondering/wondering
4. have been reading
5. have read
6. have been
7. haven't had
8. have been writing
9. have changed
10. have you been doing
11. Have you been working
12. Have you had
13. have had
14. Have you decided
B. Answers will vary.

D3: Writing a Conversation (p. 116)

Answers will vary.

D4: Connecting the Past and the Present in Discourse (p. 117)

1. I've been studying
2. for
3. I've been thinking
4. you made
5. I've applied
6. decided
7. I've been trying
8. I've been taking
9. told
10. I talked
11. I've spoken
12. She's been
13. changed
14. I decided
15. I've come
16. I've never seen

Think Critically About Meaning and Use (p. 118)

2. a 4. b 6. b 8. a
3. a 5. b 7. a

Edit (p. 119)

Life expectancy is the average number of years that a person will live. Two thousand years ago, the Romans ~~have been living~~ *lived* only an average of 22 years. In other words, they ~~have been having~~ *had* a life expectancy of 22. Since the beginning of the twentieth century, life expectancy around the world has been rising dramatically in many parts of the world. It will certainly continue to go up well into the twenty-first century. The rise in life expectancy ~~has been being~~ *is* due to the fact that people have been taking much better care of themselves. Each generation has experienced better nutrition and medical care than the one before. In 1900, people in the United States ~~have been living~~ *lived* to an average age of 47. All that has changed, however: the life expectancy in 2009 was 78.7, and it may be even higher today.

CHAPTER 6

A3: After You Read (p. 123)

2. T   3. F   4. T   5. F   6. F

Think Critically About Form (p. 124)

1. line 15: 'd admired
   line 16: had been
   line 17: 'd lumped
   line 21: 'd relied
   line 36: 'd attempted
   The contracted form of *had* in the past perfect is *'d*.
2. auxiliaries: had, been
   main verb: search
   The past perfect form is *had* + past participle.
   The past perfect continuous form is *had* + *been* + main verb + *-ing*.

B1: Listening for Form (p. 126)

2. 'd been working   10. had crossed
3. visited   11. had been trying
4. made up   12. had died
5. wanted   13. had been
6. became   14. seemed
7. hadn't flown   15. happened
8. hadn't let   16. flew
9. didn't care

B2: Working on Verb Forms (p. 127)

2. We went to school. (simple past)
   We had been going to school. (past perfect continuous)
3. They tried hard. (simple past)
   They had tried hard. (past perfect)
4. I had held my keys. (past perfect)
   I had been holding my keys. (past perfect continuous)
5. You had fun. (simple past)
   You had had fun. (past perfect)
6. He had made a mess. (past perfect)
   He had been making a mess. (past perfect continuous)
7. They thought about it. (simple past)
   They had been thinking about it. (past perfect continuous)
8. We did nothing. (simple past)
   We had done nothing. (past perfect)
9. What had happened? (past perfect)
   What had been happening? (past perfect continuous)
10. It got harder. (simple past)
    It had been getting harder. (past perfect continuous)

B3: Building Sentences (p. 127)

Had you been sick?   She had been sick.
Had you had lunch?   Who had left?
She had left.   Who had lunch?
She had lunch.   Who had taken a walk?
She had taken a walk.   Who had been working?
She had been working.   Who had been left?
She had been left.   Who had been sick?

B4: Asking and Answering Questions (p. 128)

A. 2. A: Before you started this course, had you ever studied English grammar?
   3. A: Before you started this course, had you ever spoken on the phone in English?

4. A: Before you started this course, had you ever written any letters in English?
5. A: Before you started this course, had you ever seen any English-language movies?

B. 2. A: Before you started this course, had you been learning any songs in English?
   3. A: Before you started this course, had you been practicing English with friends?
   4. A: Before you started this course, had you been watching any TV programs in English?
   5. A: Before you started this course, had you been listening to English language news broadcasts?

B5: Transforming Sentences (p. 128)

3. She had limped for the last mile.
6. Had anyone looked for us?
7. They had tried to call for help.
8. What had been happening?

Items 2, 4, and 5 cannot change because verbs with stative meanings are not usually used with the past perfect continuous.

B6: Understanding Informal Speech (p. 129)

2. had gone
3. had taught
4. had prepared
5. had, signed up
6. had, been trying

Think Critically About Meaning and Use (p. 130)

1. a. because a tree had fallen across my driveway
   b. after she had enrolled
   c. He'd been on a mountain climbing expedition
   d. Although I'd been terrified
2. past perfect
3. simple past

C1: Listening for Meaning and Use (p. 132)

2. a   4. b   6. b   8. a
3. a   5. a   7. a

C2: Expressing the Order of Past Events (p. 132)

2. *2, 1*
Before he graded the exam, he read the answers carefully.
Before he graded the exam, he had read the answers carefully.
3. *1, 2*
They had a child when they had been married for five years.
4. *1, 2*
After the car collided with a truck, someone called the police.
After the car had collided with a truck, someone called the police.
5. *2, 1*
Until the doctor said she was very healthy, she was worried.
Until the doctor said she was very healthy, she had been worried.
6. *1, 2*
By the time she slept for ten hours, I decided to wake her up.
By the time she had slept for ten hours, I decided to wake her up.

C3: Discussing Previous Accomplishments (p. 133)

1. They hadn't fixed the window yet.
   They hadn't repaired the lock yet.
2. He had already completed the English requirement.
   He had already taken the math courses.
   He hadn't passed the writing test yet.
3. She had already looked at the classified ads.
   She had already gone to an employment agency.
   She hadn't written her résumé yet.

C4: Describing New Experiences (p. 134)

A. Answers will vary. Some examples are:
1. b. They had never bathed a baby before.
   c. They had never fed a baby before.
2. a. She had never lived on her own before.
   b. She had never slept in a dormitory before.
   c. She had never cooked her own meals before.
3. a. He had never used an electronic cash register before.
   b. He had never gotten a paycheck before.
   c. He had never stocked shelves before.
4. a. She had never driven a car before.
   b. She had never been so scared before.
   c. She had never felt so nervous before.

B. Answers will vary.

Think Critically About Meaning and Use (p. 135)

1. a   2. b

D1: Listening for Meaning and Use (p. 137)

	JUST BEFORE	UNCLEAR
2.		✓
3.	✓	
4.	✓	
5.		✓
6.	✓	
7.		✓
8.		✓

D2: Talking About Continuing Past Actions (p. 137)

2. When her husband joined the company in 2011, Brigitte had been working at C & M for two years.
   When her husband joined the company in 2011, Brigitte had been working at C & M since 2009.
3. When the electricity went off, the chicken had been baking for fifteen minutes.
   When the electricity went off at 5:45, the chicken had been baking since 5:30.
4. When the phone woke Lisa up, she had been sleeping for three hours.
   When the phone woke Lisa up at 2:00 A.M., she had been sleeping since 11:00 P.M.
5. When they had their first child in 2011, Paulo and Celia had been married for two years.
   When they had their first child in 2011, Paulo and Celia had been married since 2009.
6. When she graduated from medical school in 2011, Kate had been studying for six years.
   When she graduated from medical school in 2011, Kate had been studying since 2005.
7. When he moved to Paris in 2010, Carlos had been living in Mexico City for two years.
   When he moved to Paris in 2010, Carlos had been living in Mexico City since 2008.
8. When he gave his first recital in July 2010, Eric had been taking piano lessons for seven months.
   When he gave his first recital in July 2010, Eric had been taking piano lessons since January.

D3: Expressing Reasons and Results (p. 138)

A. Answers will vary. Some examples are:
2. because she had cheated.
3. because she hadn't liked it.
4. He joined a gym because he had been gaining weight.

B. Answers will vary. Some examples are:
2. We were tired
3. she made a big mistake.
4. Because the traffic had been bad, we were late for our appointment.

D4: Expressing Contrasts (p. 138)

A. Answers will vary. Some examples are:
2. even though she hadn't done her homework.
3. Although they had dressed warmly,
4. Even though he had been making a lot of money,

B. Answers will vary. Some examples are:
2. We had no more food
3. we stopped communicating.
4. I didn't finish the project.

D5: Adding Background Information (p. 139)

A. Answers will vary. Some examples are:
2. I had been up all night packing my belongings. I had been feeling excited to move into my new apartment.
3. It had started to rain. We had been planning to meet our friends for dinner.
4. My furniture had been moved. My window had been opened.

B. Answers will vary.

Think Critically About Meaning and Use (p. 140)

2. a. F   4. a. F   6. a. F   8. a. T
   b. T   b. T   b. T   b. ?

3. a. F   5. a. ?   7. a. F
   b. T   b. T   b. T

Edit (p. 141)

In 1953, Edmund Hillary and Tenzing Norkay ~~had been~~ *were* the first climbers to reach the top of Mount Everest. Since then, many people ~~had~~ *have* climbed Mount Everest, especially in recent years. Before 1953, no human had ever stood on top of the world's highest peak, although some had tried. George Mallory and Sandy Irvine, for example, ~~had~~ died almost thirty years earlier on a perilous path along the North Ridge.

Since 1953, many more people ~~had~~ *have* set world records. In 1975, Junko Tabei of Japan ~~had become~~ *became* the first woman on a

mountaineering team to reach the top. In 1980, Reinhold Messner of Italy had become the first person to make the climb
~~became~~
to the top alone, without other people and without oxygen. In 1995, Alison Hargreaves of Scotland had duplicated Messner's triumph. She became the first woman to climb Mount Everest solo and without oxygen.

Each climber faces frigid winds, storms, avalanches, and most dangerous of all, the serious effects of the high altitude on the heart, lungs, and brain. So why had many hundreds of
~~have~~
people tried to climb Mount Everest in recent years? The only way to explain these numbers is to understand that the climb up Mount Everest represents the ultimate challenge of reaching the "top of the world."

Part 2 TEST (pp. 143–144)

1. a	9. b	15. g
2. d	10. Have you just been jogging?	16. we had bought
3. d		17. had not lost
4. c	11. How long has it been raining?	18. How long have you been in this room?
5. a		
6. b	12. b	19. Where has your sister been lately?
7. d	13. d	
8. c	14. h	20. How long have you been a student?

CHAPTER 7

A3: After You Read (p. 147)

2. c   3. b   4. a   5. a   6. a

Think Critically About Form (p. 148)

1. line 6:   might be
   line 11: might be having
   line 14: may take
   line 15: should (normally) strengthen
   line 16: could have
   line 16: may be
   line 19: might lead
   line 20: could result
   line 22: may turn out
   line 23: could prove

2. a. Modals followed by *be*
   line 6:   might be
   line 16: may be

   b. Modals followed by *be* + verb + *-ing*
   line 11: might be having

   c. Modals followed by a different main verb
   line 14: may take
   line 15: should (normally) strengthen
   line 16: could have
   line 19: might lead
   line 20: could result
   line 22: may turn out
   line 23: could prove

B1: Listening for Form (p. 150)

3. may	8. Could
4. can't	9. has to
5. might	10. may
6. must	11. could
7. Could	12. 's got to

B2: Completing Conversations with Modals (p. 151)

Conversation 1
2. can't be

Conversation 2
1. should arrive
2. won't arrive
3. ought to be

Conversation 3
1. has to be
2. couldn't be
3. must be

Conversation 4
1. has got to be
2. should be

B3: Using Short Answers with Modals (p. 152)

Answers will vary. Some examples are:
3. B: They might.   6. B: They could be.
4. B: It must be.   7. B: It couldn't.
5. B: They may.   8. B: They might be.

B4: Building Sentences with Modals (p. 152)

John must have a problem.
John might be sleeping.
John might have a problem.
John can't be sleeping.
John can't have a problem.
John has to be sleeping.
John has to have a problem.
It must be sleeping.
It must be true.
It must be a problem.
It must be broken.
It must have broken.
It might be sleeping.
It might be true.
It might be a problem.
It might be broken.
It might have a problem.
It might have broken.
It can't be sleeping.
It can't be true.
It can't be a problem.
It can't be broken.
It can't have a problem.
It can't have broken.
It has to be sleeping.
It has to be true.
It has to be a problem.
It has to be broken.
It has to have a problem.
It has to have broken.

B5: Writing Your Own Sentences with Modals (p. 152)

Answers will vary.

Think Critically About Meaning and Use (p. 153)

1. a, c, f   2. b, d, e

C1: Listening for Meaning and Use (p. 155)

	LESS CERTAINTY	MORE CERTAINTY
2.		✓
3.	✓	
4.		✓
5.		✓
6.		✓
7.		✓
8.	✓	

C2: Expressing Degrees of Certainty (p. 156)

Answers will vary. Some examples are:

Conversation 2
1. should
2. must

Conversation 3
1. has to
2. ought to

Conversation 4
1. has got to
2. could

Conversation 5
1. might
2. must

C3: Guessing with *Could, Might,* and *May* (p. 157)

Answers will vary. Some examples are:
1. They might be watching a baseball game.
   They may be enjoying an outdoor concert.
2. They could be celebrating a pay raise.
   They might be having a birthday celebration.
   They may be throwing old papers away.

C4: Making Guesses and Drawing Conclusions (p. 157)

Answers will vary. Some examples are:
2. There might not be a fire. The fire alarm was ringing all day yesterday.
3. He may be shy around new people. He doesn't seem unhappy.
4. She has to be on a diet. She didn't eat dessert yesterday, either.
5. I must be getting sick. I never sneeze unless I'm sick.
6. She could have a secret admirer. Yesterday, she received a box of chocolates without a card.
7. She may be asleep. She turns off her phone when she sleeps sometimes.
8. He has got to be exhausted. He has two jobs.

C5: Stating Expectations and Drawing Conclusions (p. 158)

3. Terry must be admitting new patients. OR Terry should be admitting new patients.
4. it must be 4:30. OR it should be 4:30.
5. Terry must be giving patients medicine. OR Terry should be giving patients medicine.
6. Terry must be discharging patients. OR Terry should be discharging patients.
7. Terry must be meeting with night nurses. OR Terry should be meeting with night nurses.
8. it must be 10:00. OR it should be 10:00.
9. it must be 2:45. OR it should be 2:45.
10. Terry must be attending a meeting. OR Terry should be attending a meeting.

C6: Expressing Understanding (p. 159)

Answers will vary. Some examples are:
2. You must be hungry. OR You must feel starved.
3. You must be nervous. OR You must feel anxious.
4. You must be relieved. OR You must feel glad.
5. You must be impatient. OR You must feel excited.
6. You must be angry. OR You must feel mad.
7. You must be disappointed. OR You must feel unhappy.
8. You must be happy for them. OR You must feel happy for them.

C7: Expressing Strong Certainty and Disbelief (p. 159)

A. Answers will vary.
B. Answers will vary.

Think Critically About Meaning and Use (p. 160)

1. a, c   2. b, d   3. a, c

D1: Listening for Meaning and Use (p. 162)

	LESS CERTAINTY	MORE CERTAINTY
2.		✓
3.		✓
4.	✓	
5.		✓
6.		✓
7.	✓	
8.		✓

D2: Expressing Degrees of Certainty (p. 162)

Answers will vary. Some examples are:
2. We may come later.
3. The flight will arrive at 8:10.
4. It could rain this afternoon.
5. It shouldn't be cold tonight.
6. He ought to get the job.
7. Video exercise games could become more challenging.
8. He might be taking the express train this evening.
9. The class will meet on Thursdays next semester.
10. She should be in Miami for the winter.

D3: Making Predictions About the Weather (p. 163)

Answers will vary. Some examples are:
Tomorrow:
Tomorrow may be cloudy.
There might be sleet in the afternoon.
It should rain overnight.
Saturday:
There will be rain and strong winds on Saturday morning.
It should clear in the afternoon, but it may rain on Saturday evening.
There could be flooding.
Sunday:
There will be sunshine on Sunday morning.
It could snow in the evening.
It probably won't snow after midnight.

D4: Making Predictions About Your Lifetime (p. 164)

A. Answers will vary. Some examples are:

3. might
4. won't
5. could
6. might
7. could
8. may not
9. will
10. will not

B. Answers will vary.

C. Answers will vary.

Think Critically About Meaning and Use (p. 165)

2. a   4. b   6. a

3. c   5. a

Edit (p. 165)

A migraine is a severe headache that can ~~to~~ affect your quality of life. Migraine sufferers often experience symptoms such as zigzag flashing lights or blind spots in their vision.

However, there are other symptoms that could signaling that a migraine is coming. You ~~maybe~~ *may be* sensitive to light, sound, or smells, or you might ~~be~~ feel overly tired. The good news is that treatment ~~must~~ *may* often relieve the pain and symptoms and prevent further attacks.

CHAPTER 8

A3: After You Read (p. 169)

2. ✓   3. ✓   4.   5. ✓   6.

Think Critically About Form (p. 170)

1.
line 9: has to have been	line 49: could have generated
line 22: could have happened	line 51: must have acted
line 25: could have launched	line 55: must have rotated
line 26: could have fallen	line 64: could have taken off
line 27: (could have) managed	line 71: could have helped
line 35: could have helped	line 73: might have developed
line 44: may have provided	

2. Past Modals with Singular Subjects

line 9: has to have been	line 44: may have provided
line 22: could have happened	line 49: could have generated
line 25: could have launched	line 55: must have rotated
line 26 : could have fallen	line 64: could have taken off
line 27: (could have) managed	line 73: might have developed
line 35: could have helped	

Past Modals with Plural Subjects

line 51: must have acted
line 71: could have helped

There is no difference in form between past modals with singular subjects and past modals with plural subjects. Past modals have only one form with all subjects.

3. The auxiliary *have* follows the modals. The form of the main verbs is the past participle.

B1: Listening for Form (p. 172)

2. could have   8. may have

3. may have   9. ought to have

4. couldn't have   10. could have

5. should have   11. may have

6. couldn't have   12. might have

7. might have

B2: Completing Conversations (p. 173)

Conversation 1
2. might not have liked
3. must have been

Conversation 2
1. shouldn't have driven
2. should have taken

Conversation 3
1. couldn't have left
2. might have forgotten

Conversation 4
1. must not have got
2. should have gone
3. could have written

Conversation 5
1. might have left
2. couldn't have
3. must have dropped
4. might have locked

B3: Asking and Answering Questions with Past Modals (p. 174)

Answers will vary. Some examples are:

3. A: Could prehistoric birds have had wings?
   B: Yes, they must have.
4. A: Could prehistoric birds have jumped from trees?
   B: No, they couldn't have.
5. A: Could prehistoric birds have run fast?
   B: Yes, they could have.
6. A: Could prehistoric birds have lived on the ground?
   B: No, they couldn't have.
7. A: Could prehistoric birds have eaten smaller animals?
   B: Yes, they could have.
8. A: Could prehistoric birds have eaten seeds?
   B: Yes, they must have.

B4: Forming Past Modals (p. 174)

2. The report should have been available on April 12.
3. He ought to have studied more for the test.
4. I could have worked harder.

5. She has to have been home.
6. I should have done things differently. I should have exercised more. I know I could have found the time.
7. I should have relaxed more. Perhaps I could have learned yoga.
8. I shouldn't have worried so much. Worrying couldn't have been good for my health.

B5: Understanding Informal Speech (p. 175)

2. could have
3. might not have
4. must have
5. should have
6. must have
7. could have
8. might have

Think Critically About Meaning and Use (p. 176)

1. a, d   2. b, c

C1: Listening for Meaning and Use (p. 177)

	LESS CERTAINTY	MORE CERTAINTY
2.		✓
3.		✓
4.		✓
5.	✓	
6.	✓	
7.	✓	
8.		✓

C2: Understanding Degrees of Certainty (p. 178)

Answers will vary. Some examples are:
2. A: He couldn't have built a fire.
   B: He might have built a fire.
3. A: He could have frozen to death.
   B: He must have frozen to death.
4. A: He must have lived in a valley.
   B: He may not have lived in a valley.
5. A: He might not have been older than 25.
   B: He couldn't have been older than 25.

C3: Making Guesses and Drawing Conclusions (p. 178)

Answers will vary.

C4: Expressing Impossibility and Disbelief (p. 179)

Answers will vary. Some examples are:
2. B: He couldn't have sent me a letter. He died a very long time ago.
3. B: It couldn't have run out of gas. I don't have a car.
4. B: I couldn't have grown three inches taller this week. I haven't grown in years.
5. B: I couldn't have lost a million dollars yesterday. I've never had a million dollars.
6. B: I couldn't have swum the English Channel last week. I don't know how to swim.

C5: Writing About Impossibility and Disbelief (p. 179)

A. Answers will vary.
B. Answers will vary.

Think Critically About Meaning and Use (p. 180)

1. b, c   2. a   3. c

D1: Listening for Meaning and Use (p. 182)

2. a   4. b   6. b   8. a
3. b   5. b   7. b

D2: Contrasting *Could* and *Could Have* (p. 182)

2. could have ridden
3. could see
4. could have taken
5. could have called

D3: Talking About Past Opportunities (p. 183)

A. Answers will vary. Some examples are:

Situation 1
2. He could have gone to medical school.
3. He could have taught science in a high school.
4. He could have directed a research program.

Situation 2
1. He could have become a cook in a restaurant.
2. He could have opened a restaurant.
3. He could have worked in a hotel.
4. He could have started his own business.

Situation 3
1. She could have been a fiction writer.
2. She could have gone to law school.
3. She could have worked for a newspaper.
4. She could have become a teacher.

Situation 4
1. He could have become an art teacher.
2. He could have gotten a job in advertising.
3. He could have done graphic design.
4. He could have opened an art gallery.

B. Answers will vary.
C. Answers will vary.

D4: Talking About Advice in the Past (p. 184)

Answers will vary. Some examples are:

Situation 1
2. A: Should he have brought an expensive gift?
   B: No, he shouldn't have. His friend didn't expect an expensive gift.
3. A: Should he have brought a traditional food from his country?
   B: Yes, he should have. It's polite. OR He could have. We like trying different kinds of food.
4. A: Should he have brought five friends?
   B: No, he shouldn't have. There was not enough food for his friends, too.

Situation 2
1. A: Should he have waited for the host?
   B: Yes, he should have. It is rude to eat before the host.
2. A: Should he have eaten more slowly?
   B: Yes, he could have. He might not be hungry anymore.
3. A: Should he have asked for more?
   B: No, he shouldn't have. He should have waited for his friend to offer him more.
4. A: Should he have waited for someone to offer him more?
   B: Yes, he should have. It's polite to wait until you are offered more.

Situation 3

1. A: Should he have whistled?
   B: No, he shouldn't have. It's not polite to whistle at waiters.
2. A: Should he have snapped his fingers?
   B: No, he shouldn't have. It is rude to snap your fingers.
3. A: Should he have clapped loudly?
   B: No, he shouldn't have. It's not common to clap loudly in a restaurant.
4. A: Should he have raised his hand when the waiter was looking at him?
   B: Yes, he could have. That is a polite way to get the waiter's attention.

Situation 4

1. A: Should he have ignored it?
   B: No, he shouldn't have. He should have brought it to the waiter's attention.
2. A: Should he have told the waiter?
   B: Yes, he should have. The waiter could have corrected the mistake.
3. A: Should he have called the manager immediately?
   B: No, he shouldn't have. He should have talked to the waiter first.
4. A: Should he have shouted at the waiter?
   B: No, he shouldn't have. It may not have been the waiter's mistake.

D5: Expressing Regret (p. 185)

Answers will vary. Some examples are:

2. I should have paid more attention to the rice. I shouldn't have left it on the stove.
3. I should have closed the car windows. I shouldn't have left them open during the rainstorm.
4. I should have insured my aunt's birthday gift. I shouldn't have been in such a hurry.
5. I should have applied for a summer job. I shouldn't have waited so long.
6. I should have obeyed the speed limit. I shouldn't have driven so fast.

D6: Writing About Regrets (p. 185)

A. Answers will vary.
B. Answers will vary.

Think Critically About Meaning and Use (p. 186)

2. a. T	4. a. T	6. a. F	8. a. F
b. T	b. F	b. T	b. T
3. a. F	5. a. T	7. a. T	
b. T	b. T	b. F	

Edit (p. 187)

2. When ~~he could~~ *could he* have called?
3. He might *have* been late.
4. I ~~ought to~~ *have* visited him at the hospital.
5. ~~May~~ *Could* he have taken the train instead of the bus?
6. She must have *had* a cold yesterday.
7. I ~~should~~ *shouldn't* have asked him. I'm sorry that I did.

8. He should have ~~taking~~ *taken* the exam.
9. You could ~~of~~ *have* called me.
10. She ~~have~~ *had* to have arrived yesterday.
11. The letter might *have* arrived this afternoon.
12. He must *have* had a cold yesterday.

Part 3 TEST (pp. 189–190)

1. c	8. c	15. d	19. must have gone
2. a	9. b	16. e	
3. a	10. c	17. b	20. I may have left
4. b	11. d	18. ought to have checked	
5. d	12. b		
6. b	13. c		
7. d	14. f		

CHAPTER 9

A3: After You Read (p. 193)

2. a	3. b	4. a	5. b	6. a

Think Critically About Form (p. 194)

1. Singular Simple Present Passive
   line 33: is (universally) recognized
   line 54: is (generally) recognized
   line 59: Is (ever) produced

   Plural Simple Present Passive
   line 22: are signaled
   line 58: Are ever produced
   line 62: are induced
   line 64: are induced
   line 72: are not understood

2. Singular Simple Past Passive
   line 38: was found
   line 47: was shown

   Plural Simple Past Passive
   line 45: were permitted

3. Present Continuous Passive
   line 52: are being studied

   Past Continuous Passive
   line 29: were being shown
   line 49: were being expressed

B1: Listening for Form (p. 195)

2. was asked
3. were being studied
4. is, understood
5. is, covered
6. are reserved
7. were reported
8. are, being published

B2: Asking and Answering Questions with Simple Present Passives (p. 196)

2. is picked up
3. is recycled
4. are the recycled items collected
5. are collected
6. are taken away
7. is done
8. is sold

B3: Working on Simple Past Passives (p. 196)

2. were melted
3. were cooled
4. were heated
5. were built
6. were removed
7. was poured
8. was formed

B4: Working on Present and Past Continuous Passives (p. 197)

A. 2. are being made
3. are being painted
4. is being replaced
5. are being built
6. is being upgraded
7. is being added
8. are being installed

B. 2. were being made
3. were being painted
4. was being replaced
5. were being built
6. was being upgraded
7. was being added
8. were being installed

B5: Working on Passive Questions (p. 197)

A. 2. How many computers are not being replaced?
3. Which software program is being installed?
4. How much money is being spent?
5. Are more employees being hired?
6. Is new furniture being purchased?
7. Is the old equipment being thrown away?
8. Are the hours of operation being expanded?

B. 2. How many computers were not being replaced?
3. Which software program was being installed?
4. How much money was being spent?

C. 6. Was new furniture purchased last semester?
7. Was the old equipment thrown away last semester?
8. Were the hours of operation expanded last semester?

Think Critically About Meaning and Use (p. 198)

1. They have about the same meaning.
2. 1a and 2a
3. 1b and 2b

C1: Listening for Meaning and Use (p. 199)

	ACTIVE	PASSIVE
2.	✓	
3.		✓
4.		✓
5.		✓
6.		✓
7.	✓	
8.		✓

C2: Using Agents and Receivers (p. 200)

3. The window was broken by the child.
4. The concert was attended by many people.
5. She made the cake.
6. We canceled the appointment.
7. The car was repaired by two mechanics.

C3: Focusing on Receivers (p. 200)

1. b. the bride and groom were being photographed.
   c. appetizers were being served.
   d. Answers will vary.
2. a. the roast beef was being sliced.
   b. the salad was being made.
   c. the table was being set.
   d. Answers will vary.
3. a. one person was being lifted into an ambulance.
   b. a man was being given oxygen.
   c. two witnesses were being questioned.
   d. Answers will vary.

C4: Choosing Verbs with Active or Passive Forms (p. 201)

2. A new theory about facial expressions was proposed by a psychologist.
3. This sentence cannot change into the passive form because *emerge* is an intransitive verb. Intransitive verbs have no passive form.
4. The new theory was being considered by the research team.
5. This sentence cannot change into the passive form because *have* is a transitive nonpassive verb. Many transitive verbs with nonpassive meanings, such as *have*, do not have passive forms.
6. Each participant is being paid by the psychology department.
7. This sentence cannot change into the passive form because *arrive* is an intransitive verb. Intransitive verbs have no passive form.
8. More equipment for data analysis is still needed by the researchers.

Think Critically About Meaning and Use (p. 202)

1. 1b
2. 2a

D1: Listening for Meaning and Use (p. 203)

2. a
3. b
4. a
5. a
6. b

D2: Describing Results (p. 204)

Answers will vary. Some examples are:
1. b. was blocked.
   c. were injured.
   d. was trapped.
   e. was actually untouched.
   f. were shattered.
2. a. was closed.
   b. was canceled.
   c. were given.
   d. were forced to stay home.
3. a. were put away.
   b. were vacuumed.
   c. was dusted.
   d. were cleaned.
   e. was swept.

D3: Omitting Agents (p. 205)

2. The prices at the farmer's market are always being reduced. (b)
3. Applications for summer employment are being accepted at the supermarket. (b)
4. Our new carpet was ruined when a pipe burst in our house. (b)

5. The report was lost sometime during the week. (d)
6. At that moment, the door was being unlocked. (a)
7. Attention, please. Tickets for the 5:00 PM show are now being sold. (c)
8. Many books about health and nutrition are being written. (b)
9. Last year, undergraduates were required to take a minimum of four courses per semester. (b)
10. Portuguese and a number of other languages are spoken in Brazil. (b)

D4: Writing Definitions (p. 205)

A. Answers will vary. Some examples are:
2. Soccer is a sport that is played by many people.
3. The tuxedo is a garment that is worn by a groom.
4. Farsi is a language that is spoken in Iran.
5. The Great Sphinx of Giza is a statue that was built by ancient Egyptians.
6. Rice is a food that is eaten by people all over the world.

B. Answers will vary.

D5: Keeping the Focus (p. 206)

A. 2. b   4. a   6. b   8. a
3. a   5. b   7. a

B. Answers will vary. Some examples are:
2. They must be prescribed by a physician.
   If untreated, they may be harmful to your health.
3. It is not difficult to learn.
   Romance languages also include Italian and Spanish.
4. It is now recorded on compact discs.
   They are collectors' items now.
5. They can understand a lot about a person that way.
   Our expressions tell what we are thinking.
6. It is more common than meat.
   A staple is a food that is eaten at almost every meal.

C. Answers will vary.

Think Critically About Meaning and Use (p. 208)

2. b   4. b   6. b   8. a
3. a   5. b   7. b

Edit (p. 209)

It is ~~claiming~~ *claimed* by psychologists that everyone lies at some time or other. Moreover, many people can lie without showing it in their facial expressions or body language. For this reason, lie detector tests are frequently ~~use~~ *used* in police investigations. The use of such tests to detect lies is many hundreds of years old.

For example, it is ~~believe~~ *believed* that in China suspected liars were forced to chew rice powder and then spit it out. If the powder was dry, the suspect ~~is~~ *was* considered guilty. In Spain, another variation for lie detection *was* used. The suspect ~~was being required~~ *was required* to swallow a slice of bread and cheese. It was believed that if the bread stuck inside the suspect's mouth, then he or she was lying. Psychologists report that these strange methods actually show a basic principle that is ~~know~~ *known* about lying: Anxiety that is related to lying is linked to lack of saliva, or dry mouth.

Modern lie detectors, which are ~~calling~~ *called* polygraphs, are used to indicate changes in heart rate, blood pressure, breathing rate, and perspiration while a person is ~~be~~ *being* examined. Questions about the validity of the polygraph, however, are frequently ~~raising~~ *raised*. Consequently, results from polygraphs are often thrown out in legal cases.

CHAPTER 10

A3: After You Read (p. 213)

2. b   3. a   4. c

Think Critically About Form (p. 214)

1. Present Perfect Passive
   line 6: has (finally) been broken
   line 30: have (just) been given
   line 34: have (recently) been told
   line 36: has been forced
   line 56: have been designed
   The three parts of the present perfect passive are: havs/have + been + past participle.
2. Future Passive
   line 38: will be canceled
   line 40: will be shut down
   line 41: won't be built
   line 46: will be fired
   line 48: will be closed?
   The three parts of the future passive are: *will* + *be* + past participle. Another way to form it is: *be going to* + past participle.
3. The three parts of the modal passive are: modal + *be* + past participle.

B1: Listening for Form (p. 215)

	ACTIVE	PASSIVE
2.	✓	
3.		✓
4.		✓
5.		✓
6.	✓	
7.	✓	
8.		✓

B2: Working on Future and Modal Passives (p. 216)

A. 2. will be posted
3. will not be announced
4. will be canceled
1. will be shipped
2. will be added
3. will be credited
4. will not be made

B. 2. cannot be refilled
3. should be kept
4. may be stored
1. needs to be insured
2. has to be reported
3. must be accompanied
4. should be sent

B3: Working on Present Perfect Passives (p. 217)

2. These products have been manufactured by the company for three years.
3. This book has been translated into many languages.
4. The furniture has been moved to the new house.
5. The recipes have been created by a famous chef.
6. A new prescription has been recommended by the doctor.

B4: Asking and Answering Passive Questions (p. 217)

A. 2. A: Should bicyclists be allowed on busy streets?
B: Yes, they should. OR No, they shouldn't.
3. A: Should violent films be banned from television?
B: Yes, they should. OR No, they shouldn't.
4. A: Should a new community center be built downtown?
B: Yes, it should. OR No, it shouldn't.
5. A: Should men be given parental leave for childcare?
B: Yes, they should. OR No, they shouldn't.
6. A: Should women be paid the same wages as men?
B: Yes, they should. OR No, they shouldn't.
7. A: Should children be punished for coming home late?
B: Yes, they should. OR No, they shouldn't.
8. A: Should animals be used for medical research?
B: Yes, they should. OR No, they shouldn't.

B. Answers will vary.

Think Critically About Meaning and Use (p. 218)

1. Agents:
1a: the instructor
1b: a team of experts
2a: Gregory Marks
2b: the author
2. The agents in 1b and 2a give important or unexpected information.
The agents in 1a and 2b seem unnecessary.

C1: Listening for Meaning and Use (p. 219)

	NECESSARY AGENT	UNNECESSARY AGENT
2.	✓	
3.	✓	
4.		✓
5.		✓
6.		✓
7.		✓
8.	✓	

C2: Including or Omitting Agents (p. 219)

3. Many car accidents in this community have been caused by teenage drivers.
(The agent is included because it adds important information.)

4. Children shouldn't be allowed to watch too much television. (The agent is omitted because it is obvious.)
5. A new tax law will be passed soon.
(The agent is omitted because it is obvious.)
6. The British government was led by Winston Churchill in World War II. (The agent is included because it contains important information.)
7. Will stronger environmental laws be passed by the city council this year? (The agent is included because it adds important information.)
8. This incredible story was written by a young child.
(The agent is included because it is surprising.)

C3: Including or Omitting Agents (p. 220)

At the hospital:
3. He'll be told whether it is broken.
4. If his arm is broken, he'll be sent back to the emergency room.
5. First his arm will be put in the proper position.
6. Then a cotton sleeve will be put over his arm, and it will be wrapped with wet bandages.
7. After it sets, he'll be told how to care for the cast.

At school:
1. Please listen carefully. The instructions are going to be read only once.
2. Each student will be given a test booklet and a pencil.
3. The students will be asked to turn to the first page.
4. Then they will be shown a set of pictures.
5. They will be told to check the correct answer in the booklet.
6. After the last picture, the booklets will be collected.
7. Finally, the students will be dismissed.

Think Critically About Meaning and Use (p. 221)

1. a. We use sulfur dioxide to produce sulfuric acid.
b. As a special benefit to on-line customers, we will ship orders free of charge.
c. You must insure your vehicle. You must present proof of insurance.
2. Passive sentences sound more formal and impersonal because the focus is on the results or the receiver of the action and not on the agent.
3. Sentence *a* would be used in an academic context such as a chemistry book; sentence *b* would be used by an Internet retailer on a website or in an advertisement; and sentence *c* would be used on a sign or list of rules at the Department of Motor Vehicles.

D1: Listening for Meaning and Use (p. 222)

A.

	ACADEMIC DISCOURSE	PUBLIC DISCOURSE	PERSONAL DISCOURSE
2.	✓		
3.		✓	
4.		✓	
5.			✓
6.		✓	
7.	✓		
8.		✓	

B. Answers will vary.

D2: Understanding Newspaper Headlines (p. 223)

A. 2. A new cancer treatment has been discovered.
A new cancer treatment was discovered.
3. The president's trip has been delayed by the weather.
The president's trip was delayed by the weather.
4. A site has been selected for the recycling plant.
A site was selected for the recycling plant.
5. The restaurant has been closed by the Health Department.
The restaurant was closed by the Health Department.
6. A golfer has been struck by lightning.
A golfer was struck by lightning.

B. In newspaper headlines, the passive is used to convey an objective or impersonal tone. The passive often sounds more formal, factual, or authoritative. In some sentences, the agent was included because it provided information necessary to complete the meaning or because it was important information.

D3: Understanding Informal Speech (p. 224)

2. might be promoted
3. may be transferred
4. was accepted
5. was caught
6. could be fired
7. was rewarded
8. was nominated

D4: Writing Rules (p. 225)

A. 2. Guest passes can be purchased at the main office.
3. The number of guests may be limited on weekends.
4. Children under 12 are not admitted unless an adult accompanies them. OR . . . unless they are accompanied by an adult.
5. Small children must be supervised at all times.
6. A shower must be taken before entering the pool.
7. The lifeguard must be obeyed at all times.
8. Diving is permitted in designated areas only.
9. Smoking, gum chewing, and glass bottles are prohibited.
10. Food may be eaten in the picnic area only.

B. Answers will vary.

Think Critically About Meaning and Use (p. 226)

2. b   4. b   6. a   8. a
3. b   5. b   7. b

Edit (p. 227)

2. The letter ought to ^be^ delivered in the afternoon.
3. The bell will be ~~rang~~ ^rung^ several times.
4. A young man has ^been^ seriously injured in a car accident. That's terrible!
5. The mail has ^been^ sent to the wrong address.
6. Will a new road ~~build~~ ^be built^ soon, or will the old one be repaired?
7. It will ~~be not~~ ^not be^ needed any longer.
8. All online orders must ~~get~~ ^be^ paid by credit card.

CHAPTER 11

A3: After You Read (p. 231)

2. F   3. T   4. T   5. F   6. T

Think Critically About Form (p. 232)

1. Gerund as Subject
line 11: driving
line 30: driving
line 33: (His) weaving
line 34: (His) putting
2. Gerund Following a Verb
line 22: weaving
line 46: using
3. Infinitive Directly Following a Verb
line 48: to relax
4. *It* is in subject position.

B1: Listening for Form (p. 234)

	GERUND	INFINITIVE
2.	✓	
3.	✓	
4.		✓
5.		✓
6.		✓

B2: Rephrasing Subject Gerunds as *It* . . . + Infinitive (p. 234)

2. It's not a good idea to study all night.
3. It takes too much time to walk to work.
4. It is important to get exercise.
5. It costs a lot of money to own a house.
6. It can be useful to know a foreign language.

B3: Working on Subject Gerunds and *It* . . . + Infinitive (p. 235)

A. Answers will vary.
B. Answers will vary.

B4: Building Sentences with Gerunds and Infinitives (p. 235)

He told me to speak Spanish.
She expects me to go more slowly.
She expects me to speak Spanish.
She expects to go more slowly.
She expects to speak Spanish.
He learned to go more slowly.
He learned to speak Spanish.
They advised me to go more slowly.
They advised me to speak Spanish.
They advised leaving.
They advised taking a driving class.
Don't delay leaving.
Don't delay taking a driving class.

B5: Distinguishing Gerunds and Infinitives After Verbs (p. 235)

2. seeing it?   7. to see it.
3. seeing it.   8. to see it.
4. to see it.   9. seeing it.
5. seeing it.   10. to see it.
6. to see it.

B6: Using Short Answers to Questions with Infinitives (p. 236)

2. B: don't expect to
3. B: would like to
4. B: doesn't want to
5. B: plan to
6. B: needs to

B7: Asking Information Questions with Gerunds and Infinitives (p. 237)

A. Answers will vary. Some examples are:
2. A: What do you enjoy doing in your free time?
   B: Reading the paper. What about you?
   A: I enjoy cooking.
3. A: What do you suggest doing after dinner?
   B: Watching television. What about you?
   A: I suggest taking a walk (after dinner).
4. A: What would you like to do on your birthday?
   B: Go to a movie. What about you?
   A: I would like to go to a club (on my birthday).
5. A: What do you want to do during your vacation?
   B: Relax. What about you?
   A: I want to go to the beach (during my vacation).
6. A: What do you avoid doing on the weekend?
   B: Working. What about you?
   A: I avoid getting up early (on the weekend).
7. A: What do you hope to do next summer?
   B: Go to Europe. What about you?
   A: I hope to buy a new car (next summer).
8. A: What do you dislike doing in the morning?
   B: Eating breakfast. What about you?
   A: I dislike waking up early (in the morning).

B. Answers will vary.

B8: Asking *Yes/No* Questions with Gerunds and Infinitives (p. 237)

Answers will vary. Some examples are:
2. A: Do you suggest we stay home or see a movie tonight?
   B: See a movie.
3. A: Do you hope to live in a big city or a small town?
   B: A big city.
4. A: Do you need to study a lot or a little?
   B: A lot.
5. A: Do you recommend eating breakfast or skipping breakfast?
   B: Eating breakfast.
6. A: Do you want to stay in your apartment or find a new apartment?
   B: Find a new apartment.

Think Critically About Meaning and Use (p. 238)

Same meaning: 2a and 2b; Different meaning: 1a and 1b

C1: Listening for Meaning and Use (p. 240)

2. b   3. a   4. b   5. a   6. b

C2: Rephrasing Gerunds and Infinitives (p. 240)

2. A: I hate driving in traffic.
   B: Then you should continue taking the bus home.
3. A: It started raining a few minutes ago.
   B: Then let's wait here. I don't like walking in the rain.
4. A: I hate to wait in line.
   B: So do I. That's why I prefer shopping late at night.

C3: Making Suggestions (p. 241)

Answers will vary.

C4: Expressing Feelings and Preferences (p. 242)

A. 1. 2. getting up
        3. to worry / worrying
        4. to do
     2. 1. shopping
        2. to watch / watching
        3. to buy
        4. to fight / fighting
        5. to go
        6. going
        7. to have / having
     3. 1. to feel
        2. to find / finding
        3. to avoid
        4. cooking

B. Answers will vary.

Think Critically About Form (p. 243)

1. In sentence b, the gerund follows a verb phrase ending in a noun. In sentence c, the gerund follows a phrasal verb. In sentence a, the gerund follows a preposition.
2. Sentence d has a phrase containing an infinitive (*to reach* their destinations). The infinitive follows an adjective (*anxious*).

D1: Listening for Form (p. 245)

2. relaxing   7. going
3. working   8. leaving
4. to finish   9. catching up
5. working   10. to relax
6. taking

D2: Using Gerunds After Prepositions (p. 245)

Answers will vary. Some examples are:
2. After finding a job, make sure to start a savings account.
3. Instead of cooking dinner, let's go out to eat.
4. Besides doing the laundry, I need to go to the grocery store.
5. By reducing stress, you will be a healthier person.
6. In addition to cleaning your apartment, you need to get your car fixed.
7. Before using a computer, make sure you know how to type.
8. After looking for an apartment, you'll need to buy furniture.

D3: Choosing Between Gerunds and Infinitives (p. 246)

A. Answers will vary. Some examples are:
2. A: What are you good at?
   B: I'm good at cooking chicken. What about you?
   A: I'm good at playing the guitar.
3. A: What are you eager to do?
   B: I'm eager to finish college. What about you?
   A: I'm eager to visit my family in two weeks.
4. A: What are you afraid of doing?
   B: I'm afraid of riding in elevators. What about you?
   A: I'm afraid of meeting new people.
5. A: What are you ready to do right now?
   B: I'm ready to go to a movie. What about you?
   A: I'm ready to eat dinner.
6. A: What are you accustomed to doing?
   B: I'm accustomed to eating dessert every night. What about you?

A: I'm accustomed to spending Sundays with my family.

7. A: What are you determined to do before you are 50?
   B: I'm determined to skydive before I'm 50. What about you?
   A: I'm determined to travel around the world before I'm 50.

8. A: What are you looking forward to doing next year?
   B: I'm looking forward to studying in Japan next year. What about you?
   A: I'm looking forward to going to college next year.

B. Answers will vary.

D4: Working on Purpose Infinitives (p. 246)

A. Answers will vary. Some examples are:
   2. to pick up my clothes.
   3. to fill a prescription.
   4. to return a book.
   5. to fill up the gas tank.

B. Answers will vary.

Think Critically About Meaning and Use (p. 247)

1. In 1a, Jane is driving. In 1b, Tom is driving.
2. In 2a, Sam might come early. In 2b, Susan might come early.

E1: Listening for Meaning and Use (p. 248)

2. b	4. a	6. b	8. b
3. b	5. a	7. a	

E2: Expressing Intentions and Desires (p. 249)

Answers will vary. Some examples are:
3. Situation A: to be the next president of the United States.
   Situation B: to be unemployed for a few months.
4. Situation A: you to give me advice.
   Situation B: you to help me.
5. Situation A: raising enough money for my campaign.
   Situation B: disappointing my family.
6. Situation A: everyone to vote.
   Situation B: you to find out the truth.
7. Situation A: to tell you why I'll make the best candidate.
   Situation B: to apologize for my mistakes.
8. Situation A: campaigning every weekend.
   Situation B: explaining my side of the story.

E3: Talking About Teaching (p. 249)

A. Answers will vary.
B. Answers will vary.

Think Critically About Meaning and Use (p. 250)

2. F	4. F	6. F	8. T	10. F
3. T	5. T	7. T	9. T	

Edit (p. 251)

Unfortunately, it is very common ^to^ encounter aggressive drivers every day. They are usually trying to ~~getting~~ get somewhere in a hurry. ~~Them~~ Their speeding can cause them ^to^ follow too closely or ^to^ change lanes frequently without signaling.

In order ^to^ avoid becoming an aggressive driver, there are a number of rules ~~following~~ to follow. First, allow enough time to ~~reaching~~ reach your destination. Second, change your schedule to keep from ~~drive~~ driving during rush hours. Third, call ahead ~~for~~ to explain if you are going to be late. Then you can relax.

If you see an aggressive driver, try ^to^ get out of the way safely. Never challenge an aggressive driver by ~~speed~~ speeding up or attempting to hold your position in your lane. Don't let others make you ~~driving~~ drive dangerously. You need ^to^ be in control at all times.

Part 4 TEST (pp. 253–254)

1. c	9. a	17. g
2. d	10. b	18. If it snows, the game will be canceled.
3. a	11. d	
4. b	12. not to do	19. The mayor has been seen at that restaurant.
5. d	13. to eating	
6. b	14. riding	
7. d	15. a	20. *The Three Musicians* was painted by Pablo Picasso.
8. c	16. f	

CHAPTER 12

A3: After You Read (p. 257)

2. F Chicken soup makes you feel better both emotionally and physically.
3. T
4. F Dr. Sackner showed that chicken soup was better at fighting congestion than hot or cold water.
5. F Chicken soup is good for colds, but Dr. Ziment thinks spicy foods are even better.
6. T

Think Critically About Form (p. 258)

1. line 26: literature   line 30: chemical
   line 27: centuries   line 31: soup
   line 28: drugs   line 33: drug
   line 29: Chicken

2. Adjective + Noun
   line 25: early medical literature

   Article + Noun
   line 28: the drugs   line 31: the soup

   Article + Adjective + Noun
   line 29: a certain chemical line 32: a common drug

3. line 27: centuries   line 29: Chicken

4. Singular   Plural
   line 26: literature   line 27: centuries
   line 29: Chicken   line 28: drugs
   line 30: chemical
   line 31: soup
   line 33: drug

B1: Listening for Form (p. 260)

2. Ø	5. Ø	8. Ø	11. the	14. a
3. Ø	6. The	9. Ø	12. the	
4. the	7. Ø	10. the	13. a	

B2: Identifying Indefinite and Definite Articles (p. 260)

Have you ever eaten coconut? You probably have, but you may not be very familiar with <u>coco palms</u> [I]. <u>Coconuts</u> [I] come from <u>coco palms</u> [I], which are <u>trees</u> [I] that grow in <u>tropical regions</u> [I]. <u>Coco palms</u> [I] are very unusual because all of <u>the parts</u> [D] of <u>the tree</u> [D] have a <u>commercial value</u> [I]. For example, <u>coconuts</u> [I] <u>are an important food</u> [I] in <u>tropical regions</u> [I], <u>and coconut milk</u> [I], which comes from inside <u>the coconut</u> [D], is a <u>nutritious drink</u> [I]. <u>Coconut oil</u> [I], <u>the most valuable product</u> [D] of all, also comes from <u>coconuts</u> [I]. Some of <u>the other parts</u> [D] of <u>the tree</u> [D] that are eaten include <u>the buds</u> [D] and <u>young stems</u> [D]. Besides <u>food</u> [I], <u>the tree</u> [D] is also used for manufacturing <u>commercial products</u> [I]. <u>The leaves</u> [D] are used for making <u>fans</u> [I] and <u>baskets</u> [I], and <u>the fibers</u> [D] from <u>the husks</u> [D] and <u>trunks</u> [D] are made into <u>mats</u> [I], <u>cord</u> [I], and <u>rope</u> [I]. Even <u>the hard shells</u> [D] and <u>the husks</u> [D] are used to make <u>fuel</u> [I], and <u>the trunks</u> [D] are used for <u>timber</u> [I].

B3: Building Sentences with Indefinite and Definite Articles (p. 261)

I ate some rice.	They had some fun.
I ate some vegetables	They had some vegetables.
I ate rice.	They had rice.
I ate vegetables.	They had fun.
I ate the rice.	They had vegetables.
I ate the vegetables.	They had the pencil.
They had a pencil.	They had the rice.
They had an idea.	They had the vegetables.
They had some rice.	They had the idea.

B4: Transforming Sentences (p. 261)

A. 2. Take some peaches. / Take the peaches.
3. This is an herb.
4. A child gets more colds than an adult.
5. We need a magazine with more information.
6. I watched some movies last night.

B. 2. Take a sheet of paper and a pen.
3. Did you eat the cookies or cake?
4. I'm taking medication and eating yogurt twice a day.
5. Did you see the movie last week?
6. I went to the store yesterday.

Think Critically About Meaning and Use (p. 262)

1. 1a
2. 2b refers to a small quantity of the underlined noun.
2a classifies the underlined noun.

C1: Listening for Meaning and Use (p. 263)

		SPECIFIC	NOT SPECIFIC
2.	apples		✓
3.	a new doctor		✓
4.	a friend	✓	
5.	some soup	✓	
6.	an appointment	✓	
7.	a book		✓
8.	cough medicine	✓	

C2: Introducing New Information (p. 264)

A. Answers will vary. Some examples are:
2. B: I bought a loaf of bread, some eggs, and a watermelon.
3. B: I take a suitcase, some clothes, and an iron.
4. B: I want some new clothes, a watch, and some CDs.
5. B: I keep chewing gum, a comb, and a pen in my pockets.
6. B: You can buy tools, nails, and lightbulbs at a hardware store.

C3: Classifying Nouns (p. 264)

A. Answers will vary.
B. Answers will vary.

Think Critically About Meaning and Use (p. 265)

1. b   2. a   3. c

D1: Listening for Meaning and Use (p. 267)

2. a   4. a   6. a   8. a
3. a   5. b   7. b

D2: Choosing Definite or Indefinite Articles (p. 267)

1. 2. a
2. 1. The
   2. a
   3. an
   4. a
3. 1. an
   2. the
4. 1. the
   2. an
   3. the
5. 1. the
   2. the

D3: Using *Another* and *The Other* (p. 268)

Answers will vary.

D4: Making Inferences Based on General Knowledge (p. 268)

Answers will vary. Some examples are:
2. The waiter gave a detailed description of the lunch specials.
3. The mechanic said that it would be very expensive to fix the problem.
4. The bank teller forgot to give me a receipt.
5. The author did an excellent job of creating suspense.
6. The receptionist said that I could make an appointment for next week.

D5: Connecting Information (p. 269)

A. 5. He cut the wire and jumped from the window into a creek.
3. No one knows exactly where he found the ladder.
1. Another prisoner has escaped from the local prison.
4. He was able to reach a high window covered with wire.
6. He swam across the creek, climbed over a wall, stole a car, and drove away.
2. Sometime during the night, the prisoner climbed up a ladder.

B. Answers will vary.

D6: Talking About Familiar Nouns (p. 270)

Answers will vary. Some examples are:

2. I went to the First National bank before I came to class.
3. I bought the *Daily News* before I came to class.
4. The mayor who was just elected is going to speak on television tonight.
5. I didn't feel well yesterday, so I went to the doctor who you recommended to me.

D7: Understanding Shared Information (p. 270)

A. Answers will vary. Some examples are:

2. One man is selling his car. The other man wants to buy the car. They are discussing the price.
3. The couple wants to buy their first home. The woman just found out that the bank will give them a loan to buy a house.
4. The three women attended a concert recently. One of the women took photographs. They want to look at the pictures together.
5. The woman is talking to her brother, who was supposed to pay the telephone bill. He forgot, and now the payment will be late.
6. The two men are brothers. One of them has just gotten tickets to see a movie.

B. Answers will vary.

Think Critically About Meaning and Use (p. 271)

1. 1b, 2a, 3b, 4a
2. 1a, 2b, 3a, 4b

E1: Listening for Meaning and Use (p. 273)

		GENERIC	SPECIFIC
2.	almonds	✓	
3.	garlic	✓	
4.	food		✓
5.	the onion	✓	
6.	a cold		✓
7.	vitamins	✓	
8.	a headache	✓	

E2: Defining Nouns with *A/An* (p. 273)

Answers will vary. Some examples are:

2. An iris is a tall flower that can be many colors.
3. An elm is a tall tree with large leaves.
4. A pineapple is a tropical fruit.
5. A crib is a bed for babies.
6. An octopus is an eight-legged sea-creature.
7. A calculator is a small mathematical device.
8. A screwdriver is a tool with a narrow blade for turning screws.

E3: Rephrasing Formal Generic Sentences (p. 274)

A. Kangaroos are Australian animals with very distinctive physical features. They have large back legs that are used for hopping very fast, and they have very large tails that help them maintain their balance. Female kangaroos carry their young around in special pockets of skin on their stomachs that are called pouches.

B. Answers will vary.

E4: Choosing Between Generic and Specific Nouns (p. 274)

A.
1. 2. a
2. 1. A
   2. a
3. 1. Ø
   2. The
4. 1. Ø
   2. The
   3. a
5. 1. Ø
   2. Ø
6. 1. Ø
   2. a

B. Answers will vary.

Think Critically About Meaning and Use (p. 276)

2. a. F	5. a. F	8. a. T
b. T	b. T	b. F
3. a. T	6. a. T	
b. T	b. T	
4. a. T	7. a. T	
b. F	b. F	

Edit (p. 277)

2. When you get to my house, you don't have to ring ^the doorbell. Just walk in.
3. We have plenty of sandwiches. Please take ~~the~~ another one.
4. My grandparents were ~~some~~ immigrants. They came to this country in 1920.
5. She graduated with a major in ~~the~~ mathematics and physics.
6. ~~The~~ life is not always easy.
7. Calcium is ^a mineral.
9. ^The Book I bought was on sale.
10. Let's sit in X^the last row so that we can leave quickly when the play is over.

CHAPTER 13

A3: After You Read (p. 281)

2. T
3. T
4. F The woman says she is "fashion-conscious."
5. F The blog is written by a woman consultant.
6. T

Think Critically About Form (p. 282)

1. line 14: which for men means suits and ties
   line 28: who dress in a neat, professional way
   line 30: who wants to make the best possible impression
   line 34: that looks good and feels good
   line 36: who is confident and capable
   line 43: who doesn't have a lot of time to worry about my wardrobe
   line 48: who want to show their stylish side
   line 51: which is written by a top-level woman consultant
   line 55: who is on her feet all day

2. line 14: which   formal business wear
   line 28: who   job candidates
   line 30: who   a male college grad
   line 34: that   a suit
   line 36: who   a person
   line 43: who   a fashion-conscious female executive
   line 48: who   female executives
   line 51: which   a blog called "execu-chic"
   line 55: who   the busy female executive

3. line 6: which supposedly have "business casual" dress codes
   line 14: which for men means suits and ties
   line 51: which is written by a top-level woman consultant

B1: Listening for Form (p. 284)

2. a   4. a   6. b   8. b

3. a   5. b   7. b

B2: Identifying Relative Clauses (p. 285)

Paul: Do you mean my new blue shirt, which is at the cleaners?

Dad: Oh. Well, what about the shirts that are hanging on the bedroom door?

Paul: Hmm… should I wear the white one or the one that has pinstripes?

Dad: Wear the one that feels more comfortable. What time is the interview?

Paul: The boss's secretary, who called to confirm yesterday, said 10:15, although the manager who originally contacted me said 10:30. I'd better be there at 10:15.

Dad: By the way, was the Department of Labor booklet helpful?

Paul: Yes, especially part 3, which had a lot of practical advice.

Dad: Is the position that's open a new one?

Paul: No. I know the person who has it now. She's leaving to work in the Boston branch, which opens after the first of the year.

B3: Building Sentences with Subject Relative Pronouns (p. 285)

We like the man who works in the bakery.
We like Gary, who works in the bakery.
We like the new phone cards, which are affordable.
We like cars that are affordable.
We like cars which are affordable.

B4: Working on Placement of Relative Clauses (p. 286)

A. 2. Some employers won't hire applicants who dress too casually.
3. Employees who oppose dress codes believe that clothing is a form of free expression.
4. Some companies restrict clothing that has sports logos on it.
5. A company dress code may not allow women to wear skirts that are very short.

B. 2. What do you think about rule number 3, which restricts very tight clothing?
3. My nephew Dan, who works for a high-tech company, often wears very unusual clothing.
4. My boss, who has been here only for a year, is trying to enforce a new dress code.
5. Casual dress, which is hard to define, has become the new standard in many companies.

B5: Working on Verb Agreement in Relative Clauses (p. 286)

1. 2. who / that asks
2. 1. which was
   2. that / which looks
3. 1. who lives
   2. who own / that
4. 1. who / that treats
   2. who has
5. 1. who finished
   2. who / that were
6. 1. which has
   2. that / which are

B6: Combining Sentences with *Who, That,* or *Which* (p. 287)

2. The professor who / that emailed me teaches Russian.
3. My sister has a cat that / which has three kittens.
4. Did you buy the socks that / which were on sale?
5. The little girl who / that hurt her knee was crying.
6. They gave us an exam that / which lasted an hour.
7. I spoke to two women who / that saw the accident.
8. The child who / that was sick went home.

Think Critically About Meaning and Use (p. 288)

1. 1b   2. 2b

C1: Listening for Meaning and Use (p. 289)

2. a   4. a   6. a   8. b

3. a   5. b   7. a

C2: Identifying Nouns (p. 290)

Answers will vary. Some examples are:

2. My car is the one that has a box on the top.
3. My boots are the ones that have a zipper.
4. My raincoat is the one that has a scarf in the pocket.
5. My backpack is the one that has a water bottle in the pocket.
6. My keys are the ones that are on a soccer ball key ring.

C3: Identifying and Defining with Subject Relative Pronouns (p. 291)

Answers will vary. Some examples are:
1. b. She is famous for painting flowers that were colorful.
2. a. Cancer is a serious condition that causes tumors to grow in the body.
   b. Radiation is a cancer treatment that can shrink tumors and prevent them from spreading.
3. a. Martin Luther King, Jr. was an African American who led the civil rights movement in the 1960s.
   b. Passive resistance is a nonviolent method of protest that was previously used by Mahatma Gandhi in the 1940s.
4. a. A phobia is an exaggerated fear that can prevent a person from leading a normal life.
   b. People who have a fear of being in open places suffer from agoraphobia. People who have a fear of being in closed places suffer from claustrophobia.

C4: Defining Words with Relative Clauses (p. 291)

Answers will vary. Some examples are:
2. A neurologist is a doctor who treats diseases of the nervous system.
3. A pediatrician is a doctor who treats children.
4. A dentist is a doctor who treats teeth.
5. A cardiologist is a doctor who treats heart problems.
6. A podiatrist is a doctor who treats foot problems.

C5: Distinguishing Between Two Nouns (p. 292)

Answers will vary. Some examples are:
2. The boy who is wearing an orange jacket./The boy wearing an orange jacket.
   The boy who is throwing a/the ball./The boy throwing a/the ball.
3. The woman who is on the phone./The woman on the phone.
   The woman who is using the computer./The woman using the computer.
4. The man who is drinking a soda./The man drinking a soda.
   The man who is reading a magazine./The man reading a magazine.
5. The hat that is hanging on the wall./The one hanging on the wall.
   The hat that is on the shelf./The one on the shelf.
6. The tea mix that has sugar./The tea mix with sugar.
   The tea mix that doesn't have sugar./The tea mix without sugar.

C6: Connecting Ideas with Relative Clauses (p. 293)

A. Answers will vary. Some examples are:
School dress codes are becoming popular again, although this doesn't necessarily mean that students have to wear uniforms. A school dress code is a set of rules that restricts certain types of clothing. Some dress codes prohibit certain T-shirts which have offensive writing or pictures on them. Other dress codes prohibit certain types of pants or shirts that are very baggy or tight. Many others prohibit skirts and dresses that are several inches above the knee. Some dress codes go even further. They don't allow sports clothing that has logos on it.

B. Answers will vary.

Think Critically About Meaning and Use (p. 294)

1. a (necessary information); b (not essential information)
2. b

D1: Listening for Meaning and Use (p. 295)

2. b   3. b   4. b   5. b   6. a

D2: Adding Extra Information (p. 296)

A. Answers will vary. Some examples are:
2. I once visited the Vatican, which is in Rome.
3. I've never met Mr. Williams, who is the president of the company.
4. I'd like to meet Bill Gates, who is an extremely successful businessman.

B. Answers will vary. Some examples are:
2. My best friend, who is the best student in her class, studies every night.
3. My birthday, which is in November, is very important to me.
4. My home, which is on the top floor of my building, has a great view of the city.

D3: Choosing Restrictive or Nonrestrictive Relative Clauses (p. 296)

2. restrictive
3. nonrestrictive — We live in Panama City, which is very warm and humid.
4. nonrestrictive — My father, who loves to play golf, lives next to a golf course. OR My father, who lives next to a golf course, loves to play golf.
5. restrictive
6. restrictive
7. nonrestrictive — I've invited my friend Jane, who works in the legal division at your company.
8. nonrestrictive — Pollution, which is still a major problem, was a political issue in the last election.

D4: Describing People (p. 297)

Answers will vary. Some examples are:
2. My uncle who owns a hardware store has three sons. His youngest son, who is a great baseball player, is my age.
3. My friend who is a medical student is always studying. Her brother, who lives in the same apartment building, never sees her.
4. The teacher that we had for biology last year is no longer at our school. Her husband, who is an army officer, was transferred overseas.
5. My neighbor who lives across the street just bought a new car. His son, who helps all the neighbors, is washing it now.
6. My classmate who sits next to me always helps me with my homework. His friend, who has a computer, lets us use it to type our essays.

Think Critically About Meaning and Use (p. 298)

1. b. F   4. a. T   6. a. T   8. a. T
2. a. T   b. T   b. F   b. T
   b. F   5. a. T   7. a. T
3. a. F   b. F   b. F
   b. T

Edit (p. 299)

What kind of clothing should people ~~which~~ [who/that] are going on a job interview wear? Is it ever acceptable to wear jeans to an interview? Should job candidates wear something that is sporty and comfortable? Or should they wear something ~~what~~ [that/which] is more professional-looking? These are some of the questions͜concern [that/which] many high-school and college students ~~which has~~ [who/that have] never been on a job interview before.

Most people agree about the type of clothing͜is [that/which] appropriate for interviews nowadays. Many employment websites advise that job applicants should try to dress in clothing͜is [that/which] appropriate for a particular job. For example, a man who͜applying [is] for an entry-level food service or factory job doesn't need to appear for an interview in a three-piece business suit and an expensive silk tie. He should wear sensible, clean, and well-pressed clothing that show͜a [shows] readiness to roll one's sleeves up and get the job done. Someone͜is [who/that] applying for a managerial position will obviously need to dress more professionally to make a good first impression. Remember, too, that personal cleanliness is something ~~who~~ [that/which] can impress an interviewer as much as your clothes. Candidates that show͜x up for an interview with bad breath or messy hair or fingernails͜are [that/which] dirty are not going to make a good impression.

CHAPTER 14

A3: After You Read (p. 303)

2. b   3. a   4. c   5. c   6. b

Think Critically About Form (p. 304)

1.
Object Relative Pronoun	Noun/Noun Phrase
line 1: which	Women's World Cup
line 7: who	Mia Hamm
line 11: that	passion
line 19: which	Title IX
line 23: that	role models
line 31: which	Mia Hamm Foundation
line 39: that	things

2. The object relative pronoun missing from each clause is *which/that*.

B1: Listening for Form (p. 306)

2. b   3. a   4. b   5. a   6. b

B2: Examining Relative Clauses with Object Relative Pronouns (p. 306)

Kay Valera used to be a "soccer mom." But now the 40-year-old mom has become a soccer player in a (women's league) which she joined last spring. One of the (things) that she has learned is how challenging it is to play a sport that requires players to think, kick, and run at the same time. As she plays, she recalls all the (advice) that she has given her kids. Everything that looked so easy from the sidelines is now so challenging.

Many kids come to the games to cheer on the moms. They can be very encouraging, but they also love to discuss the (mistakes) that mom made and the (moves) that she should have made. They might say, "Don't feel bad, you did your best, but you know that (kick) that you tried in midfield, well . . ."

B3: Using Object Relative Pronouns (p. 307)

2. Marcus, (who) we saw on Tuesday, (doesn't) work with us.
3. The bike (that / which / Ø) they bought (is) missing.
4. Ellen, (who) works with me, (is) always late for work.
5. The people (that / who / Ø) she (visits) live nearby.
6. The teacher (that / who / Ø) I like (is) not here today.

B4: Combining Sentences Using Relative Clauses (p. 308)

Answers will vary. Some examples are:
2. Here is a photo of your grandfather, who I still miss so much.
3. Our great grandfather Gus, who we loved a lot, is in this picture.
4. The dress which I wore to my wedding is in this box.
5. I'll never forget the guests who I invited to my wedding.
6. I remember my high school teacher Miss Pullman, who I liked so much.
7. Here is a poem that I wrote in her class.
8. This is an award that I received for my poem.

B5: Asking and Answering Questions with Object Relative Pronouns (p. 308)

Answers will vary. Some examples are:
2. A: What is a game that you liked to play as a child?
   B: Hide-and-seek is a game that I liked to play as a child.
3. A: Who is the relative that you look like most?
   B: The relative that I look like most is my aunt.
4. A: Who is the person that you call when you're in trouble?
   B: The person that I call when I'm in trouble is my best friend.
5. A: What is a food you have never tasted?
   B: Fried chicken is a food I have never tasted.

6. A: Who is a teacher you will always remember?
   B: My second grade teacher is a teacher I will always remember.
7. A: What is a book which you like to read over and over again?
   B: A book which I like to read over and over again is *The Great Gatsby*.
8. A: What is a thing that you can't live without?
   B: Sunshine is a thing that I can't live without.

Think Critically About Meaning and Use (p. 309)

1. 1a. The (coat) that costs $200 is on sale now.
   1b. The (coat) you wanted is on sale now.
   2a. (Megan Quann), who was only 16, was on the Olympic swimming team.
   2b. (Megan Quann), who I know, was on the Olympic swimming team.
2. In 1a and 1b, the relative clauses help identify the noun. In 2a and 2b, the relative clauses add extra information about the noun.

C1: Listening for Meaning and Use (p. 310)

2. b   3. a   4. a   5. b   6. a

C2: Identifying Nouns (p. 311)

A. Answers will vary. Some examples are:
2. that likes to garden.
3. who enjoys reading the newspaper.
4. which challenges me.
5. that has a swimming pool.
6. who goes dancing every Friday night.
7. that offer discount prices.
8. who knows how to have fun.

B. Answers will vary.

C3: Adding Extra Information (p. 311)

A. Answers will vary. Some examples are:
3. The Olympics occur every four years.
4. The soccer team Real Madrid has a lot of fans.
5. Wayne Gretzky is a famous hockey player.

B. Answers will vary.

C4: Expressing Your Opinion (p. 312)

Answers will vary. Some examples are:
2. I like teachers who are patient. I don't like teachers that give too much homework.
3. I like clothes that are fashionable. I don't like clothes which are expensive.
4. I like newspapers that have important news. I don't like newspapers which only report gossip.
5. I like friends who are loyal. I don't like friends that are late.
6. I like TV shows which are based on real life. I don't like TV shows that are silly.
7. I like foods that are light and healthy. I don't like foods which are heavy and greasy.
8. I like music that is soothing and relaxing. I don't like music that is too loud.
9. I like books which are about interesting people. I don't like books that are too long.
10. I like cell phones that are easy to use. I don't like cell phones which are too complicated.

Think Critically About Form (p. 313)

1. a. We saw the movie that everyone is talking (about).
   b. We saw the movie (about) which everyone is talking.
2. In sentence a, the preposition occurs at the end of the relative clause.
   In sentence b, the preposition occurs at the beginning of the relative clause.
   In sentence a, that is used. (You can also use which or Ø here.)
   In sentence b, which is used. (You can only use which here.)

D1: Listening for Form (p. 315)

2. b   3. a   4. a   5. b

D2: Building Relative Clauses Ending in Prepositions (p. 315)

1. A woman who/whom/that/ Ø I always talk to at the supermarket called me last night.
   A woman who/whom/that/ Ø I went to high school with called me last night.
   A woman who/whom/that/ Ø I used to live next door to called me last night.
2. The movie that/which/ Ø we went to last night was great.
   The movie that/which/ Ø you told us about was great.
   The movie that/which/ Ø I didn't want to go to was great.
   The movie that/which/ Ø you reported on in class was great.
3. Do you know the doctor who/whom/that/ Ø Young-soo lives across from?
   Do you know the doctor who/whom/that/ Ø Eva plays tennis with?
   Do you know the doctor who/whom/that/ Ø Luisa works for?
   Do you know the doctor who/whom/that/ Ø I was waiting for?
4. Have you read the book that/which/ Ø the whole class is interested in?
   Have you read the book that/which/ Ø the teacher looked for last week?
   Have you read the book that/which/ Ø Julie wrote about?
   Have you read the book that/which/ Ø I brought in?
5. Today we're going to read the story that/which/ Ø you heard a lot about.
   Today we're going to read the story that/which/ Ø you listened to a recording of.
   Today we're going to read the story that/which/ Ø I was working on.
   Today we're going to read the story that/which/ Ø the lecturer talked about.

D3: Working on Relative Clauses Ending in Prepositions (p. 316)

A. Answers will vary. Some examples are:
2. that/which/ Ø she grew up in.
3. that/which/ Ø Luisa is sitting on.
4. who/that/ Ø she spoke to on Tuesday.
5. that/which/ Ø he hasn't heard about.
6. that/which/ Ø she listened to last night.
7. who/that/ Ø he didn't talk to right after the game.
8. that/which/ Ø I'm interested in.

B. Answers will vary. Some examples are:
2. You ask her the name of the town in which she grew up.
3. A salesman recommends the one on which Luisa is sitting.
4. Today she asked for the nurse to whom she spoke on Tuesday.

Think Critically About Meaning and Use (p. 317)

Sentence b sounds the most formal.

E1: Listening for Meaning and Use (p. 318)

	FORMAL	INFORMAL	CONTEXT
2.	✓		an academic lecture
3.	✓		an awards reception or ceremony
4.		✓	a mother talking to her son
5.	✓		a courtroom
6.		✓	a cooking lesson

E2: Rephrasing Formal Relative Clauses (p. 318)

Application for Travel Insurance
2. List the city that/which/ Ø you'll depart from and the city that/which/ Ø you'll return to.
3. List the name of the tour operator who/that/ Ø you'll be traveling with
4. List the hotel that/which/ Ø you'll be staying in.
5. List the code numbers of any extra tours that/which/ Ø you've registered for.

Job Application
1. Name two colleagues who/that/ Ø you've worked closely with.
2. Name one supervisor who/that/ Ø you've worked for in the last year.
3. List two different projects that/which/ Ø you've worked on.
4. Name two decisions that/which/ Ø you've played an important role in.
5. Name the job that/which/ Ø you'd like to apply for.

E3: Reducing Relative Clauses Ending in Prepositions (p. 319)

Answers will vary.

E4: Writing an Email Message (p. 320)

Answers will vary.

E5: Using *Where, When,* and Object Relative Pronouns (p. 320)

A. 2. where / in which
3. where / in which
4. that / which / Ø
5. when
6. which
7. that / which / Ø
8. that / when / Ø / in which
9. when
10. which

B. Answers will vary.

C. Answers will vary.

Think Critically About Meaning and Use (p. 322)

1. b. T   5. a. F   8. a. T
2. a. F   b. F   b. T
   b. T   6. a. T
3. a. T   b. F
   b. F   7. a. T
4. a. F   b. F
   b. T

Edit (p. 323)

Sisleide Lima do Amor, ~~which~~ *who* soccer fans know as Sissi, was not discouraged as a child by the boys who wouldn't let her play the game ~~with~~ which she loved most. Eventually, she got her way on the streets of Salvador, Brazil, because the soccer ball that the boys wanted to play with ~~it~~ was hers. Still, she often ran home with her ball after she grew frustrated with the negative attitudes that the boys displayed. Sissi had learned to play soccer by practicing with all kinds of objects ~~what~~ *that* she found around the house. These included rolled-up socks, oranges, bottle caps, and the heads of dolls that her parents had given her ~~them~~. It was her father who finally decided that she needed a soccer ball to keep her from destroying her dolls.

Sissi showed her admiration for Brazil's male soccer heroes by choosing the jersey number ~~who~~ *that/which/Ø* Romario once wore and by shaving her head to resemble the style ~~in~~ which Ronaldo has made famous. During the Women's World Cup, Sissi displayed the type of skill fans will long remember. Left-footed Sissi scored seven goals for her team, including a goal that she kicked in with her weaker right foot. According to Sissi, her seventh goal was the one ~~about~~ which she kept thinking about / the one about which she kept thinking ~~about~~ long after the 1999 Women's World Cup was over. During a 3-3 tie, she kicked the ball into a spot the goalkeeper couldn't reach ~~it~~, and her team's 4-3 victory put them into the semifinals.

Part 5 TEST (pp. 325–326)

1. c
2. b
3. b
4. d
5. a
6. c
7. a
8. c
9. b
10. c
11. a
12. I bought the shoes made in Italy.
13. Look at the man wearing a tuxedo.
14. There are the dresses on sale.
15. d
16. h
17. e
18. a
19. a
20. an

CHAPTER 15

A3: After You Read (p. 329)

2. a   3. c   4. b

Think Critically About Form (p. 330)

1. *Selection 1*
   If there is beauty in the person
   If there is harmony in the house
   If there is order in the nation

2. *Selection 2*
   if I had it to do over again (line 13)
   If I had my life to live over (line 16)

   Selection 3
   if it were over tomorrow
   The verb form in each main clause is *would* + ve rb.

3. *Selection 4*
   Wish is in the present tense. The verb form used in each clause that follows *wish* is the past form.

B1: Listening for Form (p. 332)

2. b   4. a   6. b   8. a
3. b   5. a   7. a

B2: Working on Real and Unreal Conditionals (p. 332)

A. Answers will vary.

B. Answers will vary.

B3: Building Conditional and *Wish* Sentences (p. 333)

If I were ready, I'd leave.
If she is sick, call for help.
If she is sick, he'll take over.
If she is sick, you could come later.
If they were driving, I'd leave.
If they were driving, you could come later.
I wish I were ready.
I wish they were driving.

B4: Working on *Wish* Sentences and Unreal Conditionals (p. 333)

A. 1. 2. did
       3. 'd / would buy
   2. 1. weren't
       2. were
       3. would get / 'd get
       4. could leave
   3. 1. had
       2. had
       3. would have / 'd have
   4. 1. could
       2. didn't have
       3. would stay / 'd stay

B. Answers will vary.

B5: Completing Real and Unreal Conditionals (p. 333)

A. Answers will vary. Some examples are:
   2. I call and let the doctor know.
   3. I would stay home.
   4. I forget someone's name.
   5. I could find a better one.

6. I have enough money.

B. Answers will vary.

B6: Understanding Informal Speech (p. 334)

2. were too late
3. weren't so unfriendly
4. were ready
5. were mad
6. were going

Think Critically About Meaning and Use (p. 335)

Sentence b is a promise.
Sentence a is a statement of fact.
Sentence d is a warning.
Sentence c is an instruction.

C1: Listening for Meaning and Use (p. 337)

	FACTS OR GENERAL TRUTHS	ADVICE, WARNINGS, INSTRUCTIONS	PROMISES
2.			✓
3.	✓		
4.		✓	
5.			✓
6.		✓	
7.	✓		
8.		✓	

C2: Describing Factual Conditions (p. 337)

Answers will vary. Some examples are:
If you're between 7 and 15, it costs $150 to buy a half-season pass.
If you're 16 or older, it costs $200 to buy a full-season pass.
If you're 16 or older, it costs $125 to buy a half-season pass.
If you have children 6 and under, they ski free when accompanied by an adult ticket holder.
If you're a member, you get two free days of skiing: once before December 23 and once after March 6.
If you're a member, you get a 50% discount on lift tickets on Membership Appreciation Days.
If you're a member, you get a free lift ticket for one guest per member on Membership Appreciation Days.

C3: Making Promises (p. 338)

Answers will vary. Some examples are:
2. If I am elected mayor, I will improve education.
3. If you vote for me, I will build new schools.
4. If I become mayor, I will reduce crime.
5. If I am elected mayor, I will hire more police.
6. If you vote for me, I will expand health care.
7. If I become mayor, I will open more hospitals.
8. If I am elected mayor, I will cut taxes.
9. If you vote for me, I will employ more women.
10. If I become mayor, I will employ more minorities.

C4: Rephrasing Advice with Conditional Sentences (p. 338)

Answers will vary. Some examples are:
2. If you study hard, you won't fail the test.
   If you don't want to fail the test, (you should) study hard.

3. If you make calls at night, your telephone bill won't be so high.
   If you don't want a high telephone bill, (you should) make calls at night.
4. If you don't eat so much, you won't get indigestion.
   If you don't want indigestion, you shouldn't eat so much.
   If you don't want indigestion, don't eat so much.
5. If you read a book for a while, you'll fall asleep easily.
   If you want to fall asleep easily, (you should) read a book for a while.
6. If you call the doctor, you'll get some good advice.
   If you want some good advice, (you should) call the doctor.

C5: Giving Warnings with *If* and *Unless* Clauses (p. 339)

A. Answers will vary. Some examples are:
  2. You'll be unhealthy
  3. you won't get enough sleep
  4. you won't have strong bones
  5. you will gain weight

B. Answers will vary. Some examples are:
  2. you don't watch your step
  3. you read without the light
  4. you don't wash your hands
  5. you play with matches

C. Answers will vary.

Think Critically About Meaning and Use (p. 340)

1. 1a expresses something that is more likely to happen.
   1b expresses something that is probably imaginary.
2. 2b sounds more direct.
   2a sounds more indirect.

D1: Listening for Meaning and Use (p. 341)

2. b　　3. a　　4. b　　5. b　　6. b

D2: Asking Questions About Unusual Situations (p. 342)

A. Answers will vary. Some examples are:
  2. you met the president?
  3. you won a million dollars?
  4. you had a free plane ticket?
  5. you had a big party?
  6. you got sick?

B. Answers will vary.

D3: Giving Advice with *If I Were You* (p. 342)

Answers will vary. Some examples are:
2. If I were you, I'd find a new apartment.
   If I were you, I wouldn't pay rent.
3. If I were you, I'd cancel one of them so your friends don't get angry.
   If I were you, I wouldn't be so quick to say "yes" next time.
4. If I were you, I'd change my phone number.
   If I were you, I wouldn't list my number in the phone book.
5. If I were you, I'd try to be nice to him anyway.
   If I were you, I wouldn't put up with it.
6. If I were you, I'd call the credit card company to explain.
   If I were you, I wouldn't pay the bill.

7. If I were you, I'd take a computer class.
   If I were you, I wouldn't buy a computer yet.
8. If I were you, I'd hire an English tutor.
   If I were you, I wouldn't turn in assignments late.

D4: Asking Permission (p. 343)

Answers will vary. Some examples are:
2. A: Would you mind if I listened to the news?
   B: No, not at all.
3. A: Would it bother you if I opened the window?
   B: No, I'm hot, too.
4. A: Would it be OK if I borrowed your book?
   B: Sure, I just finished reading it.

D5: Using Conditionals with Many Results (p. 343)

A. Answers will vary.
B. Answers will vary.

Think Critically About Meaning and Use (p. 344)

1. 1b is a wish about the present moment. 1a is a wish about the future.
2. 2a expresses a complaint. 2b expresses a regret.

E1: Listening for Meaning and Use (p. 345)

		EXISTS	DOESN'T EXIST
2.	pictures		✓
3.	free time		✓
4.	a car	✓	
5.	a safety lock		✓
6.	a limit	✓	
7.	a credit card	✓	
8.	your guitar	✓	

E2: Making Wishes About the Present (p. 346)

Answers will vary. Some examples are:
2. I wish I made more money. If I made more money, I'd buy a car.
3. I wish I could change classes. If I changed classes, I'd take something more interesting.
4. I wish I weren't so busy. If I weren't so busy, I could spend more time with my friends.
5. I wish I didn't live in a big city. If I didn't live in a big city, I'd spend more time outside.
6. I wish I didn't drive to work. If I didn't drive to work, I'd be much more relaxed.
7. I wish I could get more exercise. If I exercised more, I'd be healthier.
8. I wish I had my cell phone. If I had it with me, I could call for help.

E3: Making Wishes About the Future (p. 346)

Answers will vary. Some examples are:
2. I wish you would eat healthier food!
3. I wish my sister would come shopping with me this weekend.
4. I wish you would relax!
5. I wish you would stay here until the weather improves!
6. If only you would finish college!

E4: Complaining with *Wish* and *If Only* Sentences (p. 347)

Answers will vary. Some examples are:

2. If only he wouldn't use up all the hot water in the shower.
3. If only he would replace the milk when he uses it up.
4. I wish he would talk to my friends when they visit me.
5. I wish he would clean up the kitchen.
6. I wish he wouldn't play video games for hours.

E5: Expressing Regret with *Wish* Sentences (p. 347)

Answers will vary. Some examples are:

2. I did, but I sold the last one ten minutes ago.
3. I could, but I was absent yesterday.
4. I did, but I have to work.
5. there were, but you just ate the last one.
6. it were, but it's colder than it was yesterday.

Think Critically About Meaning and Use (p. 348)

1. b. T	4. a. T	6. a. F	8. a. F
2. a. F	b. F	b. T	b. F
b. F	5. a. T	7. a. F	
3. a. T	b. T	b. T	
b. T			

Edit (p. 349)

What ~~you would~~ *would you* do if there were an earthquake in your area? Would you know what to do? Some people are too frightened to find out about safety precautions. They wish they ~~live~~ *lived* somewhere else. If you could, ~~won't~~ *wouldn't* you rather find out what to do in advance? Here is some advice about what to do before, during, and after an earthquake.

1. If you don't have a box of emergency equipment and supplies, you will need to prepare one in advance.
2. If you ~~would~~ *are* indoors during an earthquake, you should stay away from windows, bookcases, and shelves.
3. If it ~~were~~ *is* possible, you should turn off the gas, water, and electricity.
4. After the earthquake, don't walk around unless you are ~~not~~ wearing shoes to protect your feet from broken glass.

Don't wait. Don't wish you ~~are~~ *were* prepared. Be prepared!

CHAPTER 16

A3: After You Read (p. 353)

2.
3. ✓
4. ✓
5.

Think Critically About Form (p. 354)

1. line 10: . . . what would have happened if there had been no Bering Strait or English Channel or no Franklin Delano Roosevelt.

line 13: What would have happened if, in February 1933, Giuseppe Zangara's hand had not been pushed aside in Miami and his bullet had killed Franklin Roosevelt rather than the mayor of Chicago?

line 39: If Cleopatra hadn't lived, Marc Antony would have kept his mind on the affairs of state and not been eliminated from the race for Roman emperor.

line 46: If Marc Antony had done that, it would have hastened the fall of the Roman Empire by a hundred years.

line 51: If Joseph Ginoux, a café owner in Arles, had allowed Vincent van Gogh to pay for his lodging in paintings instead of evicting him, then Vincent would have had some peace and security.

2. The past perfect verb form is used in each *if* clause. *Would have* + past participle is used in each main clause.

B1: Listening for Form (p. 355)

2. a	3. b	4. b	5. a	6. b

B2: Completing Past Conditional Sentences (p. 356)

A. Answers will vary. Some examples are:

2. I would have chosen my friends more carefully.
3. I would have studied law.
4. I wouldn't have succeeded in school.
5. I would have traveled all over Asia.
6. I would have experienced a different way of life.
7. I wouldn't have come to the United States.
8. I wouldn't have seen my classmates.

B. Answers will vary.

B3: Working on Past Conditionals (p. 357)

Answers will vary.

B4: Understanding Informal Speech (p. 357)

2. might have done
3. wouldn't have been
4. could have had
5. would have been
6. wouldn't have won

B5: Working on Past Wishes (p. 358)

A. 1. 3. wishes
   4. had gone
2. 1. wishes
   2. had seen
   3. wish
   4. had shown
3. 1. Do you ever wish
   2. had learned
   3. wish
   4. had been

B. 2. he had.
3. we had.
4. they hadn't.
5. she could have.

Think Critically About Meaning and Use (p. 359)

1. Sentence a refers to a situation that was not true in the past. (In fact, she wasn't a better student, so she didn't graduate on time.)
2. Sentence b refers to a situation that is not true in the present. (In fact, she isn't a better student, so she won't graduate on time.)

C1: Listening for Meaning and Use (p. 360)

2. b   4. a   6. a   8. a

3. a   5. a   7. b

C2: Giving Indirect Advice (p. 361)

Answers will vary. Some examples are:

2. B: (If I'd been you,) I would have asked what the money was for.
3. B: (If I'd been you,) I would have complained to the manager.
4. B: (If I'd been you,) I would have asked the questions again.
5. B: (If I'd been you,) I would have asked my boss why I didn't get the raise.
6. B: (If I'd been you,) I would have demanded to speak to the supervisor.

C3: Distinguishing Fact and Fiction (p. 361)

2. Facts:
   1. Napoleon's armies didn't have proper nails for horseshoes.
   2. They didn't conquer Russia.

   Paraphrase: Napoleon's armies would have conquered Russia, but they didn't have proper nails for horseshoes.

3. Facts:
   1. *Apollo* 13 had an explosion during its flight.
   2. It didn't land on the moon.

   Paraphrase: *Apollo* 13 would have landed on the moon, but it had an explosion during its flight.

4. Facts:
   1. Mozart died young.
   2. He didn't finish his famous piece *Requiem*.

   Paraphrase: Mozart would have finished his famous piece *Requiem*, but he died so young.

5. Facts:
   1. An asteroid or meteorite crashed into Earth.
   2. Dinosaurs died out 65 million years ago.

   Paraphrase: Dinosaurs wouldn't have died out 65 million years ago, but an asteroid or meteorite crashed into Earth.

C4: Describing the Ifs of History (p. 362)

Answers will vary.

Think Critically About Meaning and Use (p. 363)

1. Present situations: 1a and 2a
   Past situations: 1b and 2b
2. 2a and 2b

D1: Listening for Meaning and Use (p. 364)

2. a   4. b   6. a   8. b

3. a   5. b   7. b

D2: Expressing Regret (p. 364)

Answers will vary. Some examples are:

2. I wish I hadn't raised my voice.
   If only I hadn't gotten angry.
3. I wish I'd told him how I felt.
   If only I'd explained my feelings.
4. I wish I'd called my doctor before I missed so many classes.

If only I'd called my doctor as soon as I started to feel sick.

5. I wish someone had called to remind me.
   If only I'd remembered his birthday.
6. I wish I hadn't accepted the first offer so quickly.
   If only the other company had called me first.

D3: Expressing Regret or Dissatisfaction (p. 365)

A. Answers will vary. Some examples are:

3. B: I wish he hadn't.
4. B: If only it hadn't.
5. B: I wish it hadn't been.
6. B: If only I had.
7. B: I wish it hadn't.
8. B: If only they had.

B. Answers will vary.

D4: Explaining Wishes (p. 365)

A. Answers will vary.

B. Answers will vary.

Think Critically About Meaning and Use (p. 366)

1. b. T   4. a. F   7. a. T
2. a. T   b. T   b. T
      b. F   b. T   8. a. T
3. a. F   6. a. F   b. T
      b. T   b. T

Edit (p. 367)

Historians love to think about the dramatic "what-ifs" of history. They have even given the name "counterfactual history" to this pursuit. How would history ~~had~~ have changed if some key event had been different? What would the consequences have been if the weather ~~has~~ had been different in a certain battle? What would ~~had~~ have happened if a famous person had lived instead of died? These are the sorts of questions that are asked in two recent books that imagine how history might have been under different circumstances: *What If?*, edited by R. Cowley and S. Ambrose; and *Virtual History*, edited by N. Ferguson.

Don't just wish ~~you've~~ you'd been alive in a different era. Go back and explore what could have, should have, or might have happened at various times in history. You won't be sorry. You'll wish ~~you'll~~ you'd gone back sooner!

Part 6 TEST (pp. 369–370)

1. a
2. b
3. d
4. c
5. a
6. d
7. b
8. c
9. would have refused
10. I would have called
11. I would have taken
12. would you have taken
13. would you have brought
14. you had known
15. e
16. b
17. c
18. instruction
19. promise
20. fact

CHAPTER 17

A3: After You Read (p. 373)

2.
3.
4. ✓
5. ✓

Think Critically About Form (p. 374)

1. a.
   line 3:   how bad your job has to be
   line 20: what opportunities are out there
   line 21: what kinds of skills and experience are required to get those jobs
   line 21: how much these positions pay
   line 28: which areas you need more experience in
   line 28: which skills you need to improve
   line 29: what opportunities are available
   line 29: what the salaries are
   line 32: what you learn during your job hunt to improve your current position

   b.
   line 1:   whether you want a new job
   line 13: whether he should continue at his present job or start to look for a new one
   line 24: if you would actually end up switching jobs
   line 35: if you can work on different types of projects to expand your opportunities

   c.
   line 10: that his managers treated him with respect
   line 12: that his managers recognized his efforts or his new skills
   line 16: that job hunting and working to improve his current job are opposites
   line 31: that you are not making enough money
   line 33: that you should present your boss with the results of your salary research and a list of your accomplishments, and then ask for a raise

2. Answers will vary. Some examples are:
   a. *Wh-* clause: opportunities are
   b. *Whether/if* clause: you want
   c. *That* clause: you are not making
   The noun clauses listed above are all in statement word order (subject, verb, object).

B1: Listening for Form (p. 375)

	WH-CLAUSE	IF/WHETHER CLAUSE	THAT CLAUSE
2.	✓		
3.		✓	
4.	✓		
5.		✓	
6.			✓
7.	✓		
8.		✓	

B2: Identifying Noun Clauses (p. 376)

Many employment counselors (believe) that your résumé is a kind of personal advertisement. It (summarizes) what you have accomplished and (describes) what kind of work you want. Hopefully, it (tells) why you should be hired. A good résumé doesn't always (determine) whether you will get an interview, but a bad one will certainly eliminate your chances.

Résumés are only one tool that you need to use in your employment search. Many employers don't even use them; employers often (decide) whether they should hire you based on other information. Nevertheless, most employment counselors (believe) that it is worthwhile to write a good résumé. It helps you get organized. Most importantly, it helps you (figure out) what kind of job you really want and whether or not you have the qualifications.

B3: Working on *Wh-* Clauses (p. 376)

2. 1. the mail didn't come
   2. happened
   3. the post office closes
3. 1. the chemistry exam will be / is going to be / is
   2. it will start / is going to start / starts
   3. it will last / is going to last / lasts
4. 1. this costs
   2. he is

B4: Working on *If/Whether* Clauses (p. 377)

Answers will vary. Some examples are:
2. 1. it is going to rain today.
3. 1. these avocados are on sale?
   2. they are
4. 1. there are any seats for the concert on May 7.
   2. there are any seats available for the eighth?
5. 1. there is a gas station/service station
   2. there is
6. 1. it is going to be warm
   2. it is (going to be)

B5: Unscrambling Sentences with *That* Clauses (p. 378)

2. They predict it will happen soon.
3. I guess that I need some help.
4. I remembered that my rent is due tomorrow.
5. He proved he could do it.

B6: Completing Noun Clauses (p. 378)

A. 2. how long you worked there?
   3. if you liked your job.
   4. what your greatest strength is?
   5. why you are changing jobs?

B. Answers will vary.

Think Critically About Meaning and Use (p. 379)

1. Noun Clause:
   what I need
   everything on your list
   whether I did or not
   if it's in the car
   Verb:
   decide
   get
   know
   wonder
   Decide, *know*, and *wonder* express mental activities.
2. 2b

C1: Listening for Meaning and Use (p. 380)

2. a
3. b
4. b
5. b
6. a
7. b
8. a

C2: Expressing Uncertainty (p. 381)

Answers will vary. Some examples are:
2. I can't remember what time it occurred.
3. I have no idea what it looked like.
4. I'm not certain how many people there were.
5. I'm not certain what the license plate number was.
6. I don't know how fast it was going.
7. I can't remember what color it was.
8. I'm not sure what he looked like.

C3: Adding *If/Whether* Clauses to Expressions of Uncertainty (p. 382)

A. Answers will vary. Some examples are:
1. b. whether or not she will have to work late.
   c. if her boss will like her.
2. a. if the owners will accept his offer.
   b. whether anyone else is interested in the house.
   c. he'll be able to afford to live there if he loses his job.

B. Answers will vary.

C4: Asking Indirect Questions with *If/Whether* Clauses (p. 383)

Answers will vary. Some examples are:
2. Do you have any idea if the library is closed during vacation?
3. Could you please tell me if the teacher is going to show a film today?
4. Do you know whether the assignment is due tomorrow?
5. Do you have any idea whether the new language lab is open yet?
6. Could you please tell me if I missed anything important yesterday?

C5: Asking Indirect Questions with *Wh-* Clauses (p. 383)

Answers will vary. Some examples are:
1. b. A: Excuse me. Could you please tell me where the baggage claim is?
      B: It's upstairs to the right.
2. a. A: Excuse me. Could you please tell me what time it is?
      B: Sure. It's 3:15.
   b. A: Excuse me. I was wondering if you know where the bus schedule is.
      B: It's next to the bus stop.
3. a. A: Excuse me. Do you have any idea what the price of this shirt is?
      B: It's $37.50.
   b. A: Excuse me. Could you tell me what size these pants are?
      B: They're medium.
4. a. A: Excuse me. Could you tell me where the manager is?

B: He's in the produce department.
   b. A: Excuse me. I was wondering how much this broccoli is.
      B: It's $1.49 a pound.
5. a. A: Excuse me. Do you know where the history department is?
      B: I think it's on the second floor in Room 217.
   b. A: Excuse me. Could you tell me where I can pay my tuition bill?
      B: You can pay it at the bursar's office.

Think Critically About Meaning and Use (p. 384)

1. 2a and 2b
2. 1a and 1b have different meanings because they have different tenses in their noun clauses. When the mental activity verb is in the present tense, such as *know* in 1a and 1b, the verb in the following noun clause can be in the present, past, or future. The meaning of the sentence depends on which tense is used.

D1: Listening for Meaning and Use (p. 386)

2. a   3. a   4. b   5. b   6. a

D2: Thinking About Tense Agreement with *That* Clauses (p. 386)

A. 2. they'll accept, they accept, they accepted
3. wouldn't be
4. had won
5. needs, needed, will need
6. will start, starts, started

B. Answers will vary.

D3: Giving Opinions Using *That* Clauses (p. 386)

A. Answers will vary. Some examples are:
2. I agree that most people are basically honest. It's common for people to tell the truth rather than a lie.
3. I agree that hybrid cars are a good idea. They help reduce pollution in big cities.
4. I agree that you can't really change someone. I think if you try, you will just be disappointed.
5. I feel that all children should leave home at 18. I think parents should only be responsible for the first 18 years of their children's lives.
6. I agree that we learn from our mistakes. I think the most valuable lessons are learned from making mistakes.

B. Answers will vary.

D4: Expressing Opinions About Work (p. 387)

A. Answers will vary.
B. Answers will vary.

Think Critically About Meaning and Use (p. 388)

2. ?   4. F   6. T   8. ?
3. T   5. ?   7. F

Edit (p. 389)

2. I asked her if I could borrow her pen.
3. I thought that she ~~is~~ was sleeping when I called.
4. I can't remember who called?
5. Do you know if ~~are you~~ you are coming with us?

6. I didn't realize ✗that she was absent.

7. She thought he ~~will~~ come later.
   would

8. Do you know if or not he's staying?/Do you know if or
   or not ✗ *whether*
   not he's staying?

9. I need John's phone number, but I don't know where
   the phone book.
   is

10. Frederica didn't understand what ~~was saying the teacher.~~
    the teacher was saying

CHAPTER 18

A3: After You Read (p. 393)

2.
3. ✓
4.
5.
6. ✓

Think Critically About Form (p. 394)

1. **Reporting Verbs**
   line 13: were asked
   line 19: were asked
   line 27: reported
   line 46: ask

2. *wh-* clause: what health problems they had
                             discussed with each patient
   that clause: that they had such problems
   if/whether clause: if they understand
   infinitive clause: to fill out a detailed questionnaire

3. **Reported Speech Clause**   **Reporting Verbs**
   line 16: to list their most serious   asked
             health problems
   line 25: that cholesterol was a major   reported
             concern
   line 29: (that) their patients were   said
             suffering from obesity,
             high blood pressure, or
             certain heart problems
   line 32: that they had an obesity   report
             problem
   line 33: (that) they had high blood   say
             pressure
   line 35: that there was concern about   said
             their heart
   line 36: that patients often   concludes
             misunderstand their doctors
   line 38: that doctors may be missing   proposes
             the most important concerns
             of their patients

B1: Listening for Form (p. 396)

2. a   4. b   6. b   8. b
3. b   5. a   7. a

B2: Identifying Reported Speech (p. 396)

1. A: You're kidding. Julia said the same thing happened
   to her on Tuesday. I wonder whether we should
   complain to Allison. She hired him.

B: I'm not sure if we should say anything yet. I asked
Tom what he thought. He said that we should wait
one more week.

2. A: Did you hear the news? Channel 7 reported that the
superintendent just resigned.
B: I know. I wonder if something happened. Everyone
says he was pleased with the way things were going.
A: Yesterday's news mentioned that he hadn't been
feeling well lately. Maybe it's something serious and
his doctor told him to resign.

3. A: Did you speak to the travel agent?
B: Yes. I asked whether I needed to change the flight.
He admitted that he'd made a mistake, but he said
that he would take care of it. He assured me that
everything would work out.
A: Let's hope so. I told you to be careful during the
holiday season. They're so busy that they often
make mistakes.

Other reporting verbs:
wonder   report   mention   admit   assure

B3: Building Sentences with *Tell, Say,* and *Ask* (p. 397)

He asked them if I had called earlier.
He asked them to leave early.
He asked if it was raining.
He asked if I had called earlier.
He asked to leave early.
I said that it was raining.
I said that I had called earlier.
She told them (that) it was raining.
She told them (that) I had called earlier.
She told them to leave early.

B4: Restating Questions with Reported Speech (p. 398)

A. Answers will vary. Some examples are:
2. What do you like to do?
3. Where do you work?
4. How old are you?
5. How long have you studied English?
6. What are your hobbies?

B. Answers will vary. Some examples are:
2. They also ask me what I like to do.
3. They usually want to know where I work.
4. They sometimes want to know how old I am.
5. Someone typically asks how long I've studied English.
6. Some people even ask what my hobbies are.

B5: Reporting Statements, Questions, and Imperatives (p. 398)

Answers will vary. Some examples are:
2. The patient asked if she could have a copy of the test
results.
   The doctor told her (that) the lab is sending one.
3. The patient asked how often she should take the
medicine.
   The doctor told her not to take it more than three times
a day.
4. The patient asked if she needed to come back.
   The doctor said (that) it wouldn't be necessary unless
there was a problem.

5. The patient said (that) she needed to be better by the weekend.
   The doctor asked her why.
6. The patient said (that) she was going out of town for a few days.
   The doctor told her she would be fine and that she should get lots of sleep.

Think Critically About Meaning and Use (p. 399)

1. a and c   2. b

C1: Listening for Meaning and Use (p. 401)

2. a	4. b	6. a	8. b
3. b	5. b	7. b	

C2: Understanding Reporting Verbs (p. 402)

2. informed	5. asked	8. promised
3. confessed	6. replied	9. told
4. explained	7. advised	10. admitted

C3: Reporting Messages (p. 403)

Answers will vary. Some examples are:
1. b. Joe's Repair Shop called on Monday. They asked you to call them back before 6:00 P.M.
2. a. Bob called on Tuesday. He said that he would call back later.
   b. Richard Smith called on Tuesday. He explained that he wanted/wants to talk to you about an insurance policy. He said that his number is 555-1221.
3. a. Rosa called on Wednesday. She said that she was just calling to say hello.
   b. Stuart Lee called on Wednesday. He remarked that he had been calling for several days. He asked if anything is/was wrong. He requested that you call him back soon.
4. a. Eric Martin called today. He asked where you are/were. He said that he has/had some questions.
   b. Gibson's called today. They said (that) they will/would be able to deliver the desk you ordered on Monday, March 27.
   c. Tanya called today. She said that she was sorry she hasn't/hadn't called. She said that she should have called sooner.

C4: Reporting a News Item (p. 404)

A. Answers will vary. Some examples are:
This report states that schools have begun to put communication skills into the curriculum.
A spokesman for the Medical Association said that the time has come to focus more on doctor-patient communication.
The latest Smith Public Opinion Poll reports that the best doctors talk with their patients.
The poll also indicates that the best doctors encourage questions, explain procedures, and discuss alternatives.
The poll reports that the best doctors also know how to listen and sometimes even use humor.
This reports says that as a result, first-year medical students are spending more time speaking and listening in retirement homes, homeless shelters, soup kitchens, and other community agencies.
The report indicates that first-year medical students are also in the classroom discussing what kinds of

communication skills they need to treat these patients, and that they are also learning how to interact with patients in a variety of situations.
The situation is in the present; therefore, the tenses are in the present.

B. Answers will vary.

C5: Reporting Advice (p. 405)

A. 1. she go to an employment agency.
   she should go to an employment agency.
2. (that) she think about getting another degree.
   that she should think about getting another degree.
   her to find out about different types of graduate programs.
   (that) she find out about different types of graduate programs.
3. (that) she quit her job and have a baby.
   that she should quit her job and have a baby.
   (that) she should try to teach part-time instead of full-time.
4. (that) she not quit but just take a leave of absence for a year.
   that she shouldn't quit but just take a leave of absence for a year.
   her to ask for a raise before she does anything else.
   (that) she ask for a raise before she does anything else.
   that she should ask for a raise before she does anything else.
5. she ask to teach a different grade next year.
   that she ask to teach a different grade next year.
   that she should ask to teach a different grade next year.
   to do whatever makes her happy.
   that she should do whatever makes her happy.

B. Answers will vary.

C. Answers will vary.

Think Critically About Meaning and Use (p. 407)

1. b. T		6. a. ?
2. a. F		b. T
b. ?		7. a. ?
3. a. T		b. T
b. T		8. a. T
4. a. ?		b. F
b. T		
5. a. ?		
b. T		

Edit (p. 408)

Linguist Deborah Tannen claims✗men and women have different conversational styles. She argues that the differences can cause miscommunication between the sexes. Here's a typical example of what Professor Tannen means.

A married couple met at the end of the day. They greeted each other, and he asked her how ~~had~~ her day ^had^ been. She replied that she ^had had^ a very busy day. She explained ^to^ him that she had attended several different meetings, and she had seen four clients. She described how she had felt and what ~~had she~~ (she had)

been thinking. After that, she eagerly turned to her husband

and asked how ~~your~~ (his) day had been. He replied that it had been

the same as usual. She looked disappointed, but quickly forgot

about it until later that evening when they met friends for

dinner. During the meal, her husband told the group that

something extraordinary had happened to him ~~today~~ (that day). He went

on to explain the amusing details. Everyone laughed except his

wife. She felt quite frustrated and confused. She didn't

understand why he hadn't told her the story earlier in the

evening.

According to Tannen, the answer relates to the difference in

conversational styles between men and women. She ~~tells~~ (says) that

women use conversation to establish closeness in a

relationship, but men consider conversation to be more of a

public activity. Men use it to establish their status in a group.

Do you agree with this distinction? Do you know men or women

like this?

Part 7 TEST (pp. 410–411)

1. c	10. c	17. what experience you have?
2. c	11. a	18. "Don't come back tomorrow."
3. b	12. d	19. "How often should I take the medication?"
4. a	13. a	20. "Are you staying?"
5. d	14. you liked your job.	
6. b	15. why you're cleaning the house again?	
7. a	16. how much this coat is.	
8. d		
9. c